New Riders' Guide to
CD-ROM,
2nd Edition

Dana Parker
Bob Starrett

NRP
NEW RIDERS
PUBLISHING

New Riders Publishing,
Indianapolis, Indiana

New Riders' Guide to CD-ROM, 2nd Edition

By Dana Parker and Bob Starrett

Published by:
New Riders Publishing
201 West 103rd Street
Indianapolis, IN 46290 USA

Printed in the United States of America   2 3 4 5 6 7 8 9 0

Library of Congress Cataloging-in-Publication Data
Parker, Dana J., 1953-
New Riders' Guide to CD-ROM / Dana J. Parker, Robert A. Starrett. -- 2nd ed.
    p.   cm.
  Rev. ed. of: A guide to CD-ROM. 1992.
  Includes index.
  ISBN 1-56205-308-6 : $35.00
  1. CD/ROM. I. Starrett, Robert A. 1954-   . II. Parker, Dana, 1953-
Guide to CD-ROM. III. Title. IV. Title: Guide to CD-ROM.
TK7895.M4P37   1994
004.5'6--dc20
94-10123

CIP

Warning and Disclaimer   This book is designed to provide information about CD-ROM. Every effort has been made to make this book as complete and as accurate as possible, but no warranty or fitness is implied.

The information is provided on an "as is" basis. The author and New Riders Publishing shall have neither liability nor responsibility to any person or entity with respect to any loss or damages arising from the information contained in this book or from the use of the disks or programs that may accompany it.

About the Authors

Dana J. Parker is Western Regional Sales Manager for Cinram, Inc. She was formerly President of CD-ROM Access, Inc. and Technical Lead and Senior Technical Support Engineer for Meridian Data, Inc. Ms. Parker is Chairman of the Editorial Board of CD:RE, Inc., and a member of The Discovery Channel's Desktop Video Advisory Panel. Ms. Parker also writes a regular column on CD-ROM standards for *CD-ROM Professional* magazine. She has worked in the CD-ROM industry since 1989.

Prior to her CD-ROM experience, Ms. Parker was a field engineer for various corporations, and was one of the first 50 female field engineers for IBM. She studied computer science at Sonoma State University.

Robert A. Starrett is an independent CD-ROM consultant and writer. He was formerly Vice President of CD-ROM Access, Inc., and an Applications Engineer for Meridian Data, Inc. Mr. Starrett has been involved with CD-ROM publishing and production since 1988.

Before his interest in CD-ROM consumed all his time, Mr. Starrett was in private law practice. He has worked as a senior systems analyst, lead programmer, and senior programmer. He received his J.D. degree from the University of Colorado School of Law, where he was Chairman of the Board of Directors of the Legal Aid and Defender program. He received a B.A. degree in Political Science from Metropolitan State College and was awarded the Colorado Scholar's Award.

Publisher	LLOYD J. SHORT
Associate Publisher	TIM HUDDLESTON
Acquisitions Manager	CHERI ROBINSON
Managing Editor	MATTHEW MORRILL
Product Development Manager	ROB TIDROW
Marketing Manager	RAY ROBINSON
Product Director	CHERI ROBINSON
Acquisitions Editor	ALICIA KRAKOVITZ
Lead Editor	JOHN SLEEVA
Editors	SARAH KEARNS
	PETER KUHNS
	ROB LAWSON
Technical Editor	ROBERT WARING
Acquisitions Coordinator	STACEY BEHELER
Editorial Assistant	KAREN OPAL
Publisher's Assistant	MELISSA LYNCH
Imprint Manager	JULI COOK
Book Design	ROGER MORGAN
Production Team Leader	KATY BODENMILLER

Production Team

AYRIKA BRYANT	KIM COFER
TERRI EDWARDS	RICH EVERS
KIM HANNEL	GREG KEMP
STEPHANIE J. MCCOMB	JAMIE MILAZZO
SHELLY PALMA	CHAD POORE
CASEY PRICE	RYAN RADER
BOBBI SATTERFIELD	ANN SIPPEL
TONYA SIMPSON	SA SPRINGER
SCOTT TULLIS	ELAINE WEBB
DENNIS WESNER	ROBERT WOLF

Indexer	CRAIG SMALL
Production Analysts	MARY BETH WAKEFIELD
	DENNIS CLAY HAGER

Dedication

This book is dedicated to the memories of my father, R.W. "Bill" Parker, who always believed that I could do anything, and my brother, Jerry Parker, who was the real writer in the family.

I would like to express my appreciation to Bob Starrett for his hard work, his faith in the project, his steadfastness through the worst times, and for being such a great guy. Thanks also to the Starrett family for their support.

Dana J. Parker

This book is dedicated to my parents, David and Grace, whose support for whatever I do is greatly appreciated.

I would like to thank Dana Parker for putting up with my two-fisted scheduling and for never being afraid to meet obscure, cryptic, ambiguous, and incorrect information head-on, sort it out, and turn it into something tangible.

Robert A. Starrett

Acknowledgments

Writing is often described as a solitary process, but our experience as authors has been one of collaboration, cooperation, and assistance from many individuals. We owe thanks to the following people for their support, encouragement, patience, and knowledge:

Wink Saville, Saville Associates, for invaluable technical information about standards and compatibility.

Matthew Leek, Trace, for believing in us and offering wise counsel and support, as well as technical information.

John Sands, Young Minds, for always being available to answer our questions, no matter how busy he was, providing that we listened to his jokes.

Mary Lynn Davis, Crowninshield Software, for her insight, straight talk, and for providing a laugh when we needed it most.

Cheri Robinson and the staff of New Riders Publishing for their editing and developmental suggestions, and for giving up their weekends when the deadline loomed.

Thanks to John Kasle of Philips, Jill Dosik of Sony, and Benita Kahn of Creative Labs for providing us with evaluation hardware and support.

For assistance in answering technical questions, thanks to Desmond Whelan and Matt Seitz of Meridian Data, Rob Van Eijk of Laser Magnetic Storage International, Alex Iida of Taiyo Yuden, Bert Gall of Philips, Dr. Ash Pahwa of CD-ROM Strategies, Katherine Cochrane of The One-Off CD Shops, Adrian Farmer of Nimbus Engineering, and Steve Soto of Todd Enterprises.

Special thanks to Scott Fast, who is indirectly responsible for this entire book—he introduced us.

The following companies assisted us by providing CD-ROM applications for review:

American Business Information, Bureau of Electronic Publishing, Britannica Software, CD Plus, CD-ROM Resources Group, Creative Multimedia Corporation (CMC ReSearch), Counterpoint Publishing, Delorme Mapping, Digital Publishing Company, Grolier Electronic Publishing, H.W. Wilson Company, Information Sources Incorporated, Institute for Scientific Information, Lotus Development Corporation, Maxwell Electronic Publishing, Meckler, Metatec/Discovery Systems, Novell, Sony Electronic Publishing, Time Warner Communications, Tri -Star Publishing, University Microfilms (UMI), UniDisc, VT Productions, Wayzata Technology, and World Library.

The following companies provided technical information:

3M, CBIS, Metatec/Discovery Systems, Hitachi, IBM, JVC, Kodak, Mammoth MicroProductions, Meridian Data, Micro Design International, Online Computer Systems, Optical Media International, Panasonic, Sony, Todd Enterprises, and Toshiba.

Finally, thanks to those individuals and companies who helped us, but who we have neglected to mention here, purely through oversight.

Trademark Acknowledgments

New Riders Publishing has made every attempt to supply trademark information about company names, products, and services mentioned in this book. Trademarks indicated below were derived from various sources. New Riders Publishing cannot attest to the accuracy of this information.

Trademarks of other products mentioned in this book are held by the companies producing them.

AutoCAD is a registered trademark of Autodesk, Inc.

CorelDRAW! is a registered trademark of Corel Systems Corporation.

Intel is a registered trademark of Intel Corporation.

Lotus and 1-2-3 are registered trademarks of Lotus Development Corporation.

Microsoft Windows 3.1, Word for Windows, and Microsoft Extensions are registered trademarks of Microsoft Corporation.

Novell and NetWare are registered trademarks of Novell, Inc.

Contents at a Glance

Table of Contents

Foreword

Finally, a fresh book on CD-ROM. Dana Parker and Bob Starrett have written a book that addresses the needs of the person who is trying to understand and use CD-ROM for business information. This book provides enough detail so that readers will understand CD-ROM, but not so much that they need to be a computer guru to comprehend it.

This book provides the most up-to-date information on CD-ROM publishing, including information about the latest CD technology, CD-WO. The primary value of this book, however, is its capacity to teach the CD-ROM novice. It provides sources and guidance on how to actually publish information on CD-ROM.

I believe that *New Riders' Guide to CD-ROM* has been written at a most opportune time. I have been in the CD-ROM business for more than eight years, and CD-ROM is just now becoming more common. We now see Kodak's Photo CD, Philip's CD-I, Microsoft's MPC, Tandy's VIS, and Sony's MMCD, to name just a few products. I believe CD-ROM will become one of the predominate information delivery mediums of the '90s, and this book provides invaluable information to help further the knowledge of the technology.

Bob and Dana, congratulations and thank you.

Wink Saville

Preface

Much has changed since *Technology Edge: Guide to CD-ROM* first appeared in print in December 1992. In a little over a year, CD-ROM went from a technology on the cutting edge to a technology of the mainstream. Everywhere you look these days, you see CD-ROM—in libraries, bookstores, computer stores, video stores, offices, living rooms, classrooms, courtrooms, hospitals, army tanks, cars, and even auto repair shops. As more people learn about the advantages of this versatile medium, more innovations appear in its applications. New products are developed; new standards are proposed; new capabilities are realized.

As with all emerging and developing technologies, it is difficult to keep up with the changes. One of the facts of life when writing a book about CD-ROM, or any dynamic technology, is that parts of it are sure to be out-of-date the instant it hits the shelves. Over the last year, we've watched as the changes accumulated—some products did not live up to their initial promise; others have been announced and have failed; many others are just now finding their place in the market.

Through all of this, the quality that has set CD-ROM apart, and that is responsible for much of its success, is still standardization. CD-ROM is still the most standardized distribution medium for data ever developed. Because of this, there are many things in the Second Edition that have not changed. We have updated chapters to reflect recent developments, added more detailed explanations in areas that we have learned more about, and expanded and updated the appendixes. We added an entire chapter about CD-Recordable technology, which adds a whole new meaning to desktop publishing.

We've been working with CD-ROM for more than five years. We've seen CD-ROM grow from a serious, cutting edge, high-technology research publishing medium to a flashy, compelling, cutting-edge entertainment publishing medium. CD-ROM has grown from the library, to the office, to the home, to Hollywood, and it will be part of the foundation of the much-vaunted information superhighway. It will become more and more a part of all of our lives, in ways we haven't even thought of yet.

We wrote this book as a friendly introduction to this fascinating technology that offers so much in the way of disseminating information. We hope it answers your questions about CD-ROM and makes the technology more accessible to you.

Dana Parker, CIS 75030,2620

Bob Starrett, CIS 73524,0102

February 26, 1994

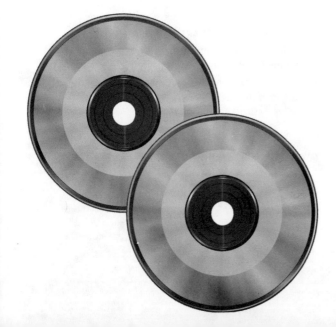

INTRODUCTION

The earliest form of written communication was probably a figure drawn in dust or mud with a twig. This form of communication was followed by cave painting, then by hieroglyphics on clay tablets and on bark, parchment, and papyrus. Centuries later, documents were still being created one at a time. Gutenberg's development of the printing press with movable type was a great advance because it permitted the printing of multiple copies of a document for distribution.

CD-ROM (Compact Disc Read-Only Memory) is possibly the greatest advance in publishing since Gutenberg. A CD-ROM disc can hold vast amounts of data—not just text, but also pictures, sound, and animation. It can be mass produced very cheaply. CD-ROM is compact, lightweight, durable, and incorruptible. Best of all, information contained on a CD-ROM disc is indexed and cross-referenced so that you can quickly find and display any piece of data on the disc.

You have probably heard of CD-ROM. It has been around since 1982, and it has been featured in articles in computer magazines and newspapers. At first, its use was limited to high-tech applications and large companies and libraries with a need to distribute large amounts of information. Recently, however, CD-ROM drives have become so affordable and CD-ROM applications have become so useful and entertaining, that many smaller companies, and even individuals, are finding that CD-ROM is within their reach. With the advent of multimedia, CD-ROM is becoming even more mainstream. Because of their durability, large capacity, small size, and capability of storing text, graphics, sound, and animation, CD-ROM discs are the medium of choice for multimedia applications.

Who Should Read This Book?

This book is written for the person who wants or needs to know about CD-ROM technology. This book is intended as a guide for IBM-compatible computer users who want to know more about CD-ROM. It answers many of the common questions about the technology, including CD-ROM's origin and how it is changing the ways we distribute and access information.

Until now, information about CD-ROM has only been available in technical books aimed at the computer industry. CD-ROM technology is still too new to be taught in computer science courses. This book is a general guide to how you can use and enjoy the technology without having to get an engineering degree. You will find that CD-ROM is an exciting way to access information, whether that information is a traditional, full-text database or a full-blown multimedia application.

The Benefits of CD-ROM

For years, large amounts of information of all kinds—databases, reference books, technical manuals, software programs, and catalogs—have been distributed on CD-ROM. The number of available CD-ROM titles is doubling every year. Many large public and university libraries are currently using CD-ROM. The United States government buys CD-ROM drives by the thousands. In 1991, over a million CD-ROM drives were sold, and by 1994, there will be over 11 million drives in use. Very soon, a CD-ROM drive will be as basic a part of a personal computer as a hard disk.

One of the things computers do best is to search through large amounts of information to find specific information. CD-ROM technology takes advantage of this capability by providing a medium that makes large amounts of information—a 24-volume encyclopedia or a national telephone directory—for example, available to anyone with a personal computer and a CD-ROM drive.

Another aspect of CD-ROM that makes it such an exciting tool for distributing information is the fact that it can hold much more than just pictures and text. A CD-ROM disc can contain any information that can be digitized—including music, speech, and even video. The information can be delivered in many forms beyond the standard linear, sequential, list management, and database report methods. It can be browsed, searched for every occurrence of a word or phrase, and the data can be completely cross-referenced and linked to graphics, sound, and related or in-depth information. Because of the large capacity of CD-ROM discs, it is possible to include tutorial programs and extensive help files on the disc to help users learn to fully realize the potential of the CD-ROM application.

How This Book Is Organized

This book is designed for the user who is familiar with basic computer principles, but who is new to CD-ROM technology. This book is divided into four distinct parts. Part I provides you with the fundamental knowledge that you need to understand CD-ROM before you can continue into the technological aspects of CD-ROM. Part II explains the hardware involved in CD-ROM. Part III provides you with the practical ways in which you can use this technology. Part IV includes several appendixes that serve as references to the various aspects of the industry.

Chapter 1: Why Use CD-ROM Technology?

This chapter explains the reasons why you should consider using CD-ROM technology. You learn that CD-ROM is a practical, cost-efficient, and large-capacity storage medium for your important data.

Chapter 2: Understanding CD-ROM

This chapter thoroughly explains what hardware you need to use the technology. This chapter includes a brief discussion of the three types of software needed to interface a CD-ROM drive with your computer and to access information from the disc.

Chapter 3: What Is a CD-ROM Drive?

This chapter discusses the features and functions of CD-ROM drives. Specifically, this chapter discusses the internal parts of a CD-ROM drive. You learn what is inside the CD-ROM drive, how data is stored and read from a CD-ROM disc, what features are important to look for as you shop for a CD-ROM drive, and the kind of computer you need to support a CD-ROM drive.

Chapter 4: CD-ROM Discs

This chapter discusses aspects of CD-ROM discs. You learn about the physical characteristics of CD-ROM discs, as well as how they are manufactured. You learn where you can purchase CD-ROM applications, how to install them, and how to take care of discs.

Chapter 5: Installing a CD-ROM Drive

This chapter not only teaches you how to install a CD-ROM drive, but also instructs you on the way to care for your CD-ROM drive. You also learn to install hardware and software.

Chapter 6: Understanding CD-ROM Networking

This chapter discusses the advantages of using CD-ROM as a networked resource. This chapter also provides a simple explanation of networking, explains the three basic methods that enable you to share CD-ROM discs over a network, and discusses the advantages, the disadvantages, and the issues involved in networking licenses for CD-ROM discs.

Chapter 7: CD-ROM Software

In this chapter, you learn about CD-ROM retrieval software. You can choose from seven types of CD-ROM discs. Some discs use no retrieval software. You learn the retrieval methods you can use. You also see how hypertext links are used and how many programs use links to sound, animation, and graphics.

Chapter 8: Types of Discs

This chapter provides an overview of some of the most popular CD-ROM discs that are available today. Two actual screen captures from each product are presented along with a complete description of the application.

Chapter 9: Scenarios

This chapter teaches, by example, how you can use CD-ROM technology to your benefit. No matter if you work in a law office, medical office, or library, this chapter can teach you how CD-ROM can help you.

Chapter 10: How to Produce a CD-ROM

This chapter answers the most common questions regarding CD-ROM production. Specifically, this chapter explains why you might want to manufacture a CD-ROM, when CD-ROM is the appropriate medium for publishing, how much it costs to produce a CD-ROM, and the steps to follow to produce a CD-ROM.

Chapter 11: The Future of CD-ROM Technology

This chapter presents predictions on the CD-ROM industry from leading industry experts.

Chapter 12: CD-ROM and Multimedia

This chapter explains how to use CD-ROM to help you develop rich applications with seamless integration of text, graphics, sound, animation, and full-motion video.

Chapter 13: Explaining Compact Disc Standards

This chapter discusses a few alternative formats and implementations of the compact disc. Because each format is based on a different standard, an understanding of each type of compact disc and standard is needed to have a good working knowledge of the industry.

Chapter 14: CD-Recordable

This chapter discusses the evolution and benefits of CD-R technology. Manufacturing CD-R discs enables users to create single, unique compact discs on the desktop.

Appendixes

The appendixes provide resources to help you find further information on CD-ROM drives, multimedia, development, and mastering. A glossary of terms also defines the most common terms used in the CD-ROM industry.

Conventions Used in This Book

Throughout this book, certain conventions are used to help you distinguish the various elements. Before you look ahead, you should spend a moment examining the following conventions:

- ✔ Terms introduced for the first time appear in *italic.*

- ✔ Information you type is **boldface**. This convention, however, does not apply to special keys, such as Enter, Esc, or Ctrl.

- ✔ Text that is displayed on-screen appears in a `special typeface`.

Throughout this book, you will find examples of special text that are designated as Notes, Tips, or Cautions. These passages have been given special treatment so that you can instantly recognize their significance and so that you can easily find them for future reference.

 A note includes extra information that you should find useful and which complements the discussion at hand, instead of being a direct part of it.

 A tip provides advice for getting the most from CD-ROM. A tip might suggest a shortcut or a technique to help you work more efficiently.

 A stop tells you when a procedure may be dangerous. Some warnings are like tying a string around your finger to remind you not to make certain common mistakes.

Publisher's Note

The staff of New Riders Publishing is committed to bringing you the very best in computer reference material. Each New Riders book is the result of months of work by authors and staff, who research and refine the information contained within its covers.

As part of this commitment to you, New Riders invites your input. Please let us know if you find this book useful, if you have trouble with any of the information or examples presented in it, or if you have a suggestion for the next edition.

If you have a question or comment about any New Riders book, please contact NRP at the following address:

New Riders Publishing
Macmillan Computer Publishing
A Division of Paramount Publishing
Attn: Associate Publisher
201 West 103rd Street
Indianapolis, IN 46290

If you prefer, you can FAX New Riders Publishing at the following number:

(317) 581-4670

New Riders Publishing also maintains a CompuServe forum. We welcome your participation in this forum (**GO NEWRIDERS**). Please feel free to post a public message there if you have a question or comment about this or any other New Riders product. If you prefer, however, you can send a private message directly to this book's product director at 75250,1431.

We will respond to as many readers as we can. Your name, address, phone number, or electronic mail ID will never become part of a mailing list or be used for any purpose other than to help us continue to bring you the best books possible.

Thank you for selecting *New Riders' Guide to CD-ROM.*

Part I

CD-ROM Fundamentals

1

CHAPTER

Why Use CD-ROM Technology?

In this chapter, you learn the advantages of using CD-ROM as a data storage and data distribution medium. You will see that CD-ROM is a durable, standardized, large-capacity medium that has the additional advantages of cross-platform compatibility and CD audio capability. In addition, CD-ROM discs are inexpensive to replicate, and single discs can be produced on the desktop. CD-ROM is a widely accepted data-distribution and publishing medium. Drive prices are low and getting lower all the time, and the CD-ROM titles available today have something to offer everyone.

In Search of Standards

The computer world is constantly in search of "standards." You may recall that at one time the operating system standard was CP/M (Control Program for Microprocessors) written by Gary Kildall. This operating system ran on the Zilog Z80 processor, and hundreds of manufacturers made computers based on this chip. Although the operating system was a standard for a short period of time before being eclipsed by the IBM PC and PC/MS-DOS, an interesting thing occurred: each manufacturer had its own floppy disk format.

A popular program at the time was Media Master, which allowed conversion between disks from 66 different CP/M machines. Although this conversion software did not cover all the floppy disk formats, it did help somewhat. The problem was that without this software, a user could not read a disk created on another machine, even though that machine used the same processor, the same operating system, and the same physical floppy disk drive.

Even with the introduction of the IBM PC, floppy disk drives were plagued by lack of standards, not in format, but in disk capacity. The first IBM PCs had one or two 5 1/4-inch 160K floppy drives. Next came the 5 1/4-inch 360K drive, then the 720K 3 1/2-inch drive, the 1.2M 5 1/4-inch drive, and now the standard is the 1.44M 3 1/2-inch drive.

Although some backward compatibility exists, remember that early 1.2M drives had trouble reading disks that had been written with a 360K drive. Many early PCs were not able to support some of the later drives without a ROM BIOS upgrade.

So what does CD-ROM offer that other removable storage mediums do not? It offers standardization, capacity, durability, cross-platform compatibility, CD audio capability, low drive prices, low replication prices, one-off capability, and a large number of disc titles.

Standardization

CD audio discs were an instant success because of standards. Any CD you buy at the record store will play in any manufacturer's CD audio player. The same is true of CD-ROM—any CD-ROM disc can be read by any CD-ROM drive.

Exchange, distribution and portability of information is one of the great boons of the PC industry. The quest for inexpensive, large capacity, removable media has been going on for a long time. Magneto optical (MO) and WORM drives seemed

to promise much toward making this a reality. Unfortunately, the promise has not been met. The industry is plagued by the same problems that it had during the CP/M days. An MO or WORM cartridge written in one manufacturer's drive cannot necessarily be read in another drive, even though in many cases the cartridge itself is physically identical. Manufacturers have each decided on their own logical format for the disc.

Although CD-ROM was originally thought of only as an electronic publishing medium, today it is used for many purposes. Companies that need to distribute large amounts of information to branch offices, affiliates, or customers use CD-ROM as the medium. Network administrators use CD-ROM to store static information that usually takes up expensive and scarce file server hard drive space. The Document Image Processing (DIP) industry, one of the fastest growing segments of personal computer use, is finding that CD-ROM can be an effective replacement for expensive WORM and MO drives and jukeboxes.

Capacity

Today, CD-ROM discs are employed for much more than their original use as a publishing medium. Many software companies find that it is more cost effective to distribute their software on CD-ROM than on floppies.

Borland, Microsoft, Lotus, Corel, and other software manufacturers are using CD-ROM to distribute programs that are extremely large. Corel-DRAW! 3.0, which is distributed on CD-ROM, includes the CorelDRAW! program, 14,000 clip art images, and 250 fonts. Distribution of this quantity of material on floppy is not cost-effective.

Lotus 1-2-3 Version 1.1 with Smarthelp for Windows is distributed on CD-ROM. The disc contains 177M of programs, data, graphics, and sound. Distributing this on 1.44M floppy disks would take 123 (pure coincidence) disks, and most users would not have the disk space, time, or patience to load it all. If you use the CD-ROM version, however, you can copy only the necessary program files to the hard disk. The extensive help functions, including many examples and audio explanations, remain on the CD-ROM disc and can be accessed as needed. Distributing the product on CD-ROM also reduces postage, duplication, and labeling costs.

If you have ever had to reload a large program or operating system (or install Novell NetWare), you will appreciate the convenience of not inserting or swapping disks or making backup copies.

Durability

CD-ROM discs and drives are durable. You cannot have a head crash on a CD-ROM drive. You cannot accidentally delete files from a CD-ROM disc. You never get cross-linked clusters or a scrambled File Allocation Table on a CD-ROM disc. CD-ROM discs are impervious to viruses and have an estimated life of up to 100 years.

Your ability to read data from a CD-ROM is generally not impaired by minor scratches, dust, fingerprints, magnetic fields, or other common computer media hazards. Because nothing touches the disc but laser light, CD-ROM discs do not wear out.

Cross-Platform Compatibility

CD-ROM drives are not restricted to use on the IBM PC. They work equally well on Macintosh, Sun, DEC, and any other system that can use a SCSI device. The drives work with any of these systems, and data in the CD-ROM (ISO 9660) format is accessible through any of these systems. One advantage of this cross-platform capability is a cost savings in data distribution. A data distributor whose customers include PC, Macintosh, and Sun users can distribute a single CD-ROM that contains a database and retrieval software for all three platforms. This compatibility produces an enormous cost savings over distributing three separate databases on other media.

CD Audio Capability

As multimedia moves from marketing department hype to real-world applications, CD-ROM becomes even more compelling as a distribution medium. Multimedia applications are necessarily large because of the size requirements of full-screen, full-color graphics, sound files, animation files, and soon, 30 frame-per-second full-motion video.

No other medium is available that allows multimedia applications to reach the personal computer user at a reasonable cost, both for the media itself, and the hardware that it takes to access it. When true CD-quality audio is a feature in an application, only CD-ROM has the capability to play it.

Low Drive Prices

As of this writing, CD-ROM drives are selling for as little as $119. It is fair to predict that within a year, drives will be selling for less than $100. At this price, CD-ROM should become a standard device in a personal computer. One in four PCs sold today contains a CD-ROM drive. Given the size of today's and tomorrow's programs and operating systems, the large base of available CD-ROM titles, and the ease with which the CD-ROM disc can be produced and distributed, a CD-ROM drive will be as necessary for the personal computer user as the floppy disk drive.

Low Replication Prices

The cost of CD-ROM replication has dropped dramatically in recent years. In large quantities, CD-ROMs can be replicated for as little as $1.00 per disc. This is less than one-fifth of one penny per megabyte. Compared to the cost of storage on paper, magnetic tape, MO cartridge, WORM, hard disk, floppy disk or microfiche, CD-ROM is by far the cheapest storage medium for computer data.

One-Off Capability

The availability of low cost, write-once desktop recorders will bring the capability of single and low volume CD-ROM production to the average personal computer user. Although the new generation of CD-ROM recorders is still too expensive for the average user, many companies can produce a single CD-ROM for you for as little as $150.

One of the many practical uses for the average PC user is to store copies of all master program disks on CD-ROM so that programs can be reloaded if necessary. A Windows user, for example, can put the contents of each Windows disk on a separate subdirectory, such as WINDISK1, WINDISK2, WINDISK3. To reinstall Windows or to change video or other drivers, just insert the CD-ROM and specify the drive letter and path for each prompted Windows floppy. This technique works with most programs, except those that expect a certain drive letter for installation or programs that insist on writing some registration information to the installation disks.

Number of Available Titles

The number of CD-ROM titles available today exceeds 6,000 and is growing daily. Although many of the titles included in this number are specialty titles that are too expensive or too esoteric for the average user, the production rate of new titles ensures that there is or will be something for everybody. Whether it is the traditional CD-ROM materials such as medical, legal, financial or parts databases, or discs that contain dictionaries, encyclopedias, programs, shareware, games, clip art, fonts, educational programs, or telephone directories, CD-ROM provides something for every user.

Summary

In this chapter, you learned many of the reasons that CD-ROM is such an accepted medium for data storage and distribution. The next chapter examines the standardization issue in detail and covers some of the physical details of CD-ROM discs and drives. It also gives an overview of CD-ROM software.

CHAPTER

Understanding
CD-ROM

This chapter explores the basics of CD-ROM. Although later chapters discuss some of these topics in greater detail, this chapter helps you understand the basics of CD-ROM technology. You learn what CD-ROM is and what hardware you need to use the technology. This chapter includes a brief discussion of the three types of software needed to interface a CD-ROM drive with your computer and to access information from the disc.

What Is CD-ROM?

CD-ROM is an acronym that stands for *Compact Disc Read Only Memory.* This name may be an unfortunate choice because Compact Disc Data more clearly describes what CD-ROM is all about. Read Only Memory (ROM) refers only to the fact that unlike floppy disks, hard disks, or tape (also known as magnetic media), you cannot write data to a CD-ROM disc. Note that CD-ROMs are called *discs,* whereas floppy and hard drives are called *disks.*

CD-ROMs are called *discs.* Floppy and hard drives are called *disks.*

The easiest way to explain CD-ROM is to compare it to CD audio. Most people are familiar with CD audio players and discs. Since they became available in 1982, they have virtually replaced the phonograph record and turntable. Both types of discs are physically identical and are manufactured at the same plants by the same process. The only real difference is that audio CDs contain only music (and sometimes graphics), and CD-ROM discs can contain text, graphics, sound, and animation or video.

The audio CD has been an enormous success. When was the last time any of your acquaintances bought a turntable for playing LPs? The audio CD quickly made the phonograph record obsolete for several reasons. The compact disc is highly resistant to scratches. It can never be scratched during play because the only thing that contacts the surface of the disc is laser light.

CDs certainly take less room to store than LPs and are easier to maintain. Although some turntables enable you to program the order of play, this feature is standard on a CD audio player, as is a shuffle play function. The smaller size of CDs has made compact disc changers and automobile players possible. An automobile LP player or changer would be impractical.

Although CD-ROM discs will never make floppy or hard disks obsolete because CD-ROM is read-only, many of the advantages that made the audio CD so popular also apply to CD-ROM. Large capacity, durability, size, easy storage, and standard-ization all join to make CD-ROM the medium of choice for electronic publishing and, increasingly, for distribution of large software packages. CD-ROM also enables

software developers to enhance their products by including extensive on-line help, and to distribute software documentation in searchable electronic form rather than paper.

As the market for audio CDs grew, player prices went down and more features became available on audio players. As replication volume increased, replication and packaging prices dropped. The same thing has happened with CD-ROM, although it has been slower to catch on. Among the reasons for the initial slow growth was the chicken and egg theory. Users do not want to invest in hardware when available applications are scarce, and developers are reluctant to invest heavily in applications without a large installed hardware base.

Even though audio CD discs and CD-ROM discs look exactly the same, they are different. What happens if you insert a CD-ROM disc into your audio CD player? Be sure that you turn the volume down! CD-ROM discs emit loud noise when you insert them into audio CD players.

The audio player is not equipped to decode the data on a CD-ROM disc into anything more intelligible than the white noise that you hear.

Developing Industry Standards

CD-ROM technology has been around for over ten years. As with all technological breakthroughs, however, the development of industry standards is an important part of the process of the technology becoming both popular and useful. Inventions such as the telephone, television, and the microprocessor did not become useful until standards for the technologies were developed.

Without standards, you cannot communicate with everybody who has a particular technology. Television, for example, would not be widespread today without the development of standards. You would not be able to watch all televised shows if industry standards were not in place.

Red Book and Yellow Book

The compact disc is a result of a joint venture by Sony and Philips. The CD audio specification, which describes the physical characteristics concerning the size of the pits and lands that represent data and their arrangement in a spiral, was announced in 1980. This standard, known as the *Red Book* standard because of the color of the binder in which it was published, was introduced as a way to ensure that any audio CD would play in any audio CD player. This specification is relatively simple because an audio CD only contains music that is played from the disc in a stream.

Searching is handled differently on an audio CD. You search for the beginning of a music track. After the track is found, the selection is played from beginning to end. The CD audio player is not required to make multiple seeks to determine the location of the data to be played as music. After the beginning of the track is found, the data is read sequentially until the end of the track is reached. If the player is not on shuffle play, the next track is played in sequence.

The CD-ROM disc is an offshoot of the CD audio disc, and the CD-ROM specification, also known as the *Yellow Book*, is an extension of the CD audio specification. This specification enabled the manufacturer to place different kinds of data on a CD-ROM. The standard, however, is concerned only with the physical characteristics of the disc. A standard was still needed to ensure compatibility in the way that data was organized into files.

To illustrate this need for standardization, suppose that you wanted to access a particular piece of data on a CD-ROM disc. Without a standard to ensure that data organization was the same from disc to disc, you would have to know the exact location on the disc of the data you needed to access. This technique would be like finding data on your hard disk by looking at a specific cylinder, head, and sector, instead of by using DOS commands or an application to read the data. Without standards, each CD-ROM software publisher was left to develop his own approach to the way in which data is organized and accessed.

To continue the analogy to magnetic disks, this approach would be similar to having one floppy drive for your spreadsheet program and another drive for your word processor. As a result, early CD-ROM applications worked in one manufacturer's drive, but did not always work in a drive developed by another manufacturer.

High Sierra Group

In November of 1985, industry leaders involved in CD-ROM research and development met at the High Sierra Casino and Hotel in Lake Tahoe and agreed to develop an industry standard. The High Sierra Group, as it came to be known,

consisted of people from Apple Computer, Digital Equipment Corporation, Hitachi, LaserData, Microsoft, 3M, Philips, Reference Technology Inc., Sony Corp., TMS Inc., VideoTools (which later became Meridian Data, Inc.), and XEBEC. The High Sierra Group's goal was to create a method to organize CD-ROM sectors into logical blocks or records, and then to arrange those blocks into files.

ISO 9660

The result of The High Sierra Group's collaboration is sometimes referred to as the *High Sierra standard*. This standard was later adopted, with a few modifications, by the International Standards Organization as *ISO 9660*. This standard ensured that any CD-ROM disc would be accessible in any CD-ROM drive attached to computers that use different operating systems.

The International Standards Organization (ISO), which was founded in 1946, is headquartered in Geneva, Switzerland. It sets international standards by working with committees from all over the world. The United States member body is the American National Standards Institute (ANSI).

The ISO 9660 standard is one of the advantages that CD-ROM has over WORM (Write Once Read Many) and magneto optical (erasable) technology. Although both of these mediums use laser optical technology, neither has universal standards.

WORM and MO drives from one manufacturer cannot necessarily read data from a cartridge written by another manufacturer's drive, even though in many cases the optical cartridge is identical. WORM and MO are discussed in Chapter 13.

If you are interested in the lower levels of CD-ROM structure, you can order a copy of the ISO 9660 file format for CD-ROM from the International Standards Organization. You should be aware, however, that the wording and depth of coverage is anything but simple. The following quote should convince you to save some postage:

Location of Optional Occurrence of Type M Path Table (BP 153 to 156)

This field shall specify as a 32-bit number the Logical Block Number of the first Logical Block allocated to the Extent which contains an optional occurrence of the Path Table. If the value is 0, it shall mean that the Extent shall not be expected to have been recorded. Multibyte numerical values in a record of this occurrence of the Path Table shall be recorded with the most significant byte first.

You do not need to be concerned about buying the right kind of disc for your drive.

In plain English, this passage means that if a number in a certain location is 0, the information, in this case, a path table, does not exist. To the average user, however, standards rarely need to be understood. All this explanation is unnecessary if the CD-ROM disc displays a directory. All that standards really do is ensure that any disc you buy can be read by any drive. Standards ensure that drive manufacturers and disc manufacturers are playing by the same rules. You do not need to be concerned about buying the right kind of disc for your drive.

The Path Table is one of two tables contained in the volume descriptor of a CD-ROM, and comprises the file management system for the disc. The Path Table contains the names of all directories on the disc and is the fastest way to access a directory that is not close to the root directory.

It is helpful to know, however, that certain information can be found in the same place on every CD made. An audio CD player uses this information to find tracks so that you can program them to be played in any order. CD-ROM drives also use this information to differentiate between audio and data discs. This standard information is what enables you to find information so quickly with CD-ROM discs.

What happens when you insert an audio disc into your CD-ROM drive? Because the disc was not recorded in the Yellow Book, or CD-ROM format, you cannot look at the music data with DOS commands. If you try to log on to the disc, you get a message such as Not High Sierra or ISO 9660 or Not ready error reading drive D:. Some software programs, however, enable you to play audio CDs in a CD-ROM drive.

The drive must have an audio jack. Most of these programs run in the background so that you can listen to an audio disc as you run other programs on your computer.

Most modern drives have an audio jack, and the small headphones that are commonly used with portable stereos work fine with them. Larger headphones also work with a conversion jack. If you want to output the audio to speakers, you need amplified speakers or an external amplifier to get the proper results.

Some discs contain tracks of both data and digital audio. These discs usually are called *mixed mode* or *multimedia* discs. Multimedia discs are explained in further detail in Chapter 12. If a disc contains music tracks and data tracks, the first track always contains data, or the CD-ROM format. If the disc has a data track, it is always considered to be a CD-ROM disc, even if most of the information on the disc is in audio format.

For more information on mixed or multimedia, see Chapter 12.

Comparing CD-ROM and CD Audio

A CD-ROM disc and a CD audio disc are both made from polycarbonate, which is the same material used in the production of motorcycle helmets and bulletproof glass. Although the material is extremely durable and resistant to damage, you should handle discs carefully and keep them clean.

On an audio disc, music is digitized using *Pulse Code Modulation (PCM)*. Figure 2.1 shows a sound wave.

In CD audio recording, the sound wave is *sampled*, or broken into a series of numbers (samples). The sampling rate is 44.1kHz. In other words, 44,100 samples are taken every second. Each sample contains 16 bits of information, which means that there are 65,536 possible values—the value closest to the signal is assigned to the sample. Sampling is shown in figure 2.2.

Figure 2.1
A sound wave.

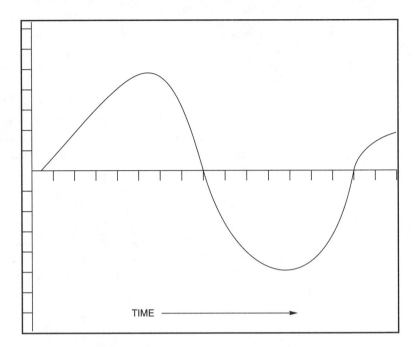

TIME ⟶

Each sample is then converted into a series of binary numbers, zeros and ones. Error correction code (CIRC, or Cross-Interleaved Reed-Solomon Code) is added to the digitized music data. This briefly can be described as performing a series of calculations on the binary numbers and including the results on the disc itself. When the disc is later decoded by the CD audio player, these calculations are performed again, and the results compared. Any errors found can then be corrected.

Cross-Interleaved Reed-Solomon Code is a complex method of interleaving and adding parity bits to data to ensure that errors produced by scratches or dirt on the surface of the disc can be detected and corrected. The entire process is far too lengthy and complicated to go into here.

Layered EDC/ECC is used on CD-ROM discs. It is an error detection and correction scheme that consists of extra error codes layered over the CIRC used by CD audio discs. ECC for CD-ROM uses polynomials and complex Galois fields to perform checksums on the data in the header and data blocks of a sector. The information generated by these calculations (a polynomial) is stored in the EDC/ECC area of each sector. When the disc is read, the calculations are performed on the data again, and the resulting polynomial is compared with the information stored in the EDC/ECC area of the sector.

If this information does not match, the error detection code can calculate the location of the error and the error correction code can generate the correct data by extrapolation.

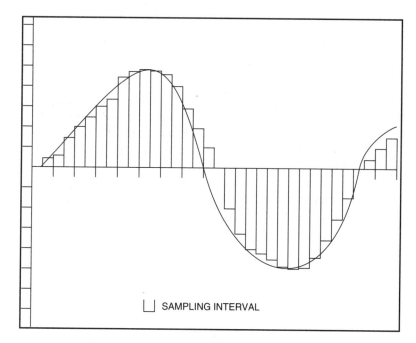

Figure 2.2
A sampled
sound wave.

SAMPLING INTERVAL

The music has now been *encoded*. The manufacturing process transfers this digital data to polycarbonate discs, where the numbers are represented as pits, or bumps. A thin aluminum reflective layer is then applied over the bumps. A transparent layer of lacquer is applied to protect the surface, and a label is printed on one side. Figure 2.3 shows a cross section of a CD audio (or CD-ROM) disc. Unlike LP records, only one side of the disc contains music, and the track starts at the center of the disc instead of the outer edge. An audio CD can contain more than 72 minutes of stereo sound.

For more details about the manufacturing process, see Chapter 4.

Figure 2.3
CD-ROM disc
cross section.

In CD-ROM recording, the process is different only up to the point of manufacturing the disc. The data, which can be text, graphics, sound, animation, or video, is encoded by a different process, which includes CIRC, *CRC (Cyclic Redundancy Check)*, *EDC (Error Detection Code)*, and *ECC (Error Correction Code)*. This process is sometimes called *layered ECC*, because it uses the CIRC method as a basis for the extended error correction of CD-ROM. The process adds numbers to the beginning and end of pieces of data, or *packets* (see fig. 2.4), to ensure that the data is read correctly despite any foreign particles or scratches on the surface of the disc. Very little error correction is performed on an audio disc in comparison to a CD-ROM disc because your ears are not sensitive enough to hear an error on an audio disc that would be catastrophic on a data disc. CD-ROM error correction is so effective that you can expect no more than one uncorrectable one-byte error in 20,000,000 CD-ROM discs. An error is not likely, even if the disc is damaged.

In CD-ROM recording, the data is divided into sectors composed of 2,352 bytes of information. Each sector of computer data consists of 12 bytes of sync, 4 bytes of header, and 2,328 bytes of information space. Normally, the information space consists of 2,048 bytes of user data, 4 bytes of Error Detection Code (EDC), 8 bytes of zeros, and 276 bytes of Error Correction Code (ECC) (see fig. 2.4). The header gives each sector a unique identification to determine how to interpret the information space. The EDC allows the drive to detect any errors in the data. The ECC attempts to correct errors detected by the EDC. The resulting 2,352 bytes of data are then encoded in exactly the same manner as 588 samples of 16-bit stereo audio samples.

Figure 2.4
CD-ROM data
packet.

Sync (12)	Header (4)	User Data (2048)	EDC (4)	Gap (8)	ECC (276)

When you play an audio CD in your home player, the player shines a laser beam on the disc, picks up the reflections made by the bumps, reverses the encoding process, applies error correction, processes and outputs audio signals, and gives you clean, clear music. The bumps that represent numbers on the CD have been decoded into a reproduction of the original sound.

When you access a CD-ROM disc on your CD-ROM drive attached to your personal computer, the drive shines a laser on the disc, picks up the reflections, reverses the encoding process, applies error detection and correction, processes and outputs the digital data (which may include audio signals), and gives you immediate access to huge amounts of data.

CD-ROM Disc Storage Capacity

A CD-ROM disc can hold 680 megabytes, or over 1,500 floppy disks, or 300,000 single-spaced typewritten pages, or 24 volumes of an encyclopedia, or 5,000 full-color images. A person reading one page per minute nonstop, twelve hours a day, would take nearly nine months to read the material contained on a single CD-ROM. At 2,400 baud, it would take 32 days to transmit the contents of a CD-ROM via a modem. Figures 2.5 and 2.6 illustrate the capacity of a CD-ROM disc.

Comparing CD-ROM Drives to CD Audio Drives

How is a CD-ROM drive different from a CD audio drive? It is usually more expensive, to begin with, because a CD-ROM drive does everything a CD audio player does and more. That is, a CD-ROM drive not only can play music, but also can search and retrieve information quickly and accurately. A CD audio player was designed only to play a stream of music from the spiral track; and, although it does have the capability to go directly to a particular track or to skip forward and backward, it cannot just go out and find a particular sound anywhere on the disc. Also, if a CD audio player detects an error, it can mask the error in many ways that are likely to be inaudible. It can play the previous 1/75 of a second of sound again, for example, and you will never hear the difference.

Figure 2.5
A stack of 1,500 floppy disks.

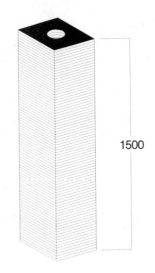

1500

Floppy Disks

Figure 2.6
A stack of 300,000 pages.

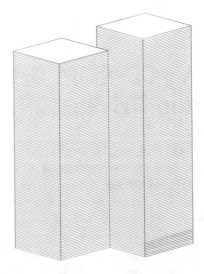

300,000 Typewritten Pages

A CD-ROM drive not only enables you to access large amounts of information quickly, it also ensures that the information is correct. How quickly can this information be accessed? Within half a second. One industry guru puts this into perspective.

John Sands, who is well-known in the CD-ROM industry, compares the piece of information to a grain of rice, and the disc itself to a football field. In less than half a second, the CD-ROM drive can retrieve the "grain of rice" from anywhere on the "field."

Physically, a CD audio player contains a laser beam mechanism, a power supply, electronics for control and remote control, various displays, buttons, output jacks, a standard 110 volt line cord to plug it in, and a case. Most of you are familiar with these units as you have used them for several years.

A CD-ROM drive contains a laser beam mechanism; electronics for control, error correction, and communication with your PC; usually an audio jack, a volume control, and an eject button; and, if the drive is external, a power supply and possibly a fan. The CD-ROM drive is controlled by your personal computer, which holds the software that enables you to access the disc's contents.

For more details about CD-ROM drives, see Chapter 3.

Understanding CD-ROM Software

Three types of software are needed when you use a CD-ROM drive. The first is the CD-ROM device driver software, the second is the Microsoft Extensions software, and the third is the retrieval software for the particular disc or discs that you are using.

Device Drivers

A *device driver* is a program that contains the information necessary for the computer to control and/or access a peripheral device such as a CD-ROM drive, a scanner, or a mouse. A mouse is a good example. When you attach a mouse to your computer, you must tell the computer certain information about the mouse so that the computer can interact with the mouse correctly. A mouse usually comes with a device driver called MOUSE.SYS. Usually, you modify your computer's CONFIG.SYS file to include the following line:

```
<PX>DEVICE=MOUSE.SYS
```

 CD-ROM device drivers are discussed in more detail in Chapter 5.

When you restart your computer, the mouse driver then tells the computer the information it needs to interface correctly with the mouse. CD-ROM drives also come with a device driver (TOSHIBA.SYS, HITACHI.SYS, SONY.SYS, to name a few) that tells the computer how to interact with the CD-ROM drive.

Floppy drives and hard drives do not require device drivers because your computer hardware and MS-DOS know what they are. When MS-DOS was written, floppy drives and hard drives were the only drives available; nobody had ever heard of CD-ROM. Nobody dreamed that someday you might be able to access 680 million bytes of information on your personal computer. This capability has created the need for Microsoft Extensions for CD-ROM.

Microsoft Extensions for CD-ROM

Microsoft Extensions for CD-ROM refers to a particular program written by Microsoft called MSCDEX.EXE. This program allows the MS-DOS operating system commands to access a CD-ROM drive. Because the capacity of a CD-ROM drive is greater than MS-DOS is used to dealing with and because CD-ROMs use ISO 9660 or High Sierra instead of MS-DOS format to store files, this special program is required.

Retrieval Software

Retrieval software (sometimes referred to as a *search engine* or *interface*) is the software that enables you to access the data placed in indexed form on the CD-ROM disc. A common (and justified) complaint in the CD-ROM world is that no standards exist for retrieval software. For ten discs, the user may have to use 10 different retrieval applications. This is not a problem in situations in which the user accesses a number of discs from the same publisher, because the interface is the same for all

of them. It is, however, a big problem for the user who wants to use several discs from several companies and finds that each has a different interface and different commands to learn. The upside of this is that different kinds of data require different access programs, and the user is not forced to use an inappropriate interface. For example, you do not use a word processor to create a spreadsheet.

Retrieval software is discussed in detail in Chapter 4.

Summary

CD-ROM technology has been around for 10 years. The CD-ROM disc is an offshoot of the CD audio specification that originally was developed jointly by Philips and Sony. The physical layout of an audio disc is governed by the Red Book, whereas the layout of a CD-ROM disc is governed by the Yellow Book. The High Sierra and ISO 9660 standards for CD-ROM ensure that any CD-ROM disc is accessible in any CD-ROM drive. The standards that are in place for CD-ROM are what give it such wide appeal.

CD-ROM and CD audio discs look alike, but they are in fact different in several ways. Error correction is essential to both types of discs. Although CD audio discs use complicated error correction algorithms, CD-ROM discs use even more error correction because of the need for computer data to be exact. CD-ROM drives and audio drives are similar, but not interchangeable. Three types of software are needed to access data on a CD-ROM. Device drivers allow your computer to see the drive. Microsoft Extensions allows your computer to see the data on the drive by using normal DOS commands. Retrieval software is the software that enables you to access the data in an efficient manner.

In the next chapter, you examine CD-ROM drives. The differences between CD-ROM drives and hard drives, read-only and read-write, and Constant Linear Velocity (CLV) and Constant Angular Velocity (CAV) are discussed. You also learn the difference between internal and external drives and SCSI and bus interfaces.

Part II

Understanding the Hardware

CHAPTER

What Is a CD-ROM Drive?

Although early CD-ROM drives were slow, expensive, and hard to find, recent improvements and the increasing number of titles have helped to make today's CD-ROM drives relatively fast, inexpensive, and readily available. In the early days of the CD-ROM industry, computer retailers looked at you in wonder if you asked for a CD-ROM drive. If they had heard of the technology, they might have been able to order a drive for you from a limited number of manufacturers. Today, however, it is likely that your computer retailer not only has heard of CD-ROM, but knows something about it. The retailer probably has drives in stock from several manufacturers and can sell you a drive at an affordable price.

This chapter discusses the features and functions of CD-ROM drives. Specifically, this chapter discusses the following topics:

- ✔ The internal parts of a CD-ROM drive
- ✔ CD-ROM drives compared to hard drives
- ✔ Purchasing a CD-ROM drive
- ✔ Hardware requirements for CD-ROM drives

You learn what is inside the CD-ROM drive, how data is stored and read from a CD-ROM disc, what features are important to look for as you shop for a CD-ROM drive, and the kind of computer you need to support a CD-ROM drive.

Understanding CD-ROM Drives

Internally, a CD-ROM drive contains an optical head, a turntable for the disc, a controller, and a signal-processing system. The *optical head*, which shines the laser on the disc surface, is mounted on a sled or swing arm and consists of a laser diode, a lens, and a photodetector that reads the laser reflections from the disc. The photodetector also contains several photodiodes that ensure the laser beam is in focus and following the disc track. The *turntable* spins the disc at a variable rate of speed, which depends on where the data is being read from the disc. The speed varies from 500rpm on the inside of the disc to 200rpm along the outside edge of the disc. The *controller*, which is a circuit board mounted inside the drive, integrates several functions that control the focus, tracking, turntable motor, rate of spin, and input from user controls. The *signal processor* demodulates, descrambles, decodes, and applies error correction to the data read from the disc.

See the section on CLV and CAV for more information on the way in which data is stored on discs.

When the drive accesses a CD-ROM disc, the drive electronics measure the reflections from the laser beam that is focused on the disc track. The reflections from the disc surface are varied, depending on whether the light is being reflected from *pits* in the surface of the disc or from *lands*, which are flat areas between the pits. The fluctuations in the intensity of the reflected light are converted to digital data that is then decoded into programs or data by the CD-ROM drive.

Comparing CD-ROMs and Hard Drives

A common misconception is that CD-ROM is a replacement for hard drives. Although CD-ROM has durability, low cost, and high capacity, the reality is that CD-ROM is complementary to hard drives. To help you understand CD-ROM better, the following section presents a comparison between the two technologies.

Read-Only Versus Read/Write

CD-ROM technology probably will not replace hard drive technology. Disc access is slow compared to a hard drive, and you cannot write data to a CD-ROM disc. Before you ask, "Then what good is it?," you must consider why this technology evolved. CD-ROM is mainly a publishing medium, just like a book, in that it is meant to hold static information for reference. The information contained on a hard drive, however, can be written over, deleted, or damaged by virus, accident, or malfunction. No matter how dependable a hard drive is, it eventually wears out and the data it contains is lost. A CD-ROM disc does not wear out from use (at least not for 50 years), the information is incorruptible by virus or accident (you cannot accidentally erase or format a CD-ROM disc), and you can access different information by changing the disc. For data that does not change frequently, CD-ROM is ideal.

See Part IV of this book for the latest developments in recordable and appendable CD-ROM.

Although rewritable CD-ROMs are in development, it is unlikely that they will ever be as fast as a hard drive because of the way in which hard drives and CD-ROMs make use of their storage space. The following section describes the differences.

Rewritable CD-ROM discs and drives are under development. These drives and discs are essentially magneto optical technology in CD-ROM form. Rewritable CD-ROM should not be confused with writable CD-ROM, which has been available since 1989. Writable CD-ROM (commonly called CD-WO or CD-R) enables you, with special equipment, to make a single or several CD-ROM discs on the desktop. The whole disc, however, must be written in one session and can never be changed. It looks and acts like a normal CD-ROM disc, except for the color of the disc, which is gold on the label side and green on the flip side. Appendable or multisession CD-ROM is a new technology that allows data to be written in multiple sessions to a CD-ROM disc on the desktop.

Drive Mechanisms and Data Layout

CD-ROM is slower than hard drives because of the way in which data is stored on a disc and the way in which the data is accessed by the CD-ROM drive. This storage method is why CD-ROM discs can hold so much more information than a hard disk or floppy disk of the same size.

CAV

A magnetic disk is divided into concentric tracks. Each track contains an equal number of sectors for storing data. Files can be stored on one track or many tracks so that additions, alterations, and deletions can be made. If you copy a new file to disk and the disk does not contain one empty space large enough to hold the file, the data is copied to several different locations. The File Allocation Table (FAT) is updated with all the locations of the pieces of the file. This process of storing pieces of the file in different locations is called *file fragmentation*. Figure 3.1 illustrates file fragmentation.

Figure 3.1
File frag-
mentation.

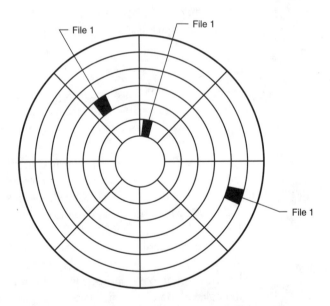

The next time you access the file, the FAT knows where the pieces of the file are located. When you access a file, the read/write head travels to the track on which the data is located and remains stationary as the data passes beneath it. The magnetic disk spins constantly at a nonvarying speed during seek, read, and write operations. This process is called *Constant Angular Velocity (CAV)*. Figure 3.2 illustrates the concept of constant angular velocity. Because the outer edges of the disk

contain sectors whose contents are less dense, the data stored on the outer edge is read more slowly than the data at the center of the disk. The speed of the rotation never changes; therefore, the locations of the concentric tracks are known in advance so that movement from one part of the disk to another is very fast.

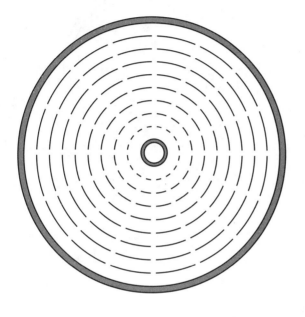

Figure 3.2
Constant
Angular Velocity
(CAV).

II

Understanding the Hardware

CLV

In contrast, a CD-ROM disc contains data in one continuous spiral track, divided into sectors of equal size and density. Files are not fragmented, but reside on contiguous sectors within the single track (see fig. 3.3). The more efficient use of space enables the CD-ROM disc to store more data than a hard disk.

A CD-ROM drive spins the disc at a variable rate of speed, depending on the optical head's position. The data is read from the disc at a constant rate of speed (about 1.3 meters per second) no matter what location on the disc it occupies. This process is called *Constant Linear Velocity (CLV)*. Figure 3.4 illustrates constant linear velocity. Information about the location of files is stored in the *path table* and the *directory table*, which are located near the beginning of the disc. These tables are created when the disc is manufactured and cannot be changed. The path table contains the file and directory information in a tree-like format, and the directory table contains the address of each directory in an index.

Figure 3.3
Contiguous
sectors.

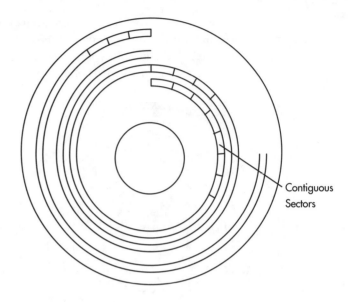

Contiguous
Sectors

Figure 3.4
Constant Linear
Velocity (CLV).

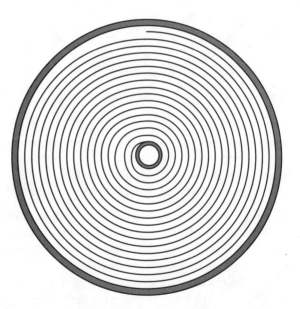

When you access a file, the optical head travels to the approximate location of the data, positions itself within the spiral track, and then refocuses to read the data. The disc's rate of spin must speed up or slow down along the way, which is why a

CD-ROM drive takes longer to find data than a hard drive. Magnetic hard disks contain several hundred concentric tracks per inch, but CD-ROMs contain up to 16,000 tracks per inch. When the optical head reads sequential sectors, it must move radially to stay focused within the spiral track as the data passes. The rate of disc spin must decrease gradually as the optical head moves toward the outer edge of the disc.

The way in which CD-ROM drives retrieve information from a disc makes the location of files an important factor in the performance of applications. Files near the beginning of the disc can be accessed much more quickly than files at the outer edge. Related files should be placed close together to decrease seek time. Installation files, which may be used only once, should be placed at the end of the spiral track. This process is called *optimization*.

For more information on disc optimization, see Chapter 10.

Most CD-ROM development software includes optimization programs that can rearrange files so that the most frequently accessed files are located at the beginning of the disc.

Although the CD-ROM is not a replacement for a hard disk, it definitely is an enhancement. One of the uses of CD-ROM is as an archival medium that is impervious to corruption. Imagine how handy it would be to have a copy of your software programs, your entire hard disk, or your network file server on a CD-ROM if your system crashes or is infected by a virus.

Buying a CD-ROM Drive

Before you purchase a CD-ROM drive you may want to consider factors such as hardware requirements, price, availability, and features. The following sections discuss the information you should know before you look for a drive.

Hardware Requirements

You do not need any special computer equipment to run a CD-ROM drive. CD-ROM drives can run on IBM PC, XT, AT, 386sx, 386, 486sx, 486, Pentium, or any 100 percent IBM-compatible computer with an open expansion slot for the CD-ROM drive interface card or an existing SCSI interface card. SCSI-based CD-ROM drives also work on Macintosh, high-end workstations such as Sun, and, with additional hardware, on some minicomputers.

You do not need a hard disk to use a CD-ROM drive. You may find, however, that the retrieval software of certain CD-ROM discs require more disk space than is available on a floppy-based system. You should always check the magnetic disk space requirements of a particular disc before you purchase it. As retrieval software becomes more efficient, more CD-ROMs may allow the retrieval software to run directly from the CD-ROM disc without much performance degradation.

Price

CD-ROM drives are made by most large electronics manufacturers. Sony, Toshiba, Hitachi, NEC, Panasonic, Magnavox, and other manufacturers all make CD-ROM drives. With so many different drives available today, you most certainly can find one that fits your needs and budget. Drive prices are constantly getting lower, and you should find a drive for between $120 and $800.

Many CD-ROM bundles are available that contain the drive and packaged CD-ROM discs. See Appendix A for a list of popular CD-ROM bundles.

You can buy a fast and reliable drive for as little as $300. You can buy a reliable but slow drive for as little as $120. Price, however, does not necessarily reflect the value of a CD-ROM drive. Just as with every commodity, the price includes such factors as a recognized name, marketing expenses, packaging, and distribution channels. Look for a fast drive that comes with lots of CD-ROM discs that contain information you want and need. Bundles such as these are readily available.

Availability

CD-ROM drives are available from a variety of sources, ranging from CD-ROM specialty houses to department stores. A current trend in CD-ROM drive marketing is to offer "bundles." These bundles are available from catalogs or computer stores. If your local computer store does not carry CD-ROM drives, it can order a

drive for you. Discount dealers that advertise in computer magazines offer great prices, but if you are buying your first CD-ROM drive, you may want local support.

For more information on obtaining CD-ROM drives, see Appendix A.

If you are concerned about installing your own drive, buy from a dealer who offers installation service. If you are interested in installing your own drive, Chapter 5 offers installation instructions.

Features To Consider

What are some of the important features to look for when you purchase a CD-ROM drive? Along with price considerations, you should consider speed and reliability. The following sections describe some of the features you should look for.

Speed

The CD-ROM drive is the slowest component of a workstation. Its speed can make a big difference in the performance of CD-ROM applications. If you plan to buy multimedia applications that contain full-motion video, speed makes a huge difference in the quality of the video playback. Modern CD-ROM drive speeds vary from 185 milliseconds to 500 milliseconds. The lower the figure, the higher the speed.

Multimedia may be the technology that makes CD-ROM a requirement for a personal computer. It makes sense to buy a CD-ROM drive that is fast enough to take full advantage of this technology.

Seek Time

Also known as *access time*, *seek time* refers to the speed at which the drive can get to the requested data. Because the disc is spinning at a variable rate of speed depending on the location of the optical read head, the access time involves the speeding up or slowing down of the turntable as well as the movement of the optical head to the desired data location. At this time, the fastest drives claim 185-millisecond access speeds, though most drives are in the 250- to 400-millisecond range.

Data Buffer Size

The CD-ROM drive contains a *buffer*, or built-in memory, that stores read-ahead data. The larger the buffer size, the more data can be accessed directly from memory, which saves a time-consuming seek. Suppose, for example, that you conduct a search for a certain term on a CD-ROM disc that contains a collection of magazine articles. The article you want to see is several pages long and does not fit on your computer screen all at once. The CD-ROM drive reads ahead and stores the entire article in memory so that when you are ready to read the next page, the data is read from the buffer rather than from the disc. The minimum size of this buffer should be 64K.

Data Transfer Speed

Another factor affecting speed is the rate at which data can be read from the CD-ROM disc after it has been located. A sustained data transfer rate of at least 150K per second is required to ensure a continuous flow of data through the buffer. This rate is also called *continuous read*. Drives that do not have this capability produce motion video displays that flicker. This feature is important for multimedia discs.

Until recently, the standard data transfer rate for CD-ROM drives was 150K per second. Recently, many drive manufacturers have introduced double-speed or "Double Spin" drives. Some, most notably NEC and Pioneer, have introduced triple-speed and quad-speed drives.

A double-speed drive spins the disc at 400 to 1000 rpm. This allows the read head to gather data faster as the spiral track passes beneath it. Data transfer rates for double-speed drives are 300K per second. This allows faster access to data and smoother video in multimedia applications. However, when the drive is requested to play a Red Book audio track, the drive must slow down or "put on the brakes" because audio must be played at 75 sectors (150,000 bytes) per second. This may cause a slight delay in starting an audio track when a program requests it.

It appears that the increasing throughput demands made by many multimedia titles are causing drive manufacturers to de-emphasize 150K per second drives. Soon, most CD-ROM drives will be at least double-speed drives. As an example, Texel, Toshiba, and NEC no longer make single-speed drives.

Triple-speed and quad-speed drives increase the disc rotation speed and the data transfer rate proportionately, so a triple-speed drive should transfer data at 450K per second and a quad-speed drive should transfer data at 600K per second. These are theoretical transfer times and in real world use, the data transfer rate may be slightly slower than these figures.

When shopping for a drive, get a double-speed or faster drive if you can afford one. Although few CD-ROM applications today require a double-speed drive, in the future many applications will be written to take advantage of increased data transfer rate.

Compatibility

Many modern drives are multisession compatible and XA ready. While this may not mean much today, these capabilities will allow you to use your existing drive, possibly with an upgraded controller or device driver, when CD-ROM XA and multisession discs become more commonplace. Many drives are called "Photo CD capable," but this does not mean that they are fully CD-ROM XA capable. Kodak's Photo CD format currently uses only Mode 2 Form 1 tracks. For true XA capability, the drive must be able to read Mode 2, Forms 1 and 2.

As of this writing, a new universal logical file format has not yet been defined for multisession, or recordable, appendable media. However, the method of appending data used today is based on the Bridge Disc standard, and the new file format, when it appears, will be backward-compatible so that today's multisession drive will be able to read finalized multisession discs. For more information about multisession capabilities and compatibility, see Chapter 13.

Reliability

No matter how fast your drive is, it is not much good if it cannot read your discs. Several factors determine the reliability of a given CD-ROM drive, but these factors can be divided into two general areas: physical and logical.

Physical failures are produced by the servo motors that control the turntable, the swing arm or sled that moves the optical head, and the tracking and focus of the laser beam. Mean Time Between Failures (MTBF) measures the likelihood of a physical malfunction of these parts. MTBF can range from 15,000 to 50,000 hours. In this case, the higher the figure, the better.

You can calculate the expected life span of a CD-ROM drive by dividing the MTBF figure by hours of daily use, then by 365. The result is the number of years before the drive will probably fail. Note that other factors, such as environment, heat, and rough handling, also can greatly reduce the life span of a CD-ROM drive.

Logical failures are produced when the drive cannot recover errors from damaged or poorly manufactured discs. Although the error-correction code on every

CD-ROM disc must conform to the Yellow Book standard, manufacturers of CD-ROM drives are not required to implement the EDC/ECC decoders on their drives to take full advantage of it. Pinholes in the reflective layer, scratches, and dust on the disc surface produce errors that can be corrected to a greater or lesser degree depending on the extent to which the built-in error-correction code is used by the drive manufacturer.

You do not need to study the manufacturer's technical documentation to discover the precise algorithm used for error correction. If you can try a drive before you buy it, lay a strip of opaque tape about one-sixteenth of an inch wide radially across the data surface of a disc (see fig. 3.5). The disc should be one you are familiar with so that you can judge how its performance is affected. Demo discs are good for this purpose because they are free and you do not lose data if the disc becomes scratched. A CD-ROM disc that is scratched and dirty is even better because it more closely represents the damage a CD-ROM disc encounters in the real world.

Figure 3.5
CD-ROM torture
test disc.

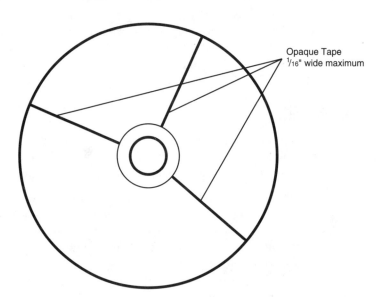

Opaque Tape
$1/16$" wide maximum

If the tape is too wide, the drive cannot read the disc at all. Make sure that the tape is narrow enough so that the disc can be read. Try two strips of tape and then three strips of tape. Make sure that the tape does not hang over the edge of the disc and that it adheres to the surface. Although the tape cannot hurt the disc, it may get stuck to the turntable or the inside of the disc caddy.

The idea is to create a *torture disc* that is just barely readable. Try this disc first with the most expensive drive you can find, then use the disc to test other drives. The error-correction electronics of the drive work to recover the data that is obscured by the tape. The access time of the disc can slow down, or you may not be able to read the disc at all, depending on how effectively the error correction is implemented by the drive. After a few tries, you will know where to look on the disc for information that is affected by the tape.

Examining Drive Specifications and Functions

Before you purchase a CD-ROM drive, you should understand the features and functions so that you can make an educated purchase. Most CD-ROM drives are available in both internal and external models. The external drives always cost more because of the additional cost of the power supply, cabinet, and the external cable.

If you have an open drive bay on your computer that you are not going to use for the addition of a tape drive or additional floppy or hard drive, an internal drive is a good option (see fig. 3.6). Internal drives save desk space and are cheaper than external drives. Even if you do not seem to have a free drive bay, you may be able to use an internal drive. Many computers have the hard drive mounted in an exposed 5 1/4-inch drive bay. Depending on your case's configuration, you may be able to mount your hard drive elsewhere in the case in an unexposed drive bay. Unlike CD-ROM drives, a hard drive does not have to be accessed to eject or insert the CD-ROM disc.

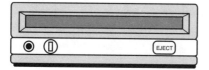

Figure 3.6
An internal CD-ROM drive (player).

You may choose an external drive for several reasons (see fig. 3.7). You may not have an exposed drive bay on your computer. If you want to move the drive to different computers, choosing an external drive makes more sense. You may want to add more CD-ROM drives later or network your drives.

II

Understanding the Hardware

Figure 3.7
An external CD-
ROM drive
(player).

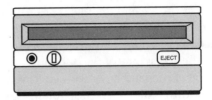

SCSI and Bus Interfaces

CD-ROM drives generally use the SCSI interface to connect them to the host
computer. *SCSI* (pronounced "scuzzy") stands for Small Computer System Interface. SCSI interface cards are made by various manufacturers and are available in
8-bit, 16-bit, and 32-bit EISA and MCA models. SCSI interface cards have a high
data transfer rate and are widely available.

The main advantage of the SCSI interface, however, is its capacity to control up to
eight computer peripherals, such as a CD-ROM drive, scanner, tape backup, and
magneto optical drive, while only taking up one expansion slot in the computer.
The devices connected to a SCSI card by the SCSI cable are referred to as the *SCSI
bus* or a *SCSI chain.* Figure 3.8 illustrates a SCSI bus.

Figure 3.8
A SCSI bus.

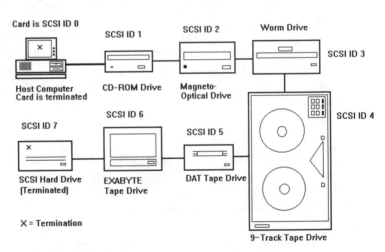

If you plan to add other SCSI peripherals to your computer, a SCSI interface is the
solution. A single card can control up to eight SCSI devices. Some SCSI cards use a
SCSI ID for themselves, while others do not. If your SCSI card does take a SCSI ID,
you can attach up to seven devices. If the card does not take a SCSI ID, you can
attach up to eight devices to the card. Because SCSI is an industry standard, all

SCSI CD-ROM drives should work with the same SCSI card. Additionally, should you need to replace an inoperative CD-ROM drive, any SCSI drive will work with the card you have. You do not need to purchase another interface card. This compatibility also extends to the SCSI card. If you need to replace your SCSI card, you can purchase a card from any manufacturer. Figure 3.9 shows an 8-bit SCSI interface card. Figure 3.10 shows a 16-bit SCSI interface card.

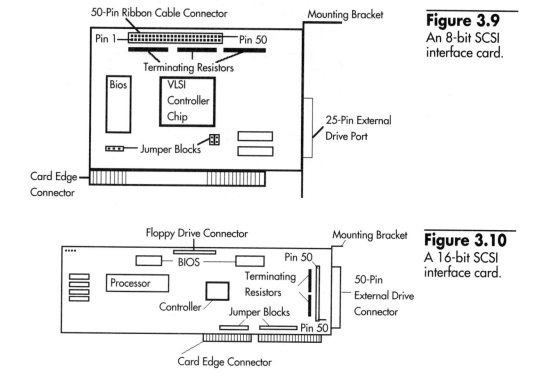

Figure 3.9
An 8-bit SCSI interface card.

Figure 3.10
A 16-bit SCSI interface card.

Many manufacturers sell their CD-ROM drives with their own proprietary interface, called a *bus interface* (see fig. 3.11). This interface card is designed by the manufacturer to work specifically with its drive. The advantage of a bus interface is that, when supplied with a CD-ROM drive, it is usually cheaper than a drive that comes with a SCSI card. Because the interface card is designed to control a particular drive, the manufacturer may be able to produce a faster data transfer rate than it can with a SCSI drive.

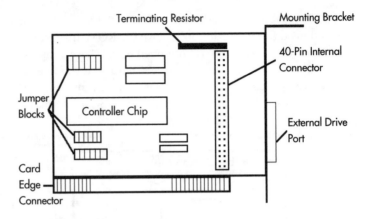

Figure 3.11
A bus interface card.

A bus interface has the following disadvantages:

✔ The card works only with the drive brand, and possibly model, for which it was designed.

✔ You may not be able to attach more than one drive to the card, even if it is from the same manufacturer.

✔ You cannot attach any device other than CD-ROM drives to the card.

Additionally, if the bus interface card goes bad, you may find it harder to obtain a new card, and the card will cost more than a SCSI card. You can replace a SCSI card with a card from any manufacturer, and it will work with your existing CD-ROM drive and other SCSI peripherals.

If you do not plan to add other peripherals to your computer and you are operating under a tight budget, the bus interface will work for you. If you want to add SCSI peripherals to your computer, a SCSI interface card is the better alternative.

Other Interfaces

CD-ROM drives are also available with IDE (Integrated Drive Electronics) interfaces. These drives make it unnecessary to add an additional interface card if your computer already has an IDE hard drive installed.

Drives that connect to your computer's parallel port are also available. These drives make it unnecessary to open the computer to add an interface card. They simply plug into the printer port on your PC. Parallel port CD-ROM drives include a pass-through connector for your printer cable.

If you need to move your drive from computer to computer, you should consider a parallel to SCSI adapter (available from Trantor Systems). This adapter allows

a SCSI drive to be connected to your computer's parallel port. It includes a pass-through for your printer cable. Be aware, though, that data transfer rates through the parallel port will be slower than the transfer rates you can obtain with a SCSI, IDE, or bus interface.

Audio Function

One of the benefits of having a CD-ROM drive is being able to listen to your CD audio discs while you work.

Most drives have a CD audio jack and volume control built in. The jack can be on the front of the drive or on the back. A jack on the front of the drive enables you to have easier access (see fig. 3.12), but a jack on the back keeps cables out of the way (see fig. 3.13). If you plan to use any discs that contain true Red Book audio, such as *National Geographic's Mammals,* or if you want to play audio CDs on your system, make sure that the drive has audio capabilities.

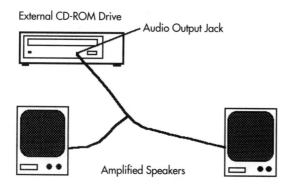

Figure 3.12
CD audio setup, front audio jack.

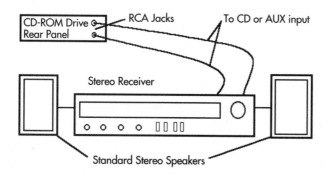

Figure 3.13
CD audio setup, rear audio jacks.

Many drives come with software that enables you to play regular CD audio discs on the CD-ROM drive. Audio software also is available from third-party vendors. You also need headphones or amplified speakers to take advantage of the audio features of a drive. The small headphones that come with portable cassette players or radios are sufficient.

Top-Loading and Front-Loading Drives

CD-ROM drives have two types of loading mechanisms. Most drives are front-loading and use a disc caddy to hold the disc (see fig. 3.14). Fortunately, with few exceptions, such as some older LMSI drives, disc caddies are standard. The caddy that comes with your drive works in other drives that use a disc caddy. The caddy protects the disc from scratches and dust. If you load a disc into a front-loading drive, an extra step is involved. After you remove the disc from its storage box (also known as the jewel case), you must place the disc in the caddy.

Figure 3.14
Front-loading drive and caddy.

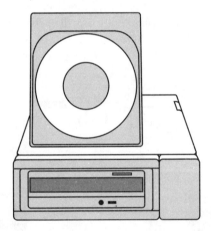

Another feature to look for in a drive is an emergency eject function. If your drive fails or your power supply quits, you may have a valuable disc stuck in the drive and no way to get it out. Some drives have a backup manual eject feature that enables you to eject a disc even if the drive is not working. Some drives eject manually so that removing a disc from a nonworking drive is not a problem.

Tip

If you must change discs often, you can buy additional caddies to hold and store your most-used discs. Extra caddies cost from $6 to $14.

Top-loading drives also are available (see fig. 3.15). These drives accept discs without caddies and save a step in loading a disc. Note, however, that with many of the top-loading drives, the whole drive mechanism slides out to accept the disc. Make sure that you have enough clearance between the drive and your keyboard to ensure unobstructed opening of the drive. With top-loading drives, you must handle discs more than if you store the discs in individual caddies.

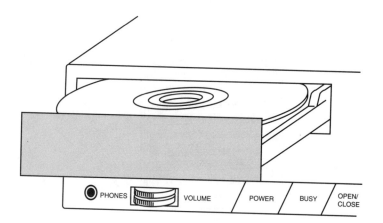

Figure 3.15
Top-loading drive.

Autochangers and Multiple Drive Units

Autochangers or "jukeboxes" are available for CD-ROM drives that accept from 6 to 240 discs. An autochanger is useful if you must access multiple discs frequently and do not want to constantly change discs. The Pioneer DRM 600 and DRM 604X six-disc autochangers are the most practical for the personal computer user. These changers come with additional software that controls the switching of discs, and they use a standard six-disc cartridge, just like the ones used for CD audio players (see fig. 3.16).

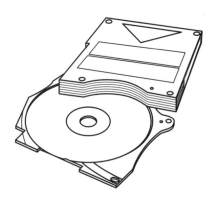

Figure 3.16
A six-disc cartridge.

II

Understanding the Hardware

Multiple drive CD-ROM subsystems also are available from several manufacturers (see fig. 3.17). These systems are useful if the CD-ROM application extends over more than one disc (some applications require as many as 100 discs), and are most useful and cost-effective in the network environment.

Figure 3.17
A four-drive
subsystem.

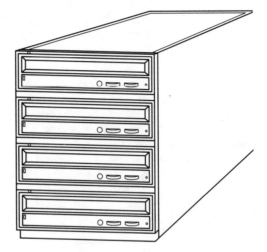

Summary

In this chapter, you learned the way in which a CD-ROM drive functions, the read-only nature of CD-ROM discs, the way data is laid out on the disc, and how the drive reads data from the disc. You also learned about drive specifications and functions, SCSI and bus interfaces, front-loading and top-loading drives, and the audio functions of a CD-ROM drive. CD-ROM jukeboxes and multiple drive units, which are mentioned in this chapter, are covered in more detail in Chapter 6.

Chapter 4 discusses CD-ROM discs. You learn how discs are manufactured, where to get discs, and how to install them. This chapter also discusses the Microsoft Extensions, a program that you must use to access most CD-ROM discs on the IBM PC platform.

CHAPTER

CD-ROM Discs

This chapter discusses aspects of CD-ROM discs. You learn about the physical characteristics of CD-ROM discs, as well as how they are manufactured. You learn where you can purchase CD-ROM applications, how to install them, and how to take care of discs.

Many people think that information is stored on a compact disc in the same way that audio information is stored on LPs. Actually, LP records and compact discs store information in completely different ways. Both are circular platters that spin and contain audio signals in a spiral track, but that is where the similarity ends.

An LP record stores audio signals as analog data, which is as a representation of a continuous and variable process. As the needle on the phonograph follows the groove, the phonograph's cartridge converts the mechanical movements of the needle into an analog signal that is amplified and played through speakers. If the sound of a loud drum were recorded on a record, for example, you could see the physical variations in the groove.

Compact discs, whether audio or CD-ROM, store information digitally, as numbers. These numbers are represented by *pits*, or bumps, and flat places, or *lands*, laid out in a spiral track that starts near the center or hub of the disc. Pits are always the same depth and width, although their length and the length of the spaces that separate them may vary. When the laser beam inside a CD audio player or CD-ROM drive shines on a CD audio or CD-ROM disc, the pits and lands scatter the light or reflect it directly back. The variations of the reflected laser light are interpreted by the electronics within the drive and converted into numbers, which are then converted to a representation of the original sound or data.

Have you ever wondered why a compact disc appears to reflect light in a spectrum, or rainbow effect? This division of light is because of the thousands of tracks on the disc. These tracks disperse light rays as a diffraction grid, or prism, breaking white light into different wavelengths. A compact disc contains up to 16,000 revolutions of the track per inch, or 20,000 revolutions per disc. All CDs, whether audio or data, contain a spiral track. This track starts at the center hub of the disc and continues until it reaches the outer edge of the disc—a distance equal to three miles.

Physical Characteristics

Compact discs are 12 centimeters (4 3/4 inch) in diameter, just over a millimeter thick, and weigh about half an ounce. A disc's physical composition consists of clear polycarbonate, a very thin layer of aluminum, and a lacquer protective coating. A CD-ROM disc can hold up to 680M of data—text, images, graphics, sound, and animation. Data is stored in the form of microscopic pits arranged in a single spiral track. A *pit* is about a half-micron wide—about the size of 500 hydrogen atoms laid end-to-end—with a single CD-ROM containing approximately 2.8 billion pits. Figure 4.1 shows the size of a CD-ROM track compared to a human hair.

A disc's physical composition consists of an injection-molded platter of polycarbonate, a very thin layer of aluminum, and a lacquer protective coating on top.

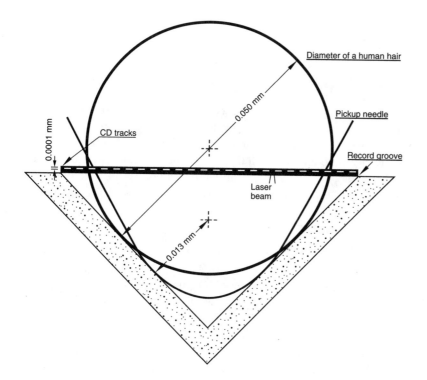

Figure 4.1
Size of CD-ROM tracks.

Understanding the Manufacturing Process

Most of the manufacturing process for CD audio and CD-ROM discs is identical. A preliminary step, called premastering, converts audio or data into a format that can be recorded to compact disc, and differs slightly according to the type of data to be stored on the mass-produced disc. Many discs, called mixed-mode discs, contain both CD audio and CD-ROM data. If a disc has both kinds of data, the first track will always be CD-ROM, and the disc will be treated as a CD-ROM disc. Quality control and testing are more stringent for CD-ROM than for CD audio, for the same reasons that error detection and correction are more complex for CD-ROM. The manufacture of a CD can be broken down into five steps:

✔ Premastering

✔ Mastering

✔ Electroforming

✔ Injection molding

✔ Spin coating and printing

Audio Premastering

Audio premastering is the first step in the process of placing audio data on compact disc. Audio programs arrive on analog or digital master tape, and are transferred to U-matic tape using a digital audio processor. Using a CD subcode processor/editor, the audio engineer will then enter the preliminary required data such as title, artist, catalog number, UPC number, index points (indicate the beginning of tracks), and track titles. The end result is known as a CD tape master.

CD-ROM Premastering

Data to be published on CD-ROM may arrive at the manufacturing plant in many different formats. Among the most common are 9-track, 8mm Exabyte, and DAT tape, but many mastering facilities also accept MO (magneto optical) cartridges and SCSI hard drives. Before this data can be used to create a compact disc, it must be put into the correct format for CD-ROM, CD-I, CD-ROM XA, or CD Video. In addition, EDC/ECC (error detection code/error correction code) must be added where necessary. Increasingly, data arrives already recorded in its final CD format, complete with error detection/correction, on CD-Recordable media. Either U-matic tape or CD-R discs can be used as input for the next step, which is the creation of a glass master.

Mastering

Mastering is the process of using an LBR (Laser Beam Recorder) to etch the audio or computer data, in the form of microscopic pits, into either a layer of photoresist or plastic on a glass master disc, which is then electroplated with silver or nickel to form a metal stamper.

Photoresist mastering requires several steps. First, a highly polished glass disc is coated with adhesive and an even layer of photoresist, and then baked to "cure" the photoresist. Then, the photoresist is exposed to the laser beam, which etches a pattern of pits and lands into the photoresist layer. The glass master is then "developed" in a chemical bath, which cuts away areas exposed to the laser beam. Finally, a metal coating is evaporated onto the etched, developed, photoresist layer. At this point, the master can be tested on a master player. This method is very difficult and time-consuming, with many critical steps and stringent humidity, temperature, and air quality requirements. Despite the difficulties of this method, it produces high-quality masters and is used in most first-, second-, and third-generation plants.

NPR (Non-Photo Resist), also called DRAW (Direct Read After Write) mastering, also starts with a glass master, but the glass is coated with a layer of plastic, which is then vaporized in a pattern of pits and lands by the LBR. A reading laser follows the cutting laser to check the integrity of the cut directly after it is made. This eliminates the chemicals used in adhesive and photoresist, and the baking and development processes, as well as the necessity for a master player to test the disc. Masters can be created two to three times faster than with the photoresist method, and any errors can be detected immediately. The NPR process assures improved efficiency, yield, and productivity over photoresist mastering and is more environmentally friendly. As in photoresist mastering, the final step is to evaporate a metal coating onto the etched layer of plastic. The metal layer makes the glass master electrically conductive.

Electroforming

Once the glass master has been written, tested, and silvered, it is ready to be electroplated. The now-electrically conductive disc is placed in a reservoir holding an electrolyte solution (nickel sulphamate). Electrical current is applied at a low level and gradually increased, producing a metal part of sufficient thickness in about two hours.

If the number of replications of this particular disc is expected to be 10,000 or less, this nickel copy, called the metal "father," can be used as a stamper to replicate CDs. Otherwise, the metal father is returned to the electroplating process to create metal "mothers," which are in turn used to generate metal "sons," which are the stampers used in molds to replicate CDs. Often, the metal "family" is stored for future reorders. Glass masters can be washed and reused many times.

Replication

Injection-molding techniques are most commonly used to stamp out thousands of copies of a disc in polycarbonate. Polycarbonate was chosen because of its transparency, dimensional stability, impact resistance, and freedom from impurities.

Polycarbonate, in the form of pellets, is heated to about 350 degrees centigrade to achieve smooth flow properties when injected into mold cavities. The molds themselves are finely machined so that the resulting disc is flat, centered, and free of optical distortion and impurities. Because the molded polycarbonate would harden slowly at room temperature, channels are carefully designed as part of the molds so that the formed disc can be cooled and hardened quickly and evenly. At this stage of the process, the compact disc is a clear plastic platter with microscopic pits molded into one side.

Metalization, Spin Coating, and Printing

For the disc to be readable by a laser beam, it must reflect laser light. Four metals are inert to polycarbonate and have sufficient reflective properties to be used as a reflective layer: gold, silver, copper, and aluminum. Aluminum is the most cost-efficient, although CD-R discs use gold for its greater reflectivity. An extremely thin layer of metal (50 to 100 nanometers) can be applied to the plastic disc via vacuum evaporation, sputtering, or wet silvering. To protect the metal from scratches and oxidation, a thin layer of acrylic plastic is applied by spin-coating and then curing in ultraviolet light. The molded, metalized, spin-coated disc can now be silk screen-printed in up to five colors, or labeled with a special non-impact offset printing process. The disc is now finished and ready to be packaged and shipped. The time from raw polycarbonate to labeling is under two minutes, and a single replication line is capable of producing two million discs per year.

Quality Control

Discs are tested at various points in the manufacturing process for correct dimensions, birefringence, reflectivity, flatness (skew), and appearance. The pit surface is checked for pit depth, volume, form, and dimensions. Modern manufacturing plants achieve the highest possible quality control by combining 100 percent automated inspection of discs with human visual inspection for cosmetic defects.

Figure 4.2 shows the manufacturing process for a CD-ROM.

 Birefringence, also called *double refraction,* occurs when a light wave breaks into two perpendicular waves upon entering the clear polycarbonate. A birefringent disc would scatter laser light and be very difficult to read.

When a CD-ROM drive reads a disc, the drive's photodetector measures reflections from a laser beam focused on the track. Reflections vary in intensity when the light hits the pits and the alternating flat areas that lie between the pits called *lands.* The fluctuations in the reflected light are converted to digital data that is decoded by the CD player or CD-ROM drive into music or data. Figure 4.3 shows how the light is dispersed.

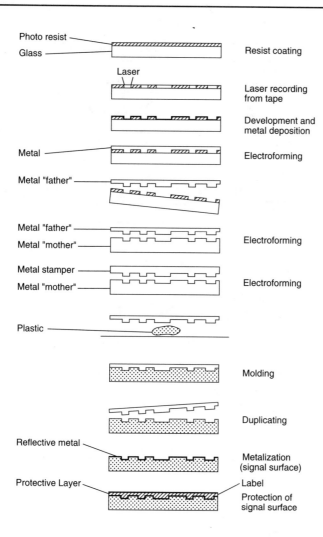

Photo resist
Glass — Resist coating

Laser
Laser recording from tape

Development and metal deposition

Metal — Electroforming

Metal "father" —

Metal "father" —
Metal "mother" — Electroforming

Metal stamper —
Metal "mother" — Electroforming

Plastic —

Molding

Duplicating

Reflective metal — Metalization (signal surface)

Protective Layer — Label
Protection of signal surface

Figure 4.2
The manufacturing process.

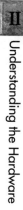

II

Understanding the Hardware

Figure 4.3
Reflection from
pits and lands.

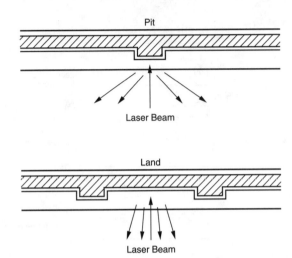

Pit

Laser Beam

Land

Laser Beam

Information Available on Disc

CD-ROM discs are usually referred to as applications or titles. Their contents can
be anything—a full technical manual, complete with a parts catalog for the Boeing
757, the complete works of Shakespeare, pornographic pictures, a pollution and
toxicology database, clip art, games, bankruptcy law, computer operating systems,
maps—virtually anything. Currently, more than 6,000 CD-ROM titles are available,
with new titles coming out every day. There are so many existing titles that it would
take an entire book in itself—or a CD-ROM—to list all the discs on the market. If
you can imagine it, you can probably purchase it on CD-ROM. Some popular discs
are reviewed in Chapter 8.

Currently, more than 6,000 CD-ROM titles are available. New titles
are announced every day.

Most CD-ROM applications fit easily into the 680M of space available on a single
CD-ROM disc. Some applications, however, span over 100 discs. These applications
generally are not commercially available because they are used to hold data such as
government engineering specifications or geophysical information. Almost all
commercially available titles are limited to one-, two-, or possibly three-disc sets.
You do not usually need a CD-ROM drive for each disc. The search and retrieval

software usually is written to request the insertion of the correct disc if the data you are seeking is not the disc currently in the drive.

Although CD-ROM discs are available for all kinds of computers, this book covers only CD-ROM titles for IBM and compatible personal computers.

Buying Discs

The most common sources for CD-ROM titles are catalogs distributed by CD-ROM publishers and distributors. Chapter 8 contains a list of publishers, distributors, and catalogs of CD-ROM titles. Many computer stores, and even bookstores, now carry CD-ROM titles. Many software vendors are starting to make their programs available on CD-ROM.

Setting Up a CD-ROM Application

Each CD-ROM application includes its own search and retrieval software that usually must be installed on your PC before the information on the disc is accessible. If your CD-ROM drive is not yet installed, see Chapter 5 for instructions and tips on installing a CD-ROM drive.

Assigning a Microsoft Extensions Drive Letter

First, you must install Microsoft Extensions for CD-ROM, which assigns a drive letter to your CD-ROM drive. Most CD-ROM drives come with this program and an automatic installation program for it, and Microsoft Extensions is now included in versions of MS-DOS 6.0 and over. This simple process is done once, when the CD-ROM drive itself is installed. However, since every drive supplier writes their own version of the installation program, it is impossible to explain each one here. Read the instructions that come with the Microsoft Extensions disk, or with MS-DOS. You may need to know the type of computer you are using, the make and model number of the CD-ROM drive, and possibly the make and model number of the interface card. If you still cannot get things to work, call the technical support number provided with the Extensions package, the CD-ROM drive, or one of the CD-ROM titles you may already have.

Installing a Disc

A CD-ROM disc comes with an installation program that either resides on the disc itself or on a floppy disk that comes with it. Usually there are instructions on a liner inside the jewel case and README files on the disc that contain help, hints, and technical support phone numbers. In some cases, an installation and reference manual is included.

If you want to wing it, try this: Insert the disc in your drive. The label goes up, so you can read it through the clear side of the caddy, if you are using one. Wait a few seconds for the disc to "spin up," then change to the drive letter assigned by Microsoft Extensions to the CD-ROM drive. (If you did not specify a drive letter in the installation, the letter is the drive letter following the last hard drive letter. For example, if your hard drive is C:, your CD-ROM drive will be D:.) Now type **DIR** and press Enter. A listing of the disc's contents appears, containing files and directories, just as if it were a magnetic disk. Figure 4.4 shows an example of a CD-ROM directory.

Figure 4.4

Directory of a CD-ROM disc.

```
D:\>dir

 Volume in drive D is MOV_CAT
 Directory of D:\

ASI           <DIR>      02-20-90    1:37p
ASI     BAT    103 02-20-90    1:22p
BIBLE         <DIR>      02-20-90    1:39p
BIBLE   BAT     47 02-20-90   11:50a
MOVIE         <DIR>      02-20-90    1:35p
MOVIE   BAT     46 02-20-90   12:20p
PCGUIDE BAT     52 02-20-90    1:21p
PC_GUIDE      <DIR>      02-20-90    1:37p
RWINTRO       <DIR>      02-20-90    1:39p
RWINTRO BAT    344 02-20-90    1:29p
        10 file(s)         592 bytes
                             0 bytes free

D:\>
```

Notice that the file names are in alphabetical order. This order, which is unrelated to the actual location of files on the disc, is required by the ISO 9660 format. The ISO 9660 format specifies that files be presented in alphabetical order. Also, look at the bottom of the screen where bytes free appears. The information supplied here always indicates there are 0 bytes free on the CD-ROM disc. This inaccuracy is a result of the relationship between Extensions and DOS. Extensions enables DOS commands to access the disc and, because DOS is unaware of the existence of CD-ROM, Extensions fools DOS into treating the CD-ROM as one big write-protected

hard disk. All DOS knows about the CD-ROM disc is that the system cannot be written to and assumes that it has no free space.

Before proceeding, be aware that the installation program could do any of several things to your system that you may not like. The program may add lines to your CONFIG.SYS and AUTOEXEC.BAT files, write files to the subdirectory you are currently in or to a directory of its own creation that may have the same name as a directory that already exists. Be particularly cautious with Windows applications— some multimedia discs can produce problems when installed in 386-Enhanced mode. Try installing Windows applications while running Windows in Standard mode first with no other programs open. To do this, at the command prompt, type **win/s**. To be safe, read the directions first.

Now look for a file called "INSTALL," "SETUP," or anything with an EXE, COM, or BAT file extension. "INSTALL" is most common. Type **INSTALL** and press Enter.

If the disc contains a Windows application, you get a message such as, "This application requires Microsoft Windows." In this case, start Windows and choose "RUN" from the File menu, and type "D:\SETUP" (where D: is the CD-ROM drive letter), or open the File Manager, select the CD-ROM drive letter, and double click on the install or setup program.

You may be prompted to enter the letter of your hard drive, the letter of your CD-ROM drive, the Microsoft Extensions CD-ROM device driver name (see Chapter 5), the type of computer, the type of monitor, the name of the subdirectory in which you want the software installed, or even the name of the batch file to be created to run the program. When in doubt, take the default. You may not be asked for any input at all. The installation program normally proceeds to write all the necessary files to a subdirectory on your hard disk (or wherever you specify), create a batch file, and possibly alter your CONFIG.SYS and AUTOEXEC.BAT files, with or without asking your permission. Titles that run in the Windows environment will usually create a program group. To be safe, make copies of your AUTOEXEC.BAT and CONFIG.SYS files before you install any CD-ROM disc.

The last thing the installation program usually does is tell you what to do to access the disc—usually enter the name of the .BAT file or click on the icon in Windows. Most applications include help and on-screen directions, but if you get in trouble and cannot get out, reboot and try again.

II

Understanding the Hardware

If you find no installation program and no README file, be really daring and type the name of a batch (.BAT) or executable (.EXE or .COM) file. This step usually starts the program running directly from the CD-ROM, with or without using the hard drive for temporary files. If no executable files are on the disc, the search software and installation program are probably on a floppy disk that accompanies the CD-ROM disc.

Avoiding Problems

Many CD-ROM developers incorrectly assume that once people have a CD-ROM drive, they will use only one application in it, buy applications from only one CD-ROM publisher, or use only one search software. The installation programs from these CD-ROM developers frequently have unusual requirements—they may change path statements, insert unique parameter settings, take up huge amounts of hard disk space, or insist upon a specific drive letter, subdirectory location, or device driver name that would make it difficult to run other applications. These requirements are not intentional acts designed to discourage purchasers from using other CD-ROM applications, merely a lack of foresight on the part of the CD-ROM developers. The bottom line is this: the best discs are those that install flexibly, run cleanly and quickly, do not demand large amounts of disk space or memory, and do not interfere with other applications. The world's most fascinating data is only as good as its accessibility.

Many of the larger CD-ROM publishers make demo discs available so that you can get an idea of what a program is like before you buy it. Free "sampler" discs are available as well. These items are good not only because you can "try before you buy," but because they can demonstrate the incredible versatility and capacity of CD-ROM with very little investment on your part.

Many of the larger CD-ROM publishers make demo discs available so that you can get an idea of what a program is like before you buy it.

Using Magnetic Media To Run CD-ROM Applications

Even though a CD-ROM holds much information, floppy or hard disk space is still necessary. As the indexed data and indexes are delivered on the CD-ROM, search software sometimes is delivered on floppy disks. This practice was established during CD-ROM's early days and is continued by some disc publishers today, although most disc publishers now include installation, search, and retrieval programs on the CD-ROM disc. To access the data on the CD-ROM, the search program must be run from the floppy disk or copied from the floppy disk or CD-ROM disc to a subdirectory on your hard drive. While the data can be accessed by running the search software from the floppy disk, there are several good reasons to run the search software from the hard drive.

First, if the search software is located on your hard disk, loading and accessing the search software is faster because of the speed of a hard disk relative to the speed of a CD-ROM drive or floppy drive. Most modern hard disks have access times of 12–28 milliseconds, whereas the fastest access time on a CD-ROM drive is 185 milliseconds. Many of the lower-priced drives have access times of up to 500 milliseconds (1/2 second).

Second, many search softwares must be able to write temporary files to some magnetic disk—files which may later be erased or overwritten. These files are used by the search software to store temporary search results and search strategies. If you want to try your search several ways, or if you want to do several searches and compare them or print them out, these files are stored for you until you stop using the CD-ROM. Since you cannot write to the CD-ROM disc, the search software writes these files on the hard disk where it is located, or to any specified magnetic disk.

Third, if a CD-ROM disc is completely full, supplying the search software on floppies that are subsequently loaded to the hard drive leaves more room on the CD-ROM for data.

Fourth, if a CD-ROM contains only the data files and the floppies contain the search software, it is easier for the publisher to control access to the data. Some publishers put several databases on a CD-ROM and charge for software to access each one. This service is very cost effective for publishers because they can mass-produce one disc instead of several different discs. If a customer wants to pay to access another database on the same disc, new floppies can easily be sent with the access software. By the same token, the same CD-ROM disc could run under different operating systems (DOS, Apple Macintosh, UNIX) by distributing the appropriate retrieval software on floppies.

Determining Disc Capacity

You might have noticed that older CD audio discs hold less music than newer ones. If you have read any older literature about CD-ROM, you also might have noticed that the data capacity has increased as well—from 550M to 680M. A CD originally was designed to hold 74 minutes of audio data, but the outside 5 millimeters of the disc, which hold the last 14 minutes of music, were difficult to mold. As a result, older CDs were limited to 60 minutes of music or data. In order to comply with the Red and Yellow Book specifications, each CD is read by the optical head at a constant rate of speed—75 sectors per second—and there are 2,048 bytes of user data in a CD-ROM sector. The capacity of a disc was figured this way: 60 minutes × 60 seconds × 75 sectors × 2,048 bytes = 552,960,000 bytes or 552M, usually rounded up to 553 or shortened to 550. Because a kilobyte is not actually a thousand bytes, but 1,024 bytes, and a megabyte is not actually a million bytes, but 1,048,576 bytes $(1024)^2$, the capacity also could be figured as 527M (552,960,000/1,048,576).

Because the manufacturing process of compact discs has improved over the years, the full 74-minute capacity of a disc now can be utilized. 74 minutes × 60 seconds × 75 sectors × 2,048 bytes = 681,984,000 bytes or 681M. Or, if you divide by 1,048,576, 650M.

Most CD-ROM discs are not nearly full. Some contain as little as 10M of data, but would use up 10M of hard disk space or require a dozen high-density floppy disks to hold the same data. (Storing data on hard drives is much more expensive than storing it on CD-ROM. Hard disks cost about $1.20 per megabyte, but CD-ROM discs cost about one-fifth of one cent per megabyte. If you want to know how much data is on a CD-ROM disc, you must use a method other than the directory command. Although the DOS directory command shows how much space is free on a hard disk or a floppy disk, if you use the DOS directory command to look at a CD-ROM disc, it will always show 0 bytes free. Although this reading indicates that the disc is full, that is usually not the case. This reading means only that there is no space on the CD-ROM to which you can write. There are two ways to find out how much data is on the disc; the first is exact, the second is rather primitive but gives you a good approximation.

To find out exactly how much information is on a disc, you can use a utility such as PC Tools, Xtree, or Xtree Gold to log the current drive as the drive letter of your CD-ROM drive. These utilities will show the file structure of the CD-ROM and how many bytes are used. Some directory-maintenance programs cannot recognize the disc correctly because some CD-ROMs have more subdirectories or files than these programs normally handle.

The second, more primitive way to find out how much data is on a CD-ROM is to physically look at the disc. Hold the disk, label side down, and look at the surface. Remember that data on a CD-ROM always starts at the center of the disc and is written outward. If you move the disc just right in the light, you can see a line

where the data ends. If a disc has 100M, for example, the line will be about 3/8 of an inch out from the center of the disc.

You may notice a large discrepancy between the number of bytes reported by a utility program and the size of the data surface that appears to contain data. This difference is because Red Book audio does not appear as data to the utility program.

When a CD-ROM is produced, the total amount of data on the CD must be estimated by the developer or the mastering facility. In most cases, a hard drive partition large enough to accommodate the data—with room to spare—is created. The contents of the entire partition are put into ISO 9660 format, output to a tape or CD-Recordable disc, and shipped to the mastering facility. The data now is called an ISO 9660 image. At the mastering facility, the image is loaded to a partition on a hard drive, or transferred to tape. (If the data arrives at the mastering facility on CD-R, it can be used as is.) From tape, hard disk, or CD-R, the information is sent to the LBR, which transfers it to the glass master. The entire contents of the partition then are written to disc. If the partition is much larger than the actual data it contains, a gap exists between the end of the data and the end of the spiral track. This gap contains nothing but zeroes. A good practice is to "zero out" a partition before copying new data to it. If you zero out a partition, you change all bits on the partition to zeros.

However, if the developer or the mastering facility is inattentive or in a hurry and does not "zero out" the partition, residual data from a former application may be written to the new disc. This information cannot be read in the conventional way because the directory table and path table on the new disc are only aware of the locations of their own files. However, if you have a utility that can perform a hexadecimal dump of a CD-ROM, you can read the data. You might be amazed at what you find. Figure 4.5 shows a raw dump of CD-ROM data.

Some discs contain data in both ISO 9660 and HFS (Hierarchical File System) formats, and work on both IBM and Macintosh platforms. These discs are referred to as hybrid discs, or *Janus discs*, after the Roman god Janus, whose two faces looked in opposite directions. Some discs contain both CD-ROM and CD audio tracks— *Compton's Multimedia Encyclopedia* and the very popular *National Geographic Mammals*, for example. These discs are called *mixed-mode discs*. If you can see two distinct data areas on a disc, you probably have a Janus disc or a mixed-mode disc. Figure 4.6 shows the layout of a Janus disc, and figure 4.7 shows a primitive size estimation.

II

Understanding the Hardware

Figure 4.5
Hexadecimal
dump.

```
000690: 20 40 1D 0B 0D 00 00 00 40 20 20 20 20 20 20 20    @......@
0006A0: 20 20 20 20 20 20 20 20 20 7C 20 20 44 75 6C 61             | Dula
0006B0: 63 2C 20 41 72 74 68 75 72 20 20 20 20 20 20 20    c, Arthur
0006C0: 20 20 20 20 20 20 20 7C 20 7E 20 46 72 65 6E 63 68         | ~ French
0006D0: 20 57 61 69 74 65 72 20 20 20 40 1C 0D 00 00 00 00    Waiter   @......
0006E0: 01 20 01 1D 0D 01 00 00 00 45 20 20 20 20 20 20    . ......E
0006F0: 20 20 20 20 20 20 20 20 20 20 31 2E 20 20 20 49             1.   I
000700: 6D 6D 65 6E 73 65 6C 79 20 70 6F 70 75 6C 61 72    mmensely popular
000710: 20 63 6C 61 73 73 69 63 20 74 68 61 74 20 67 6F     classic that go
000720: 65 73 20 70 61 73 74 20 6A 75 73 74 20 61 20 45    es past just a E
000730: 1D 0D 02 00 00 00 23 20 20 20 20 20 20 20 20 20    ......#
000740: 20 20 20 20 20 20 20 20 20 20 20 20 63 75 6C 74                cult
000750: 20 63 6C 61 73 73 69 63 2E 20 20 23 1D 0D 03 00 00    classic. #.....
000760: 00 44 20 20 20 20 20 20 20 20 20 20 20 20 20 20    .D
000770: 20 20 32 2E 20 20 20 54 68 6F 75 67 68 20 74 68      2.   Though th
000780: 65 20 70 6C 6F 74 20 68 61 73 20 6D 6F 72 65 20    e plot has more
000790: 68 6F 6C 65 73 20 74 68 61 6E 20 61 20 70 69 65    holes than a pie
0007A0: 63 65 20 6F 66 20 44 1D 0D 04 00 00 00 41 20 20    ce of D......A
0007B0: 20 20 20 20 20 20 20 20 20 20 20 20 20 20 20 20
0007C0: 20 20 20 73 77 69 73 73 20 63 68 65 65 73 65 2C       swiss cheese,
0007D0: 20 74 68 65 79 20 64 6F 6E 27 74 20 73 65 65 6D    they don't seem
0007E0: 20 74 6F 20 62 6F 74 68 65 72 20 74 68 65 20 41    to bother the A
0007F0: 1D 0D 05 00 00 00 1D 20 20 20 20 20 20 20 20 20    .......
```

Figure 4.6
A Janus disc.

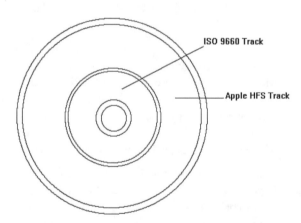

ISO 9660 Track

Apple HFS Track

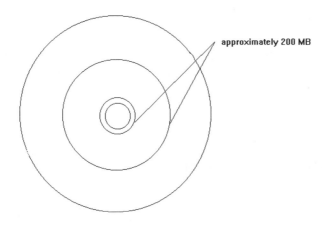

Figure 4.7
Primitive size estimation.

Caring for Your Discs

Although CD-ROM discs are sturdy, they are not indestructible. If you play Frisbee with them, stack them, or use them as coasters or Christmas tree ornaments, do not be surprised if they become scratched and unreadable. A scratch on the label side of the disc actually is more damaging than a scratch on the data side because the protective coat of lacquer is thinnest on the label side and a scratch there can damage the pits and lands. A scratch on the data side can often be compensated for by error correction.

 A scratch on the label side of the disc actually is more damaging than a scratch on the data side because the protective coat of lacquer is thinnest on the label side and a scratch there can damage the pits and lands.

Solvents, such as nail polish remover, cloud the clear polycarbonate, making portions of the disc unreadable because the laser beam cannot focus. Solvents can also penetrate the lacquer coating, causing it to separate from the polycarbonate. Even a minute opening can let in oxygen that can interact with the aluminum and cause it to corrode. This process is called disc rot.

Also protect your discs from strong sunlight, heat, humidity, and extreme cold. Store your discs in the containers in which you purchased them.

A good way to protect your discs when they are not in use is to use a "CD Muffin" made by DiscHotel. CD Muffin is a molded white plastic disc with raised center and edges that protects the data surface from scratches and dirt. For a collection of discs, you can use one of the many products designed to store and transport CD audio discs.

Cleaning a CD-ROM Disc

Always handle your discs by the outside edges to avoid fingerprints. If your discs become dirty, clean them with water or with water and a *mild* detergent. Do not use window cleaner or solvents, as they may cloud the clear polycarbonate or permeate it. Using a soft cloth, always wipe a disc radially, from the center to the edge, rather than in a circular motion. A scratch in the shape of an arc would make sequential data in a track unreadable, whereas a scratch that goes perpendicularly across the tracks only affects a few bytes in each track, and can be easily compensated for by the error correction code. Keep your discs clean and unscratched, store them in their jewel cases, and they will last for years. Playing the discs does not damage them, because nothing touches the disc but laser light, so their longevity has a direct correlation to how well you take care of them when they are not in use. Figure 4.8 shows the proper way to clean a CD-ROM disc.

Figure 4.8
Cleaning a disc.

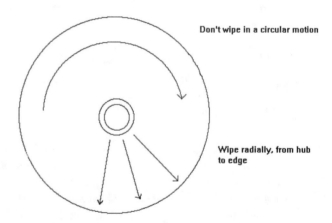

Don't wipe in a circular motion

Wipe radially, from hub to edge

How To Destroy a CD-ROM

Compact discs are so attractive, with their shiny silver rainbows, that even if they are outdated or unreadable they are rarely thrown away. There are times when you might want to purposefully destroy a CD-ROM disc. For example, if you subscribe to a CD-ROM publisher who provides updates to your discs, the publisher often requests that you either mail back your outdated discs or destroy them. Discs can be destroyed by cutting them in two, drilling a hole through them near the hub, or applying nail polish remover. Government agencies, particularly overseas, find it necessary to render sensitive information on CD-ROM inaccessible. The fastest way to accomplish this goal is to zap the CD-ROM in a microwave oven. This step is not recommended, however, if you value your microwave. The most ecological solution is to take your old discs to a mastering facility that accepts and grinds up old discs. This process saves landfill space because a powdered CD-ROM takes up very little room.

If you cannot bring yourself to part with your old discs, they can be framed, hung from the ceiling as a mobile, used as Frisbees, coasters, Christmas tree ornaments, or stacked and glued as modern sculpture. Some enterprising people have made jewelry and clocks from old discs. Mastering facilities sometimes offer "dummy" discs, which are usually extra or defective audio discs printed with a company's logo, for use as business cards.

Summary

Physically, CD-ROM discs are identical to CD audio discs. They contain a single spiral track of data three miles long. They are manufactured by the same process as CD audio discs, at the same manufacturing plants.

Installing a disc is a straightforward procedure. Installation programs and procedures vary from excellent to unworkable, although most discs today have good, flexible installation programs. CD-ROM capacity has increased, due to better manufacturing methods. CD-ROM discs are as durable as CD audio discs and should be handled and cared for in the same manner.

CHAPTER

Installing a CD-ROM Drive

I nstalling a CD-ROM drive is a straightforward procedure—a little more difficult than installing a floppy drive but less difficult than installing a hard drive.

If you buy a CD-ROM drive from a computer dealer, the dealer might offer to install the drive in your computer for a nominal charge. If, however, you buy a drive through mail order or from a store that does not have service facilities, you might have to install the drive yourself. This chapter is meant to help you get up and running as smoothly as possible. For best results, read through the procedures before you perform the steps.

Specifically, this chapter discusses the following topics:

✔ Caring for your CD-ROM drive

✔ Installing hardware

✔ Understanding SCSI basics

✔ Installing software

Caring for a CD-ROM Drive

Most CD-ROM drives that use a disc caddy function fine in either a horizontal or vertical position—in any way but upside down. Check your drive manual for vertical mounting instructions.

Sad to say, CD-ROM drives are not as robust as floppy drives. These drives are more susceptible to dirt and rough handling. By using the proper care, however, you can avoid these pitfalls. The lenses and photodetectors in a CD-ROM drive are fragile and might not survive a lot of bouncing around. Be gentle when handling your CD-ROM drive. If you drop it, it may not work.

Some new CD-ROM drives include a lens cleaning brush that is built into the drive that helps to remove contaminants.

If you mount a CD-ROM drive directly in front of the power supply fan in a computer chassis, the fan draws air in through the drive. The air contains airborne contaminants such as dust and smoke. These contaminants can settle on the lens and prism, reducing the life of your CD-ROM drive. You can prevent this problem by making sure that the drive you purchase is sealed and has a door or flap on the front. Alternatively, you can put a piece of tape over the slot where the disc is inserted. Be sure to remove the tape when you eject a disc, however.

Many of the newest CD-ROM drives not only have these doors, but also include a lens cleaning brush built into the drive that helps remove contaminants. If you have an internal CD-ROM drive, install it as far away from the fan as possible. The best solution is to reverse the fan and put a filter on it so that clean air blows out through the drive. This option is only currently available in some custom CD-ROM cabinets, however.

If a CD-ROM drive stops working, it can be cleaned. Some manufacturers accept drives for cleaning as well as repair. Your computer dealer also can refer you to a technician who can properly clean and repair your drive.

Do not try to clean the drive yourself unless you are prepared to buy a new drive. The lens and prism are very delicate, and the electronics and cables inside the drive are very susceptible to damage if you do not know what you are doing. Cleaning a drive usually requires disassembling the drive.

You can clean the lens of a CD-ROM drive with a CD-Audio cleaning disc, but always check to make sure that the manufacturer approves of this, especially if your drive is still under warranty.

On the positive side, CD-ROM discs are much more damage-resistant than hard or floppy disks. This durability results from the error-correction code as well as from the fact that the optical head never actually touches the discs' surface. Magnetic disks are susceptible to damage from magnetic fields and excessive use. Your CD-ROM drive—in fact, your entire computer system—will wear out long before your CD-ROM discs do.

Installing Hardware

The hardware elements you need include the CD-ROM drive and controller as well as the cable that connects them. If you are installing an internal or external drive, a SCSI controller or a bus controller card, the installation process begins by inserting the controller card into your motherboard.

See Chapter 3 for a full explanation of the hardware elements that you need with a CD-ROM drive.

If you are installing a drive with a parallel to SCSI adapter, such as a Trantor Mini-SCSI, you will begin by attaching the adapter to your parallel port. If you are connecting a drive to a laptop with a PCMCIA card slot, using an Adaptec SlimSCSI(TM) or similar PCMCIA adapter, you will begin by inserting the card into the laptop's PCMCIA slot. Many of the sound cards available today come with a SCSI or bus interface on the card so you can connect your CD-ROM drive to the sound card. Many multimedia upgrade kits that include a CD-ROM drive have the drive interface on the sound card. If you are installing one of these kits, follow the manufacturer's instructions.

Installing the Controller Card

First, of course, turn off your computer and disconnect the power, keyboard, monitor, printer, mouse, and any other cables. Next, you need to remove your computer's cover. This procedure used to be a simple matter of removing five screws on the back. Today, however, with many different case styles available, screws are in various places, and covers might slide off from the back, from the front, or from the top. Check your computer's manual for instructions on removing the cover. If you cannot find instructions, remove the appropriate screws, and take the cover off the case.

Depending on your computer model, its *motherboard* has 8-bit, 16-bit, or 32-bit slots, or some combination (see fig. 5.1). Compare your controller to those illustrated in figures 5.2 and 5.3 to determine if you have an 8-bit or a 16-bit controller. If you bought a low-priced or bundled drive, you probably have an 8-bit controller. You can install the controller card in any open slot of the appropriate size. Some motherboards have a proprietary memory expansion slot that might not work with your controller even though the controller fits into it. This slot, if your computer has one, is usually the last slot toward the outside of the motherboard. If you have a 16-bit controller, you must insert it in a 16-bit slot. 32-bit slots accept 8- and 16-bit cards, but have special connectors that accept 32-bit cards as well.

Figure 5.1

Expansion slots.

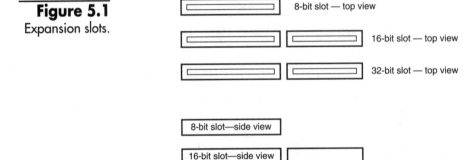

Before you install your controller card, check to see that the jumpers on the card are in the default configuration as specified in the controller manual. Remove the slot cover behind the open slot you intend to use and push the card firmly into the slot. In many cases, the card's mounting bracket does not line up perfectly with the screw hole. You can bend the mounting bracket slightly if necessary to make it line up. Insert and tighten the screw.

If you are installing an external CD-ROM drive, you can now replace the computer case and reconnect your monitor, keyboard and power cable.

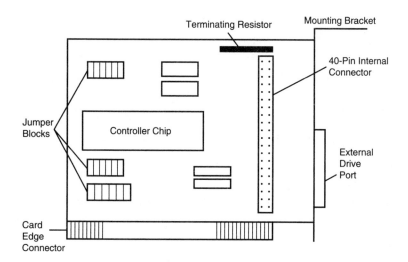

Figure 5.2
An 8-bit controller.

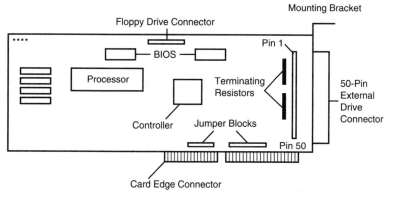

Figure 5.3
A 16-bit controller.

Installing an Internal Drive

If you are installing an internal drive, attach its cable before you insert the card—especially if you are using a slot between other cards. If you insert the card first, you might not be able to attach the cable because of space limitations. You might, in fact, need to rearrange the other cards if the drive's cable is not long enough to reach from the controller to the intended drive bay.

When you attach the cable, check your instructions carefully. Although most cables have a key that prevents the cable from going into the drive or controller card the wrong way, some do not. In addition, many cards do not have a keyed socket for the cable. Figure 5.4 shows connectors that include these keys. Locate the connector on your controller card.

Figure 5.4
Male and
female
connectors.

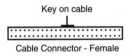
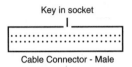

The connector should indicate where pins 1 and 50 or 1 and 40 are. It might be marked at one end only; it might indicate pins 1, 2, 49 and 50, or 1, 2, 39, 40 or it might not be marked at all. Check your instructions for proper placement of the cable. If they are not clear, follow the diagram in figure 5.5.

Figure 5.5
50-pin pinout.

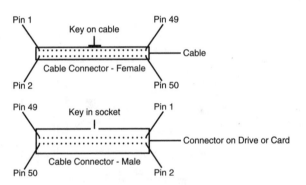

Notice a red or blue stripe on one side of the cable. This stripe indicates the side of the cable that connects to pin 1. If the connector on your controller card is not marked, pin 1 is usually toward the top of the card if the connector is vertical. The red or blue stripe on the cable should then go toward the top. If the connector on your controller card is horizontal, pin 1 is usually toward the front of the card and the red or blue stripe in the cable should face the front.

If you cannot determine where pin 1 is, and your cable is not keyed, look closely at the connector on the cable. Even though there is no key, there should be a visible molding impression in the middle of the connector. Use this impression instead of the key to align the cable correctly with the key in the drive connector.

Most computer cases use drive rails, screws, or both to mount a drive. If your case uses drive rails, mount the rails on the CD-ROM drive using the screws supplied in the kit.

Be sure to use the screws that are supplied in your installation kit. Screws that are too long can damage the drive. When in doubt, look at the drive's holes and, with a paper clip, measure the depth to which a screw can go without striking any drive components.

After you have installed the drive rails, slide the drive into an open drive bay and secure it according to the case's configuration. Some cases have locking tabs in front of the drive rails and some use friction rails that secure the drive without any additional screws. Most newer cases use only screws to hold their drives—use the same precautions concerning screw length as noted earlier. After you secure the drive, connect the power lead (because the lead is keyed, it can only go in one way).

If you do not have an available power connector, you can purchase a power-splitter cable from your local electronics or computer store.

Next, attach the cable to the drive and make sure that the cable is inserted correctly (see fig. 5.6). If the drive and cable are keyed, it can only go in one way. If no key exists, check on the back of the drive for markings similar to the card (1, 2, 49, 50, or 1, 2, 39, 40 or some such indicators), or look for a small arrow on the cable connector that should match another arrow on the drive connector. Again, if no key exists, examine the cable for a molding impression on one side. This will be the side that would normally contain the key. The red or blue stripe on the cable designates the pin-1 side of the cable; the striped side should go closest to the pin-1 markings.

You now can replace the computer case and reconnect your monitor, keyboard, and power cables.

Installing an External Drive

If you are installing an external drive, follow the same steps to install the controller card into the correct slot. The external drive's cable, however, attaches to the connector on the controller card's mounting bracket from outside of the case. Connecting the cable between the drive and the interface card is simple: if the cable has two identical connectors, it does not matter how you connect it; if they are different, you can only attach them one way. Plug in the cable and the power cord. Your physical installation is now complete.

II

Understanding the Hardware

Figure 5.6
Expansion slots.

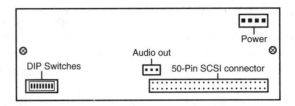

Understanding SCSI Basics

The SCSI bus is a great boon to computer users for various reasons. You can connect a SCSI device, whether a hard drive, CD-ROM, Magnet-Optical, or WORM drive, to any machine that has a SCSI controller. This flexibility has a price, however—the SCSI bus is a little more complicated than the connection between hard and floppy drives and their controller cards, and has specific conditions that must be met for it to function correctly.

 For more information on MO and WORM drives see Chapter 13.

Cable Length

A *SCSI bus* is composed of the SCSI controller, the cable, and the devices attached to the cable. The entire bus, or cable length, must be no longer than six meters, or 19.5 feet. This maximum length includes all internal and external cabling. This length is not an issue if you are using the SCSI bus to connect one internal or external CD-ROM drive to one SCSI controller because the necessary cables come with the drive and SCSI controller. If you are attaching your CD-ROM drive to an existing bus that already has devices attached, however, make sure that the total cable length is no longer than specified. A SCSI cable that is too long can cause errors. Figure 5.7 shows a simple SCSI bus.

Assigning SCSI Identification Numbers

The SCSI bus protocol allows a maximum of eight members, including SCSI devices and the SCSI card itself. Each device has an identification number (ID) from 0 to 7. Some SCSI cards take no ID for themselves, and therefore can control eight devices, while others do take an ID, leaving seven available IDs for devices.

Each device must have a unique SCSI ID number. Duplicate IDs can result in malfunctions, such as neither device being recognized by the host computer, or devices being recognized intermittently. Your CD-ROM drive is probably preset to ID 0. If the SCSI controller uses an ID, it is usually set to 7. If you have an existing SCSI bus with one or more devices, you need to find an unused ID number for your CD-ROM drive. You can set ID numbers by using a DIP switch, jumpers, or a rocker switch on the drive or on the SCSI controller card. Consult your CD-ROM drive's documentation to determine which method your device uses. Figure 5.8 shows a SCSI bus with many devices.

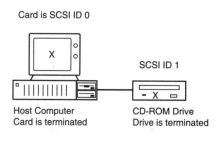

Figure 5.7
Expansion slots.

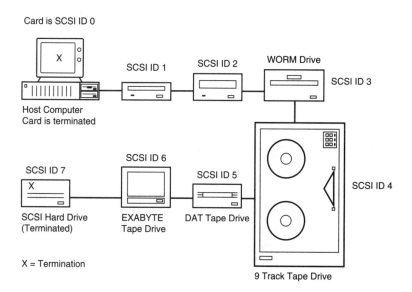

Figure 5.8
Several SCSI devices.

Understanding the Hardware

Terminating the SCSI Bus

A SCSI bus must be terminated on both ends and nowhere else. In the simplest case, your CD-ROM drive is the only device on the bus, and both the CD-ROM drive and the SCSI card are terminated (as you saw in fig. 5.7). *Termination* is accomplished by using resistors on the card, the CD-ROM drive or other device, or a cable connector. If you intend to add your CD-ROM drive to the end of an existing SCSI bus, you must terminate it and you must remove the termination from the preceding SCSI device. Do not terminate the bus if the device is installed somewhere in the middle, however. If you do, the host computer does not recognize any devices attached beyond the first terminator encountered. Missing termination on either or both ends of the bus also causes malfunctions. The documentation that accompanies the drive should describe the terminators and where to put them.

Improper termination is the most common cause of SCSI bus failure. If your SCSI device is malfunctioning and you cannot find the reason, check for incorrect termination first.

If you have an existing SCSI bus attached to external devices and you want to add an internal CD-ROM drive, you must remove termination from the SCSI controller card and add termination to the internal CD-ROM drive. The documentation that came with your SCSI card should explain this procedure. Figure 5.9 shows the type of terminating resistors that are commonly used on controller cards and on some drives. Other drives have various termination methods, and their terminators take many different shapes.

Installing Software

After you have installed your CD-ROM drive, reconnect your keyboard, monitor, and any other cables to their respective cards and ports. Plug in the power cord and turn on your computer. (If you have an external CD-ROM drive, remember to turn it on, too.) You now need to install the Microsoft Extensions program and your drive's device drivers. The device driver allows your computer to communicate with the CD-ROM drive. This process, as described in your CD-ROM drive documentation, should be a simple one.

In case your documentation does not offer software installation information, the next section describes Microsoft Extensions and explains its installation.

Terminating Resistors

Figure 5.9
Terminating
Resistors.

If your controller software has a BIOS chip, expect a slight delay at boot up while the controller card BIOS initializes the SCSI bus. You might see messages like the following:

```
1986-1988 Future Domain Corp.

CD-ROM Loadable Driver Version 1.0 Supporting

SCSI 0 LUN 0 Drive 1 Toshiba CD-ROM Drive

C:\MSCDEX

MSCDEX Version 2.00

Copyright © Microsoft Corporation 1986, 1987. All rights reserved.

         Drive D: = Driver MSCD001 unit 0
```

If you see these or similar messages, you are ready to go. Insert a CD-ROM disc. Change to the drive letter reported by Microsoft Extensions (drive D in the last line of the sample message), then enter **DIR**. The light on the CD-ROM drive flashes momentarily, then a directory listing of the CD-ROM disc appears on the screen.

Remember that a CD-ROM drive is slower than a hard drive. If you change the disc and ask for a directory right away, you might get the error CDR101: `Not ready reading drive X`. Wait a moment before you enter DI**r**. If you get the error, press **R** to retry.

Introducing Microsoft Extensions

Early versions of the IBM-PC personal computer family were very limited compared to the PCs and compatibles available today. The MS-DOS operating system software was written by Microsoft to work with these early personal computers and has proven to be flexible enough to grow and adapt as the speed, volume, and power of the hardware increases. The first hard drive for the personal computer was announced two years after the original IBM PC. This hard drive had a capacity of only 10M, but, even then, MS-DOS was capable of handling files as large as 32M. This limitation did not become a problem until hard disks larger than 32M

II

Understanding the Hardware

became available. It was not until MS-DOS 4.0 was released in 1989, however, that the 32M barrier was broken.

Although MS-DOS 4.0 and higher can handle partitions and files larger than 32M, Microsoft Extensions is necessary to access files in High Sierra or ISO 9660 formats.

Microsoft Extensions for CD-ROM was written to overcome the 32M barrier in versions of MS-DOS before 4.0, and to provide a way to access CD-ROM discs recorded in High Sierra or ISO 9660 formats by using regular DOS commands. Because of the amount of data a CD-ROM disc can hold, chances are good that one or more large files (over 32M) is present on a disc. Microsoft Extensions and device drivers serve as interpreters between a computer's operating system and the unique file format of a CD-ROM disc.

If your computer runs using DOS, you access the floppy disk drives and hard disk drives by entering **A:**, **B:**, **C:**, and so on. Because MS-DOS does not provide built-in support for CD-ROM drives as it does for magnetic drives, however, MS-DOS cannot assign the device a drive letter. Therefore, you cannot access your CD-ROM driver by using DOS commands. Fortunately, Microsoft Extensions, provides this capability. Extensions assigns a letter to a CD-ROM, and the CD-ROM looks to the user like a very large, read-only magnetic disk. Most, but not all, CD-ROM discs available today require Microsoft Extensions.

Selecting Compatible Versions

The version of Microsoft Extensions you use must be compatible with the version of DOS on your PC. The latest version of Extensions, 2.23, should be compatible with all versions of MS-DOS and PC-DOS as well as with Versions 5.0 and 6.0 of DR-DOS. Extensions 1.01, however, only works with MS-DOS 3.3 and earlier. Extensions Version 2.20 works with MS-DOS 5.0, but only if you add the statement **DEVICE=SETVER.EXE** to your CONFIG.SYS file. (See your MS-DOS manual for instructions for using SETVER.) Extensions 2.21 works with MS-DOS 5.0 without the use of SETVER. DR-DOS has no equivalent command to SETVER and runs Extensions without any additional commands. If you have MS-DOS 6.0 or 6.2, Extensions is included with the operating system and you should use the version that is supplied with these versions of MS-DOS. Table 5.1 helps you ensure that MS-DOS and Extensions are compatible.

Table 5.1
Microsoft Extensions and MS-DOS Compatibility

If you have MS-DOS Version	You can use Microsoft Extensions Version
3.1-3.34	1.01, 2.0, or higher
3.1-4.01	2.10 or higher
5.0	2.10, 2.20 with SETVER, or 2.21 (SETVER not required)
6.0	2.22 (Comes with DOS)
6.2	2.23 (Comes with DOS)

Purchasing Microsoft Extensions

If you buy a CD-ROM drive from a computer store or a CD-ROM vendor, Microsoft Extensions should be included in the package, along with a device driver. If you buy a used CD-ROM drive, be sure to get a copy of Microsoft Extensions and the device driver from the person who sells it to you. If you cannot get Extensions any other way, you can order a copy from the drive manufacturer or an authorized reseller of Microsoft Extensions.

If you obtain a copy of Extensions and drivers from an independent source, make sure you check the license agreement for the terms of any transfer.

Some CD-ROM discs and CD-ROM networking systems provide their own programs to access the disc and do not require Microsoft Extensions. These data providers usually include the required data retrieval and installation programs on magnetic floppy disks because you obviously cannot access the CD-ROM disc itself without them.

Installing the Device Driver

You must complete two steps to install the software to access the CD-ROM drive on a personal computer. The first is to install the proper device driver, the second is to install the executable program MSCDEX.EXE, which uses the device driver. Remember that the device driver goes in your CONFIG.SYS file and the executable file, MSCDEX.EXE, goes in your AUTOEXEC.BAT file or can be run separately from the command line.

If you prefer, you can run MSCDEX.EXE from the command line.

Most CD-ROM drives are shipped from the manufacturer with their own device driver. If not, thc Microsoft Extensions program available from an authorized dealer usually includes a collection of device drivers for the most popular CD-ROM drives. If the CD-ROM drive comes with its own device driver for Extensions, use it, as it is probably the drive manufacturer's latest version. Check the CompuServe CD-ROM forum for driver updates (GO CD-ROM).

If you buy a used CD-ROM drive, you run the risk of buying a drive that is no longer supported by the manufacturer. This obstacle is not insurmountable, but it might take some effort to find someone who still has a copy of the device driver you need. (See Appendix A for a listing of CD-ROM drives and manufacturers.) Also, you cannot tell if the drive is operational if you do not have the device driver and if you do not test the unit before you buy it. Unless you like a challenge, buy a drive from a dealer who can provide the necessary software to run it.

The device driver allows the CD-ROM drive to be recognized by your computer. Floppy drives and hard drives have their device drivers built in to the operating system in DOS. Like floppy disk and hard disk drives, a CD-ROM drive has a controller card. Sometimes these cards are proprietary and drive-specific. Often, however, the CD-ROM drive is a SCSI device and is controlled by a SCSI controller card. Either way, the device driver is specific for the controller card and to the CD-ROM drive. Sometimes the card and drive each require a separate device driver.

Insert the device driver name on the first line of the CONFIG.SYS file so that it is the first to load when the computer boots. Otherwise, other device drivers (such as memory managers, mouse drivers, etc.) can prevent the device driver from loading, and Microsoft Extensions might not recognize it. Contained within the device driver file, which should use the three-letter extension SYS, is the device driver default name. These two terms (device driver and device driver default name) are often confused. Remember that the first one contains the second, and that the *device driver default name* is used to call the device driver after it has been

loaded at startup. For example, a device driver for a Philips CD-ROM drive might be CM153.SYS. The device driver name contained within the CM153.SYS file might be MSCD001. This name must be used with the executable program MSCDEX.EXE when Extensions is loaded—when a drive letter is assigned to the CD-ROM drive.

In CONFIG.SYS, for example, the first line reads as follows:

```
DEVICE = CM153.SYS (CM153.SYS is the device driver)
```

and the command line entry or AUTOEXEC.BAT file reads as follows:

```
MSCDEX /D:MSCD001 (MSCD001 is the device driver default name)
```

In effect, this data tells your computer, "Find the hardware device that uses this name (MSCD001), then assign a drive letter to it."

If you do not know what the default name is, you can assign one by using a /D switch in the "DEVICE=" line in your CONFIG.SYS file. A *switch* is a parameter that modifies a command. In this case, it specifies the device driver name, when a name other than the default is being used. In this case, your CONFIG.SYS might read as follows:

```
DEVICE = C:\CM153.SYS /D:CDROMDRV
```

The corresponding command line entry or AUTOEXEC.BAT file should reflect the same information:

```
MSCDEX /D:CDROMDRV
```

You are not required to use the default name, even if you know it. You can call your CD-ROM drive "George" if you want, but the same name must appear on the device driver line in CONFIG.SYS and when MSCDEX.EXE runs.

```
DEVICE = C:\CM153.SYS /D:GEORGE
```

and

```
MSCDEX /D:GEORGE
```

If the wrong device driver is loaded, if the names do not match, or if you have an extra space or a reversed slash somewhere, you get the error message, "No valid CD-ROM device drivers found," when Microsoft Extensions tries to load. Make sure also that the name you assign to your CD-ROM device driver is not used by any other file on your system. If you name your CD-ROM device driver **CDROM**, and then try to access a file called CDROM, the operating system gets confused and cannot open the file. Likewise, do not give the device driver a name that is identical to a subdirectory name.

Other switches might be included with the device driver that comes with your drive, such as /U, /N, /P, or others. You can use these switches to tell your system how many CD-ROM drives to assign letters to, which SCSI ID to use, which I/O base address to use, and other configuration information. If you do not include these switches, the computer automatically chooses the default settings. In most cases, the defaults work fine, and you can leave out all switches. See your CD-ROM drive documentation for complete instructions on using these switches, because they are drive and device driver-specific.

Using the MSCDEX.EXE Program

You can load Microsoft Extensions from your AUTOEXEC.BAT file or from the command line. After Microsoft Extensions is loaded, it stays in memory until the computer reboots. Extensions takes up about 27K of memory, which you might need to run other programs. Thus, you might want to consider leaving MSCDEX.EXE out of the AUTOEXEC.BAT file so that it does not load every time you start your computer. When you want to access your CD-ROM drive, you can load Extensions by entering **MSCDEX /D:<*drivername*>** at the command line or you can create a batch file that will load it. Because it is a terminate-and-stay-resident (TSR) program, however, you cannot unload Extensions without rebooting your computer.

If you load Extensions by using a utility such as PC Magazine's INSTALL.COM or some similar program intended to load and unload TSRs, you can reclaim the memory that Extensions takes up by unloading it using the companion program REMOVE.COM. If you plan to load and unload Extensions in this manner, however, note that some strange behavior might result. INSTALL and REMOVE, for instance, loads Extensions and removes it from memory, but each time the program is loaded, it assigns the next highest drive letter to the CD-ROM drive until you reach the letter designated in your LASTDRIVE statement. Your CD-ROM drive still works, but the third time you install Extensions, your drive letter becomes F, while D is, in fact, the next available drive designator. If you plan to use a utility of this type, test it first and remove it if you experience problems.

Memory Considerations

Because CD-ROM applications notoriously require large amounts of free memory to run (some need as much as 540K), you might be tempted to load Extensions into high or extended memory by using a memory manager such as QEMM or 386 MAX. Do not do it—it does not work. Future versions of Extensions will take advantage of the high-memory features of DOS 5.0, but current versions (up to 2.21) cannot be loaded high. You can, however load Microsoft Extensions' buffers into high memory by using the /E switch when Extensions is loaded:

```
MSCDEX /D:CDROMDRV /E
```

Extensions uses six buffers of 2K each by default. If you load these buffers into high memory, you can save 12K of memory for use by other programs. You can also decrease or increase the number of buffers allocated by using the /M switch:

```
MSCDEX /D:CDROMDRV /M:8
```

More buffers mean faster performance because the buffers allocate memory to cache reads from the CD-ROM. Fewer buffers mean more memory available to run programs.

An additional switch is related to memory usage: the /V switch. (The *V* stands for verbose.) If you add this switch to the MSCDEX command, Extensions prints information to the screen regarding memory usage during installation:

```
MSCDEX /D:CDROMDRV /M:8 /E /V
```

Assigning the Drive Letter

As discussed earlier in this chapter, Microsoft Extensions provides the switches /D, /E, /M, and /V, which enable you to assign a device driver name, load buffers into high memory, allocate the number of buffers to be used, and print memory usage data to the screen, respectively. Yet another switch, the /L switch, enables you to assign a specific drive letter to the CD-ROM drive. You must use this option if you have a CD-ROM application that requires the CD-ROM drive to be identified by a particular letter. If the drive letter desired is M, for example, the MSCDEX command line should read as follows:

```
MSCDEX /D:CDROMDRV /L:M
```

You can, of course, include all of these switches on one line:

```
MSCDEX /D:CDROMDRV /L:M /M:12 /E /V
```

The preceding line, therefore, requests your operating system to find the device controlled by the device driver named CDROMDRV, assign the drive letter M to it, allocate 12 buffers in memory, load them into high memory, and inform you of the memory usage.

If all this information seems hopelessly technical, do not despair. Hardware manufacturers and software publishers provide technical support, and many have toll-free numbers. The companies who sell CD-ROM drives and Microsoft Extensions are happy to help you get Extensions running on your computer. All you really need to do is get Extensions to assign a drive letter—then you can forget about it. You do not need to become an expert in order to use it.

Special Notes to Microsoft Windows Users

You should load Microsoft Extensions before you run Microsoft Windows, *not* from a Windows DOS window. If you load Extensions from a DOS window, it appears to load and assign a drive letter as usual. You cannot access the CD-ROM from within Windows, however. The error messages vary according to the version of Windows and what mode it is running in.

If you are using Windows Version 3.0 with Multimedia Extensions in standard mode and load Extensions from a DOS window, Extensions assigns the drive letter and you can call for the disc's directory. You can even run the application if it does not require too much memory. When you go back to Windows and try to access the CD-ROM drive by using the File Manager, however, it appears as a network drive. File Manager tells you that drive D:\ does not contain any files. Then, if you go back to your DOS window and try to access the CD-ROM drive, you get the error message "Volume in drive D has no label. Invalid function." If you exit Windows and try to access the CD-ROM drive, you get the same error message.

In an enhanced-mode DOS window, Extensions appears to load, but if you call for a directory of the disc, the following error message appears:

```
CDR103: CDROM not High Sierra or ISO 9660 format reading drive D.

Abort, Retry, Fail?
```

Different operating systems, device drivers, and different versions of Windows produce other error messages. Of these messages, the scariest one is internal error code 001.

Do not confuse Microsoft Extensions for CD-ROM with Microsoft Windows with Multimedia Extensions. Microsoft Extensions for CD-ROM specifically refers to the program MSCDEX.EXE, which allows a PC to access a CD-ROM drive. Microsoft Windows with Multimedia Extensions is a special version of Windows 3.0 that enables the user to access sound boards, motion sequences (MMM, AVI files), WAVE audio files (WAV), and CD audio from the CD-ROM drive. Microsoft has

discontinued this version of Windows as most of its features have been incorporated into Windows 3.1. No existing version of Windows to date has built-in CD-ROM support. You still need to run MSCDEX first so that you can access the CD-ROM drive.

Windows displays a small CD-ROM disc as an icon for a CD-ROM drive, but it only recognizes the CD-ROM drive if MSCDEX.EXE is loaded before you start the Windows program. You also should, if you want to use Windows, include the command **DIR X:** (where *X* is the drive letter of your CD-ROM drive) after you load MSCDEX and before you start Windows.

It might seem strange that these two products from the same software company are so particular about the order in which they are loaded. It certainly is odd that Microsoft does not include CD-ROM support in Multimedia Windows or Windows 3.1 when Microsoft has been instrumental in creating the MPC specification, which requires Multimedia Windows or Windows 3.1 and a CD-ROM drive.

Troubleshooting Error Messages

Any error message that begins with the letters CDR is generated by Microsoft Extensions. These messages range from CDR100 to CDR104, and the accompanying messages are rather terse:

Number	Errors
CDR100:	Unknown error
CDR101:	Not ready
CDR102:	EMS memory no longer valid
CDR103:	CDROM not High Sierra or ISO 9660
CDR104:	Door open

Other error messages also might be generated by the operating system or by the application. Here are some other common error messages that you might encounter when you install or use Microsoft Extensions, and what they really mean:

✔ Not enough drive letters available.

DOS reserves A, B, C, D, and E as local drives (as opposed to networked drives). A and B are usually reserved for floppy disk drives, and you can divide or partition your physical hard drive (usually C) into several smaller logical drives, each assigned a letter. Extensions automatically assigns the next available drive letter to the CD-ROM drive (or drives) after all floppy- and hard-drive letters have been assigned. If the preceding message appears, Extensions is attempting to assign a drive letter higher than E, or higher than the drive letter in the LASTDRIVE statement in the CONFIG.SYS file.

The solution is simple: add the line LASTDRIVE=X to the CONFIG.SYS file, where X is the highest letter used. For example, if A and B are floppy drives and C, D, and E are hard drives or partitions, make the line LASTDRIVE=F for one CD-ROM drive, LASTDRIVE=G for two, and so on.

For networked PCs in a Novell NetWare environment, the first networked drive is the first drive letter after the letter in the LASTDRIVE statement. If your LASTDRIVE statement is LASTDRIVE=F, for example, the first network drive is G (unless the network software has assigned another letter for you).

✔ CDR101: Not ready reading drive X. Abort, Retry, Fail?:

This error can have many causes. You might not have allowed a disc enough time to "spin up" before you entered a command. In this case, wait a few seconds and press **R** to retry. If it still does not work, the disc might be unreadable: an audio disc, a CD-I or CD-ROM XA disc, no disc in the drive, an upside-down disc, or a damaged disc. If you are certain that the disc is the right format, try cleaning it. Look for scratches. When you reinsert it, make sure that the caddy is closed completely, is not damaged, and that no foreign objects (such as labels) are stuck in the caddy or the drive. Try another caddy, then try another disc. If it cannot read the second disc, there might be a problem in the software setup. Restart your computer. If it still does not work, reinstall Microsoft Extensions.

✔ CDR103: CDROM not High Sierra or ISO 9660 format reading drive D. Abort, Retry, Fail?

This error can result from attempts to read a CD-ROM disc recorded in the native Macintosh file system (HFS) or in the UNIX file system. It might also be produced if you attempt to load Extensions from Windows. Check that the disc is in the ISO 9660 or High Sierra format, and be sure to run Extensions before you run Windows.

✔ `Device driver not found: CDROMDRV`
`No valid CD-ROM drivers selected`

This message indicates a problem with the device driver and Microsoft Extensions software. Some possible problems might include the following:

✔ The SCSI device driver or the CD-ROM device driver failed to load

✔ The driver is corrupted

✔ A syntax error exists in the CONFIG.SYS file's DEVICE= line (extra space, reversed slash, spelling)

✔ The wrong device driver name was specified when MSCDEX was loaded

Check your CONFIG.SYS and AUTOEXEC.BAT files for errors. If you don't find any, reinstall Microsoft Extensions.

You may also receive the following error messages from Microsoft Extensions:

✔ `Expanded memory not present or not usable`

When using the /E switch, the program could find no expanded memory. Check that an expanded memory manage is present.

✔ `Illegal option "X"`

You have entered an incorrect command-line parameter. Check the syntax of the parameter.

✔ `Incorrect DOS version.`

You are using a version of MSCDEX with DOS 6.0 or 6.2 that is not 2.22 or 2.23. If you are using DOS 6.0 or 6.2, use the copy of Microsoft Extensions that came with your operating system.

✔ `MSCDEX already started`

Microsoft Extensions is already in memory. If you want to change the parameters, you will have to reboot your computer and start MSCDEX again.

Summary

Installing a CD-ROM drive should be a relatively straightforward procedure. If problems do arise, however, the information in this chapter can help you get through the process smoothly. These suggestions are not a substitute for the documentation that you receive with your drive and controller card, however. Manufacturers frequently update drivers and change installation procedures. Hopefully, they document these changes and all material is up-to-date. However, the reality is that drivers change frequently. Check the CD-ROM forum on CompuServe for the most up-to-date drivers for your drive. Most drives and bundles include an installation program that makes installation easy and trouble-free. If you follow the manufacturer's instructions, make use of their technical support personnel (if necessary), and go through the recommended installation procedure step-by-step, you should have no problems installing your CD-ROM drive.

Understanding
CD-ROM Networking

This chapter discusses the advantages of using CD-ROM as a networked resource. It provides a simple explanation of networking, explains the three basic methods that enable you to share CD-ROM discs over a network, and discusses the advantages, disadvantages, and issues involved in networking licenses for CD-ROM discs.

Before the advent of CD-ROM technology, the only way to store and access massive amounts of data was to use a mainframe computer. Users of computer terminals could share this information and communicate with each other.

CD-ROM gives the personal computer user the power to access massive amounts of data that formerly existed only on a large mainframe computer. Individual computers do not have the storage potential that CD-ROM provides. Personal computer users have overcome this lack of connectivity by installing LANs (Local Area Networks), which permit PCs to share information and resources. The combination of a LAN and CD-ROM drives gives individual PC users the advantages of communication, shared resources, and access to large amounts of information.

Some of the advantages of providing network access to CD-ROMs are as follows:

✔ Lower hardware and software cost than stand-alone CD-ROM drives

✔ Faster and more efficient use of CD-ROM applications

✔ The ability to share access to large amounts of information

Why Network CD-ROMs?

Installing CD-ROM drives on a network makes sense for several reasons. In a law office, for example, several attorneys may need to access several discs. They may need to see discs that contain data on bankruptcy law, statutory law, and Supreme Court cases. None of the attorneys will use one disc all of the time, but each of them may need to look at all three discs during the course of a day. Buying each attorney a CD-ROM drive and a copy of the discs would be costly. This setup also would force the attorneys to load and unload different applications every time they needed to consult a different database. If you had one computer with three CD-ROM drives, the attorneys would still have to take turns using the discs. If you attach the CD-ROM drives and computers to a network, however, the attorneys can look at all of the discs at any time—in fact, the attorneys can look at the same disc at the same time.

Libraries pioneered using and networking CD-ROMs. When reference works became available on CD-ROM discs, libraries installed individual computers with a single CD-ROM drive and dedicated each computer to a particular CD-ROM database. Librarians soon found that students were lining up at some computers and other computers were rarely used. Just as they did with printed reference books, students had to make appointments to research the information they needed. The solution was to give every computer access to every CD-ROM. Many libraries installed networks just so that the information from the CD-ROM discs could be shared among the users.

Local Area Networks

Because a CD-ROM disc can hold so much information and make it readily accessible, it's only natural that businesses and libraries want to share CD-ROM applications on a Local Area Network (LAN). It is simply a way to connect personal computers so that information can be shared.

A LAN can exist in many forms. It can encompass software and hardware that enable individual personal computers to communicate with each other and with other devices, such as printers. LANs also can be elaborate systems that connect PCs, terminals, and remote dial-in users to file servers and mainframe computers, which contain vast amounts of information.

Basically, however, a LAN consists of individual PCs (sometimes called *workstations*) that contain a *network interface card* (NIC). This card is attached to a network cable, which connects to a file server, if one is present. A *file server* is another, usually faster and more powerful, PC that contains one or more large hard disks to store shared files. A *network interface card,* or network adapter, is a circuit board that is installed into an open slot of a personal computer. This card, along with network software, translates data from a personal computer into a form that can be transmitted across the network cable to the file server, to another workstation on the network, or from the file server to the workstation.

Software that runs on the workstations and the file server enables the individual users of the PCs connected by the network cable to share the programs and data that reside on the file server's hard disk(s). To a personal computer user, programs and data on the file server can be accessed as readily as programs and data residing on the computer's local hard drive, and all users connected to the network can share the same information and communicate with each other.

LAN hardware and software to connect two or more personal computers can be found at software stores. For large networks that connect computers in an office, an entire building, or a campus, the hardware and software is installed by a network consultant, a company that specializes in installing networks, or the computer services department of the company. The process of installing a network includes running the cables to connect individual workstations and other network resources, installing a network interface card in each workstation, and installing software on each workstation and the file server. Figure 6.1 illustrates a typical LAN.

II

Understanding the Hardware

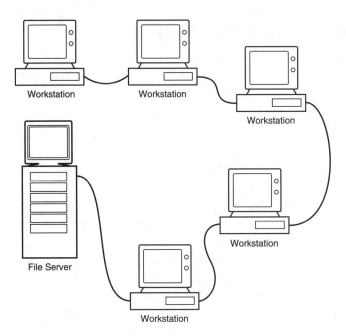

Figure 6.1
Local Area
Network (LAN).

CD-ROM Networking Solutions

Sharing CD-ROMs on a network can be accomplished in several ways. Many CD-ROM networking products are available. The three most common methods for CD-ROM access over a network are as follows:

✔ Peer-to-peer network operating systems with CD-ROM support

✔ Dedicated CD-ROM servers

✔ NetWare Loadable Modules (NLMs)

Peer-To-Peer Networking

A *peer-to-peer network* treats all computers attached to it as equals. Subject to any restrictions imposed by the network administrator, each computer on the network can access the hard drives and other devices attached to the other computers on the network. Figure 6.2 illustrates the setup of a peer-to-peer network.

Suppose that you and a coworker each have a computer. Both computers contain two floppy drives (A: and B:) and one hard drive (C:). With network software, you can access her drives as well as your own. Her drives would appear to you as drive

letters D and E (her floppy drives A: and B:) and drive F (her hard drive C:). A third workstation's drives would appear as G, H, and I.

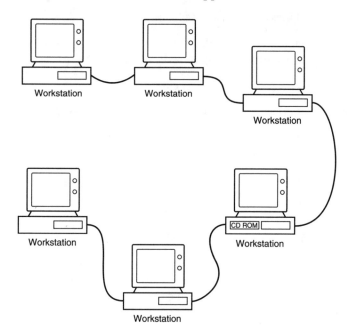

Figure 6.2
Peer-to-peer network.

If you have a file on your hard drive concerning an account that your coworker needs, you do not have to copy it on a floppy disk and walk it over to her. Your coworker can access the F: drive and look at the account on your hard drive or copy it to her hard drive. This process may sound invasive, especially if you have personal files on your system.

Certain security features in the network software permit access to certain drives, directories, and files, and prohibit the access to others. You can designate one computer on the network as a *dedicated server*. The dedicated server's task is to control devices that all users can share, such as printers.

Some peer-to-peer network operating systems offer built-in support for CD-ROM drives. The CD-ROM drive or drives can be attached to any computer on the network, including the server, and shared by all other computers. The CD-ROM looks the same to each user. The drive looks as if it were a local CD-ROM drive on each workstation.

The advantages of using peer-to-peer networks with built-in CD-ROM support are as follows:

✔ They are easy and inexpensive to install and configure.

✔ Microsoft Extensions and the CD-ROM device driver are not required on every workstation, just the workstation with the CD-ROM drive.

The disadvantages of using peer-to-peer networks are as follows:

✔ They make CD-ROM access, which is already slow, even slower.

✔ They are not really practical for large numbers of users or for several CD-ROM drives.

Please see Appendix F for a listing of companies that offer peer-to-peer networks with built-in CD-ROM support.

CD-ROM Servers

Dedicated *CD-ROM servers* are computers attached to the network that do nothing but control CD-ROM drives. CD-ROM servers can be specially designed cabinets that contain a CPU, network interface card, SCSI controller, and CD-ROM drives, or just another standard computer with a network card and an installed CD-ROM drive.

Special software runs on the CD-ROM server to make the CD-ROM drives available to workstations on the network. Each workstation must have software installed that enables it to access the CD-ROMs. Each workstation usually has a device driver and Microsoft Extensions or a redirector, which serves the same purpose, but which may not be compatible with all applications.

After the CD-ROM server is running the server software, it cannot be used as an ordinary workstation. CD-ROM servers usually include a way to use available memory to cache data so that performance can actually be faster than local CD-ROM drives. CD-ROM drives appear to the user as local. Figure 6.3 illustrates the use of a CD-ROM server.

The advantages of using a dedicated CD-ROM server and software are as follows:

✔ They are fast and efficient at handling large numbers of users and CD-ROM drives.

✔ They do not slow the functions of the file server. Some do not even require a file server to be on the network at all.

✔ If there is an extra computer available, all that is necessary to make it a CD-ROM server is the addition of a network interface card, controller card, CD-ROM drive(s), and the software. Custom-built CD-ROM network servers including a CPU, network card, CD-ROM drives, and controllers also are available.

✔ Almost all CD-ROM applications will run well on this kind of system.

✔ Most CD-ROM networking software will work on any kind of network operating system, including peer-to-peer.

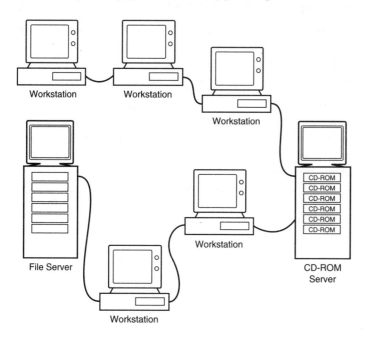

Figure 6.3
LAN with dedicated CD-ROM server.

II

Understanding the Hardware

The disadvantages of using a dedicated CD-ROM server and software are as follows:

✔ Custom CD-ROM server hardware can be expensive because it is designed specifically for holding CD-ROM drives. A few feature locking doors and special air-filtration systems, although CD-ROM manufacturers have started sealing their drives to keep dust out.

✔ Software must be installed on both the server and the workstation, which can use up RAM.

See Appendix F for a listing of companies that supply hardware and software for dedicated CD-ROM servers.

NetWare Loadable Modules (NLMs)

NLM stands for NetWare Loadable Module. NLMs are a feature of Novell NetWare Version 3.0 and above. Novell NetWare is a popular LAN operating system that uses a file server to hold shared data. The NLM feature allows CD-ROM drives to be installed as part of the file server, rather than as a part of a workstation or as part of a dedicated CD-ROM server. Novell NetWare versions 3.12, 4.0, and 4.01 come with an NLM that supports the attachment of CD-ROM drives to the file server. For earlier versions of NetWare, you must purchase an NLM or VAP (Value Added Process) separately if you want to attach CD-ROM drives to your file server.

NLMs make use of a network's file server to provide access to a CD-ROM drive or drives. A SCSI controller and CD-ROM drive are installed in a file server rather than in an individual workstation. The file server software makes the CD-ROM drive appear as another network hard drive (read-only) to the user.

Suppose that you have your hard drive (C:) and both floppy drives (A: and B:). This setup enables you to log on to the network and access the drives (including the CD-ROM drive) in the file server, which can be any letters from D through Z. Your coworker can do the same. Fortunately, a network administrator assigns access rights and keeps the drive letters straight. The CD-ROM drive attached to the file server has a drive letter, and the network software installed on the file server controls it. Figure 6.4 illustrates a network that contains a file server with NLMs and an installed CD-ROM drive.

Figure 6.4
LAN with file server with NLMs and CD-ROM drive.

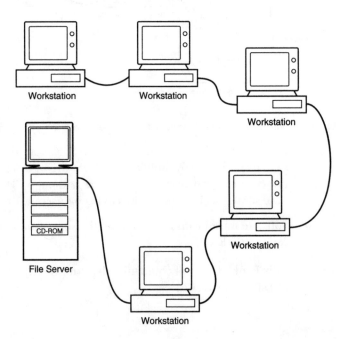

The advantages of NLMs are as follows:

✔ They are fast and inexpensive.

✔ They require no additional software on the workstation, which saves memory.

The disadvantages of NLMs are as follows:

✔ NLMs only work with Novell NetWare Version 3.0 and above.

✔ Because NLMs use Novell NetWare instead of Microsoft Extensions to assign a drive letter, many CD-ROMs do not work with NLMs.

✔ NLMs can slow down the entire network because the file server must handle the CD-ROM drives as well as the hard drives in the file server.

✔ If one part of the file server (which includes the CD-ROM drives) fails, the whole network must be brought down while it is fixed.

Please see Appendix F for a listing of companies that provide NLMs and VAPs for CD-ROM support on Novell NetWare.

Licensing and Limitations

Because CD-ROMs were not originally intended for network use, many publishers have only recently addressed the issue of network licenses. Obviously, it is in the publisher's best interest to require that each user of an application buy a disc; therefore, many publishers choose to charge exorbitant fees for the right to network their discs. Three basic methods are used to allow network licensing of CD-ROMs—site licenses, concurrent users, and licensed workstation users.

Site License

The site license enables an end user to pay a one-time fee for a CD-ROM application that can be networked and accessed by any user on the network. This method is a great idea, except that it may not be practical for a very large or very small network. A very large network can experience application slowdown from too many simultaneous users if no access restrictions are set by the network administrator. If a second copy of the disc is purchased to share the load usage, it will cost as much as the first disc. A small network, by the same token, must pay as much as a large network for the application, regardless of the number of users.

Concurrent Users

Licensing for concurrent users limits the number of users who can access the disc at any one time. If the network consists of 20 workstations and is licensed for 10 concurrent users, for example, all 20 workstations have the potential to access the disc, but only 10 workstations can access it at any one time. If an 11th user tries to access the disc, that user gets a busy message. This solution is good if a timeout is built-in. Too often, people walk away from a workstation and leave an application running.

A timeout terminates the application automatically when no activity is detected for a given period of time, freeing the application for another user.

Licensed Workstations

If you license workstations, you must specify the number of workstations that you plan to configure for access to the CD-ROM. Out of 20 workstations, you may decide to grant access to only 10 workstations. If these 10 workstations are busy accessing other applications, a user wanting access to the CD-ROM must wait until one of these designated workstations is free.

This scheme is not popular with libraries, whose workstations must be shared, because libraries pay for the number of workstations, not the numbers of users. For corporations, however, this scheme may be preferred because each workstation is usually only used by one person. It is easier to buy a license for each person who needs access to the application.

Methods of License Enforcement

Of course, there are instances in which a single copy of a disc that is intended for a single user is used in a network environment. Most libraries are scrupulously honest about paying for and honoring the licensing agreements, but as CD-ROM networking spreads beyond libraries, publishers must address the issue of authorized use without putting unreasonable constraints on end users.

Some CD-ROM publishers have come up with methods to limit the number of users. Some publishers use a device, called a *key* or *dongle*, that plugs into the printer port (see fig. 6.5). The search software looks for the presence of the key and does not run if it is not there.

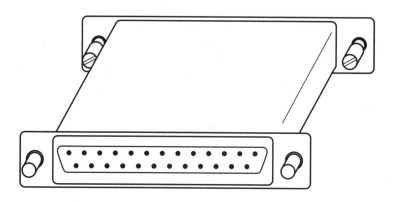

Figure 6.5
Dongle
(hardware key).

Another method of enforcement is to assign an access code to each user. After all the access codes are assigned, no more users are allowed access to the disc. Another method is to write the search software intended for a stand-alone disc to detect the presence of network software. If the software is present, the application will not run.

CD-ROM Networking Problems

A common problem encountered as you network CD-ROMs is the limited amount of memory that is available on a workstation. Because a file server can allow individual workstations to take advantage of its superior speed and storage capacity, the workstation can afford to be slower and smaller in terms of clock speed and magnetic disk space than a stand-alone computer. Some workstations on networks contain no floppy or hard disks at all. These workstations are called *diskless workstations*, and they boot from a special chip that is installed on the network interface card, which is called a *boot PROM*.

Many workstations contain only 640K of RAM. Programs, including CD-ROM applications, can be loaded from the hard drives in the file server, but they still must use the memory in the workstation to run. Network software takes up some of the memory so that it can create a communications link with the file server. Device drivers and Microsoft Extensions take up still more memory so that a communications link with the CD-ROM drive and other devices is created. By the time a network user is ready to start searching an application, there may be less than 500K of memory available; many CD-ROM applications require 540K or more of available memory.

You can, of course, install more memory on the workstation, but it is costly. You can use a memory management program that will enable you to more efficiently use existing memory. Configuring each workstation, however, is time-consuming.

If the CD-ROM networking software does not require a file server to be present, then some of the network software can be eliminated, but then the application must be run from the local magnetic drive of the workstation. The best solution is for the developers of CD-ROM search software to require less workstation memory. Many developers are responding to this need.

Summary

CD-ROM is a natural storage medium to use with a Local Area Network. The possibilities and ramifications of networking CD-ROMs are so vast that the subject deserves a book in itself. This chapter is an overview of the advantages, methods, and issues you face when you put CD-ROMs on a network.

Now that you have learned the parts that make up CD-ROM technology, Part III teaches you how you can use the technology.

Part III

Practical Uses

CD-ROM Software

CD-ROM's capability to store vast amounts of information is not worth much if the specific information you want is not readily accessible. A CD-ROM that contains a year's worth of the *Wall Street Journal,* for example, does not provide much of an advantage if you must read it page-by-page on your computer screen to find the information you need. You must have a way to find specific information quickly and reliably. *Retrieval software* is the interface between you and the data on a CD-ROM disc. Retrieval software enables you to search electronically for a word, phrase, name, subject, or date—or for whatever specific information you want—that is buried in the mass of data on a CD-ROM. Besides searching indexed text, the software can "link" to a glossary, a picture, an audio track, or related subjects.

In this chapter, you learn about CD-ROM retrieval software. You can choose from seven types of CD-ROM discs. Some discs use no retrieval software. Specifically, you learn the following:

- ✔ The retrieval methods you can use. These methods include browsing, phrase searching, word searching, and Boolean and proximity searching.

- ✔ How hypertext links are used and how many programs use links to sound, animation, video, and graphics.

Retrieval Software

The retrieval software (also called the *user interface, retrieval engine,* or *search software*) is the part of the CD-ROM software that you see. The other part of the software, used by the database developer, is usually called a *build engine* or *build software.* This software indexes the data, and you will never come in contact with it. The retrieval engine is sometimes referred to as the *run-time* version of the build software. The data on a disc, indexed in a certain way by a particular build software, must be retrieved by using the run-time version of that software, just as documents written under WordStar cannot be opened using Lotus 1-2-3. *Run-time software* is specifically designed to access data that was indexed in a particular manner.

Standardization

CD-ROM is a standardized media. All discs have a standard format, and any manufacturer's drive can read anybody's disc. In fact, CD-ROM is the most standardized data storage medium available. The user interface for retrieval of data, however, is not standardized.

CD-ROM is the most standardized data storage medium available.

The lack of a standard interface is a common complaint in the CD-ROM world. For ten discs, you may have to use ten different retrieval softwares. You do not have this problem if you use discs from the same publisher because the interface usually is the same for each one. If you want to use discs from several different publishers, however, you may find that each has a different interface and a different set of commands to learn. The advantage of this is that different kinds of data require different access programs, and you are not forced to use an inappropriate interface. Just as you do not use a word processor to create a spreadsheet, you do not look at a CD-ROM that contains geographical information—such as a world atlas— by using an interface designed for looking at text. The most important feature of retrieval software, whether you use one or several, is its capability to find the data you need quickly and easily.

Several major retrieval software vendors and CD-ROM publishers are currently working together to define a standard method of indexing information so that you

can access data by using whatever interface you prefer. Although it is extremely unlikely (and not necessarily desirable) that only one method to index CD-ROM data will be implemented, this move toward standardization is promising for librarians and professional researchers. It will enable them to use their favorite interface on discs from different publishers.

Using Retrieval Software

Unfortunately, you currently have little or no choice as to what retrieval software to use for a particular application, unless you want to produce your own disc or are only interested in data that is provided by one publisher. The disc publisher supplies the retrieval software; it is an integral part of the CD-ROM disc. You must use the retrieval software associated with the build software used to index the database. The information indexed by the retrieval software is usually licensed exclusively to the publisher of the disc by the owner or author of the information and is available only through the retrieval software supplied. In the case of multimedia applications, some of the information often is original material created by the disc's publisher.

You currently have little or no choice as to what retrieval software to use for a particular application.

If you are interested in a database produced by a government agency, such as NTIS (National Technical Information Service), ERIC (Educational Resources Information Center), MEDLINE (from the National Library of Medicine), or others, you can choose from among several different interfaces from several different publishers. Information from these agencies is considered public domain, and the agencies may license the information to several CD-ROM publishers. The publishers then index the data by using their own retrieval software.

The information is the same in each case, but the method by which it is indexed and accessed is different. Some of the larger CD-ROM publishers that offer this kind of information are Dialog, SilverPlatter, Compact Cambridge, UMI, Wilson, Compact Discovery, and EBSCO.

III

Practical Uses

The number and variety of discs that you buy determines the number and kinds of interfaces you use. If you like the challenge of learning new computer programs, you will enjoy the diversity of CD-ROM retrieval software. If you are more interested in quickly accessing and easily disseminating the information on CD-ROM to as many people as possible (librarians, health care workers, and other professionals are in this category), you will want to learn as few methods of searching for data as possible. CD-ROM is versatile enough to satisfy the needs of both groups.

Most retrieval software does an excellent job of finding the data you are looking for quickly. To learn how to use the different types of retrieval software is another matter. How can you tell the good from the bad? You will know. A good retrieval engine is a pleasure to use; a bad one is a constant frustration. You should be able to perform a simple search in a full text database or navigate through the different elements of a multimedia disc by using commands or buttons displayed on the screen. Good user interfaces provide tutorials and help, as well as on-screen commands. Of course, as with any method or application, the one that you learn first or most completely will probably be your favorite.

Distinguishing Disc Types

Different types of databases are available on CD-ROM, and different retrieval requirements exist for each of them. CD-ROM databases can be classified in three types: full text, fielded, and multimedia. Additionally, five kinds of CD-ROMs do not fit into the database category: data-only discs, program discs, indexed data-only discs, software library discs and game discs.

Full Text Databases

Full text retrieval has been and still is the main use for CD-ROM. You can search the full text of up to 300,000 pages and get results in seconds. Some examples of full text information on CD-ROM are as follows:

✔ The Congressional Record

✔ State or federal statutes

✔ Medical journals

✔ Newspapers

✔ Magazines

✔ Literature

✔ Supreme Court decisions

Full text indexing means that every word (with a few exceptions) of the data (text) is indexed so that you may search for any word or combination of words in the database. Most full text databases use a *stopword* list. Stopwords are commonly used words that are not indexed. A standard stopword list looks like this:

> a, about, above, after, again, all, along, also, am, an, and, any, are, as, at, away, back, be, been, begin, both, but, by, can, cannot, come, could, did, do, does, doing, done, down, end, even, far, for, from, get, go, good, had, has, have, having, he, her, here, herself, high, him, himself, his, how, however, if, in, into, is, it, its, itself, know, large, let, like, little, long, low, me, mean, more, mr, mrs, ms, must, my, near, need, never, new, next, not, nothing, now, of, off, old, on, one, open, or, order, other, our, out, over, own, put, same, say, seem, set, she, since, so, some, still, such, take, than, that, the, their, them, then, there, they, this, those, to, together, too, up, us, use, very, want, was, we, well, went, were, what, when, where, while, with, without, would, yet, you, your

A stopword list usually can be edited by the database producer so that certain words that occur frequently in a specific application, but are unlikely to be used as search criteria, can be added. Words usually included in a stopword list, but that may be necessary for searches in a specific database, can be deleted.

The preceding list , for example, contains the words "high" and "low." Suppose that this stopword list was used in a database that included climatological data. Searches for "high pressure" and "low pressure" would not yield the desired results because most search engines would simply ignore the words "high" and "low" and proceed to search on the word "pressure." Although you would still find all occurrences of "high pressure" and "low pressure," you also would find extra records that included the word "pressure" but not "high" and "low." To search efficiently, you must be able to narrow your search so that only the most relevant records are retrieved. As you can see, the stopword list here is not appropriate for the climatological database and would have to be edited to allow for effective searching.

Most databases enable the database producer to remove all the stopwords and to index every occurrence of every word, but indexing words such as "a" and "the" takes additional space and is costly in terms of indexing overhead, which is a concern to CD-ROM publishers. *Indexing overhead* refers to the amount of disc space that the index uses. Many different indexing schemes are used on CD-ROMs and, depending on the software used to build the CD-ROM, indexing overhead can range from 25 percent (using data compression) to 100 percent.

III

Practical Uses

If a publisher has 100M of ASCII text to index, for example, the completed database can range in size from 75M to 200M. A reasonable indexing overhead is 25 to 35 percent. ASCII text of 100M usually produces a 125M to 135M database.

Fielded Databases

Fielded data is data easily broken up into separate small parts or "fields." A good example of this type of disc is a disc that contains certain data about all the businesses in the United States, such as name of business, address, phone number, number of employees, and company description. Each of these elements is a *field* in the database; each complete set of fields is called a *record*. A database such as this can contain millions of records. Examples of fielded databases are as follows:

✔ **Business information.** Names, addresses, phone numbers, and other information about businesses in the United States

✔ **Bibliographical information.** Title, author, date of publication, and publisher of books

✔ **Auto parts catalogs.** Make, model, year, body style of cars, part numbers, manufacturer, and ordering information for parts

By using this kind of database, you can search for all the companies that manufacture ball bearings in Biloxi, or the books written by a given author, or what parts you need to order if the shocks go out on your 1968 International TravelAll.

Multimedia Databases

Richard Bowers, executive director of the Optical Publishing Association, recently pointed out that the confusion over the term "multimedia" is due to the word itself. He notes that CD-ROM is a single medium that has the capability to deliver "multiformat" information. Sound, video, text, animation and graphic images are merely many formats of information delivered together in one medium, the CD-ROM.

Multimedia discs can really be divided into two categories. The first category is discs that can be considered multimedia because they contain more than one type of information. Many full text databases contain graphics and sound. These discs can legitimately be called multimedia discs.

The second category consists of discs that use the standards for sound and animation that are part of the MPC specification. These discs are referred to as Multimedia discs. The following list gives examples of Multimedia discs:

✔ ***Audubon's Multimedia Birds of America.*** High resolution illustrations, birdcalls, and text

✔ ***National Geographic's Mammals.*** Full-color photographs, video, animal sounds, and text

Examples of Windows Multimedia Discs are as follows:

✔ ***Beethoven's Ninth.*** Red Book audio, MIDI audio, graphics, and text

✔ ***Compton's Multimedia Encyclopedia*** (**Windows Edition**). PCM audio, graphics, text, and animation

Data-Only (Archive) Discs

Recently, many companies have discovered that CD-ROM is an excellent archival medium. These companies use CD-ROM to store data normally kept on a file server hard disk, archived on tape, printed on paper, or transferred to microfiche. Because of the low cost of CD-ROM drives, many drives can be run simultaneously on a network at low cost. Essentially, a network administrator determines what information on the network needs to remain there for user access but does not need to be changed. The administrator then produces or has produced a *one-off* (write-once) CD-ROM that she mounts into one of the network CD-ROM drives. Users still have instant access to the information, but 680M of space on the file server hard drives is freed.

Many companies have discovered that CD-ROM is an excellent archival medium.

For more information on one-off and write-once discs, see Chapter 14.

III

Practical Uses

If a company must distribute information to affiliates or branch offices, it is much more efficient to produce and mail a CD-ROM disc periodically than to disseminate the information via printed matter or modem. In addition, if the information is of the sort that must be retained, but does not need to be available at all times (such as medical and financial records), CD-ROM storage is much more efficient and secure than paper, magnetic tape, or microfiche storage.

Another application for data-only discs is in the fast growing Document Image Processing (DIP) market. *Document imaging* is an expanding market because it has the potential to make the paperless office a reality. In document imaging, all documents are scanned as images, then indexed by key information contained in the document. In some systems, the images are written out to optical disc, and the index remains on the hard drive.

Because document imaging applications assume that a printed document scanned into the application is an archival document and will not be changed, the document images can be written to WORM (Write Once-Read Many) or Write Once CD-ROM (CD-WO) and placed on the network for user access. Again, because CD-ROM drives are relatively cheap, many drives can be on-line on the network at the same time. Networking can produce a great savings in access time because—unlike WORM jukeboxes, which swap a cartridge to one or two drives as a user requests a file (this can take eight seconds or more)—all data is on-line at all times. This is especially effective when multiple, simultaneous user requests occur for data on different discs.

Program, Clip Art, Typeface, and Graphics Discs

Some discs contain data that is not indexed at all. Good examples of this type are discs that contain shareware programs and their associated files, clip art discs that contain graphic images you can copy to your hard disk and use in a desktop publishing program, and discs containing fonts. Demonstration discs that contain samples and demos of many different programs also fall into this category. Some software vendors, such as Apple, Microsoft, and Borland, are currently distributing programs and operating systems on CD-ROM because of its low-cost manufacturing and distribution, imperviousness to viruses, and durability. Examples of program, clip art, graphics, and typeface discs are as follows:

- ✔ Win Platinum
- ✔ Shareware Gold
- ✔ Clipart Heaven
- ✔ Comstock Desktop Photography

- ✔ CorelDRAW!
- ✔ Font Fun House
- ✔ ColorBytes Mini Sampler

Indexed Data-Only Discs

Some discs contain indexed data that is retrievable from several different programs. The data is supplied in a common format, such as dBASE, so that you can retrieve the data from dBASE, Clipper, or any program that accesses dBASE files. This format gives the user flexibility in manipulating that data. It enables the user to create an interface best suited to the user's data retrieval needs. A good example of an indexed data-only disc is the U.S. Imports and Exports of Merchandise disc from the U.S. Department of Commerce.

Software Library Discs

Recently, many companies have begun offering discs that contain fully functional software packages from different vendors or from their own product line. These discs usually allow the user to try out software before he or she decides to purchase it. Usually, the user can run a version of the program that is limited in some way. To purchase the software, the user will call a toll free number and place an order using a credit card number. The user is then given an access code that allows a full working version of the software to be installed from the CD-ROM.

Depending on implementation, this is an easy and convenient way to try and purchase software. These discs are being produced by IBM, Microsoft, Apple and several independent producers who contract with software companies to place their software on the disc and make it available to users. Some of these discs are given away free or included with the purchase of a computer; others are distributed on a paid subscription basis. Examples of these types of discs include:

- ✔ Microsoft & More (CD-Select)
- ✔ Merisel Sampler (Merisel)
- ✔ Ambra CD-ROM (IBM)

Game Discs

Because of their intensive storage needs for graphics backgrounds, audio, animation, and video, many game producers now distribute their games on CD-ROM. CD-ROM games are consistently in the top seller list for CD-ROM retailers. The

III

Practical Uses

CD-ROM format, with its capacity for sound, animation and full motion video allows game producers to enhance their products in ways that would not be possible with traditional floppy disk distribution. Some examples of current best-selling game discs are:

✔ Dracula Unleashed

✔ Sherlock Holmes, Consulting Detective

✔ The 7th Guest

✔ King's Quest 6

✔ Quantum Gate

✔ Rebel Assault

✔ Jump Raven

✔ Busytown

✔ Day of the Tentacle

Exploring Data Retrieval Methods

The capability to find a single word among 300,000 pages of text in seconds certainly makes finding data easier, but different search strategies built into most CD-ROM retrieval packages make it fun, even remarkable. Multiple word, phrase, Boolean, and proximity searching, or a mixture of all of them, makes it possible to find exactly what you want in seconds. Retrieval engines for multimedia applications can link related pictures, sounds, animations, and video to text.

Browse

A basic way to find information on a CD-ROM is to browse through the database. This can be interesting, but not efficient. Most search software has a browse feature. Browsing the database shows you the first record of the database, and you then can move sequentially to each subsequent record.

Note   A basic way to find information on a CD-ROM is to browse through the database.

Phrase Searches

Phrase searching is a simple way to find exactly what you need, but you must know exactly what you are looking for to make it an effective search method. If you are looking for a specific phrase from the United States Constitution—"cruel and unusual punishments," for instance—you must enter this phrase exactly as it appears in the text. Figure 7.1 is from the *Colorado Revised Statutes on CD-ROM*, a disc that contains the complete text of the Colorado state statutes with annotations and the Colorado and United States Constitutions. Figure 7.1 shows the search screen with the phrase entered. Note that when you initiate the search, the program tells you it has removed the stop word "and" (see fig. 7.2).

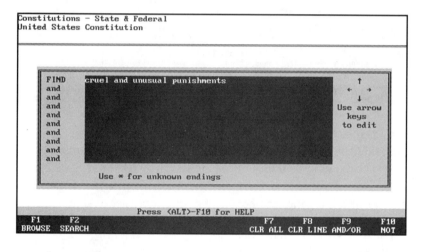

Figure 7.1
The search screen.

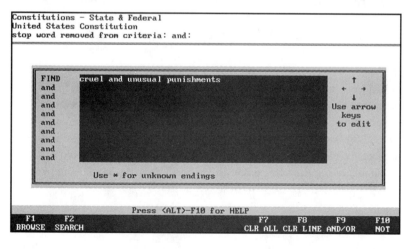

Figure 7.2
The stop word removed prompt.

III

Practical Uses

Figure 7.3 shows the results of the search. You find the words "cruel and unusual punishments" in the Eighth Amendment. Note the exactness required for a phrase search.

Figure 7.3
Successful
phrase search.

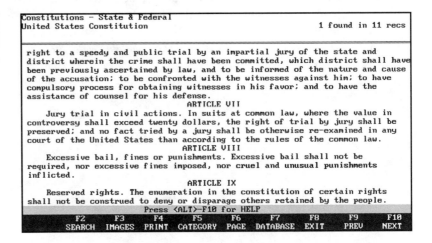

```
Constitutions - State & Federal
United States Constitution                              1 found in 11 recs

right to a speedy and public trial by an impartial jury of the state and
district wherein the crime shall have been committed, which district shall have
been previously ascertained by law, and to be informed of the nature and cause
of the accusation; to be confronted with the witnesses against him; to have
compulsory process for obtaining witnesses in his favor; and to have the
assistance of counsel for his defense.
                              ARTICLE VII
     Jury trial in civil actions. In suits at common law, where the value in
controversy shall exceed twenty dollars, the right of trial by jury shall be
preserved; and no fact tried by a jury shall be otherwise re-examined in any
court of the United States than according to the rules of the common law.
                              ARTICLE VIII
     Excessive bail, fines or punishments. Excessive bail shall not be
required, nor excessive fines imposed, nor cruel and unusual punishments
inflicted.
                              ARTICLE IX
     Reserved rights. The enumeration in the constitution of certain rights
shall not be construed to deny or disparage others retained by the people.
                     Press <ALT>-F10 for HELP
        F2      F3      F4      F5      F6      F7      F8      F9     F10
      SEARCH  IMAGES  PRINT  CATEGORY  PAGE  DATABASE  EXIT   PREV   NEXT
```

If you search for "cruel and unusual punishment," you receive the message "none found" because that complete phrase does not exist in the text. Wild cards help somewhat, as "cruel and unusual punishment*" finds the phrase.

Tip

A *wild card* is a character that matches any character or characters found in a document. Most CD-ROM retrieval software uses the asterisk (*) as a wild card for multiple characters, much as it is used in MS-DOS. For example, "punish*" matches "punish," "punishment," and "punishments," while "pun*"—depending on the database—gives you too many hits, finding such words as "pun," "punctilious," and "pundit."

In the "cruel and unusual punishments" example, you can probably use "pun*" safely because other "pun" words probably do not occur in the United States Constitution. A better strategy, however, is to search for "cruel and unusual." This yields the same result because the words only appear once in the Constitution. If you keep the phrase short, you are more likely to find it because you avoid some of the potential for misstating the phrase. On the other hand, the shorter the phrase, the more "hits" you will get. Phrase searching is a double-edged sword.

Word Searches

A simple word search is the most basic kind of search, but it usually gives you too many hits to make the retrieved data useful. The disc *United States History on CD-ROM,* for example, contains 107 books about U.S. history, as well as over 1,000 photographs and maps. If you want to find the date that Germany surrendered in World War I, and you search for the word "war," you will get many hits. In fact, the word occurs 1,118 times within the database (see fig. 7.4).

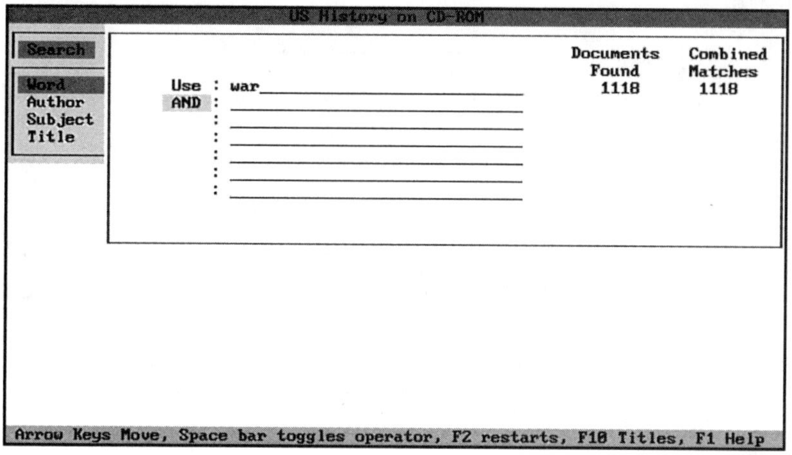

Figure 7.4
U.S. History, searching for "war."

You can narrow the search somewhat by searching for both "world" and "war" and get 675 hits, that is, 675 articles that contain both words (see fig. 7.5).

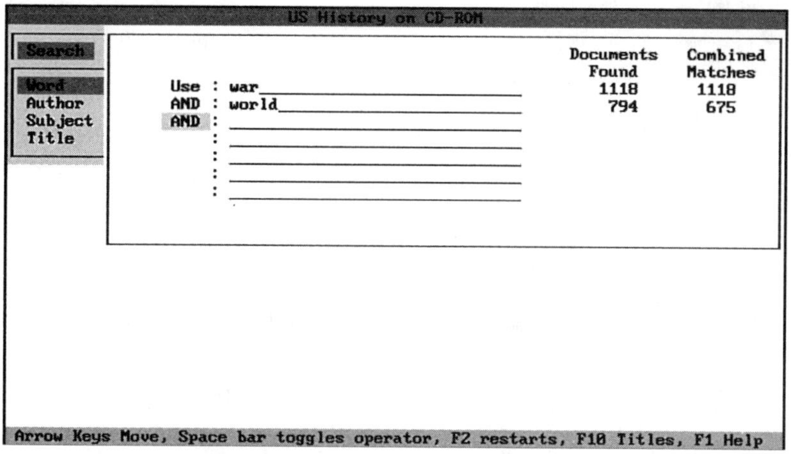

Figure 7.5
A search for "war" and "world."

This is still too broad, so you add another search word, "Germany." Now you get 194 matches, but this is still too many to consider the search successful (see fig. 7.6).

Figure 7.6
A search for "war," "world," and "Germany."

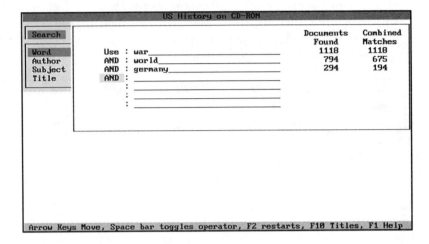

If you add "surrender," you narrow the number of hits to 42. Obviously, the search so far is applicable to both World Wars. You need to add something that can get more specific results (see fig. 7.7).

Figure 7.7
A search for "war," "world," Germany," and "surrender."

When you add "Pershing" to the list, you come up with only two hits. When you display them, you see that only one of the articles concerns World War I; you have found what you are looking for (see fig. 7.8). The armistice was signed on November 11, 1918, as shown at the top of figure 7.9.

```
                    US History on CD-ROM
 ┌─────────┐                              Documents   Combined
 │ Search  │                               Found      Matches
 ├─────────┤
 │ Word    │   Use : war_____   1118        1118
 │ Author  │   AND : world_____    794         675
 │ Subject │   AND : germany_____    294         194
 │ Title   │   AND : surrender_____    208          42
 └─────────┘   AND : pershing_____     33           2

 Introduction. . . . . . . . . . . . . . . . . . . . . .
      Air Force Combat Units of World War II
 Chapter 18  World War I:  The U.S. Army Overseas. . . . . .
      American Military History




     Arrow Keys Move, Enter Key Selects, ESCape to prev menu, F1 for Help
```

Figure 7.8
A search for "war," "world," Germany," "surrender," and "Pershing."

```
Chapter 18  World War I:  The U.S. Army Overseas. . . . . . .
      The fighting ended at the eleventh hour of the eleventh day of the
 eleventh month, 1918.

      Men died right up to the last, but finally, after more than four grim
 years, it was over.  Of the men of all nations in uniform, more than 8,500,000
 died, and total casualties exceeded 37,500,000, a price that would forever
 invite criticism of the way commanders on both sides fought the war.  American
 casualties alone totaled 320,710.

      So ended the first adventure of the United States in departing from its
 traditional policy of noninvolvement in European affairs.  That the nation
 could make such a decisive contribution in so short a time hardly could have
 been conceived in advance.

      That there would be mistakes, blunders, shortcomings under such a rapid
 expansion and commitment was perhaps inevitable.  Until mid-1918, for example,
 when separate replacement training camps were at last established, units both
 in the United States and overseas had to be broken up to provide replacements.
 This practice was damaging to morale and damaging too in that it sent many
 poorly trained men into the lines.  So close did the American supply system in
 France come to breaking down that in the summer of 1918, under threat of
 intervention from Washington, Pershing had to exert special efforts to rescue
 it.  Pershing himself was overburdened with command responsibilities –
 F3 Next, F7 Print, F8 Copy, F9 Figures, F10 Search (shift=rev), ESC Back, F1-?
```

Figure 7.9
Search results.

III

Practical Uses

Boolean Operators

Boolean operators are the words "and," "or," and "not." They derive their name from the 19th century English mathematician and logician George Boole. Boolean logic defines the relationship between groups or sets. In the case of multiple-word searching with Boolean operators, the words "and," "or," and "not" define the relationships in the database of the words you are searching for. Just as you use addition, subtraction, multiplication, and division in arithmetic, in Boolean logic, "and," "or," and "not" are the operators that you use to solve a problem. The problem is where the information is located, and the Boolean operators enable you to determine the relationships of words within the database.

You used the "and" operator in your search in the U.S. History database. The "or" operator is easy to use because it enables you to search for alternative words or phrases. If you are unsure of how something might be phrased, use "or" with several words or phrases. While this increases your chances of finding the correct information, it also has the potential to increase the number of hits that you get and may well return too many records.

The "not" operator is used to exclude certain words or phrases from your search. To search the *Complete Works of William Shakespeare* for scenes in which only Macbeth and Lady Macbeth appear, for example, enter "Macbeth" and "Lady Macbeth," not "Banquo," not "Messenger," and not "Doctor" as search criteria (see fig. 7.10).

Figure 7.10

Macbeth search.

```
      The Complete Works of William Shakespeare:  American English
                                                  Documents    Combined
 Search                                             Found       Matches
                                                      30          30
 Word        Use : Macbeth_____            10          10
 Author      AND : Lady Macbeth_____            13           4
 Subject     NOT : Banquo_____            128           3
 Title       NOT : Messenger_____             38           2
             NOT : Doctor_____
                 : _____
                 : _____



 Arrow Keys to Move, Space bar toggles operator, F2 restarts, F10 for Titles.
```

Notice the results. Act I, Scene VII and Act II, Scene II are the only scenes in the play where no other characters appear (see fig. 7.11). You have successfully used the "not" operator to narrow your search and obtain the desired results.

Note   With practice, you can gain the search skills necessary to get quick, accurate results.

These searches are simple. Be aware that in many applications, specifically large medical, legal, and financial applications, searches must be constructed with care and with a great deal of knowledge of the material being searched to achieve

satisfactory results. In these fields, proper search techniques are a necessity. Missed information can be costly. Too broad a search criteria returns so many hits that the material is unmanageable; too narrow a criteria does not return all the information you seek. Skilled searching is sometimes an art, sometimes a science, and sometimes a mixture of both. With practice, you can gain the search skills necessary to get quick, accurate results.

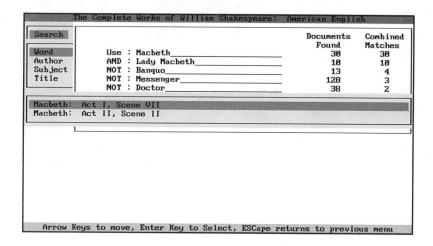

Figure 7.11
Search results.

Proximity Searches

Proximity searching is a powerful feature found in many databases, and it can, either by itself or in combination with Boolean operators, be a powerful search tool. A *proximity search* enables you to find the relationship of words by their proximity to, or distance from, each other. You can search the U.S. Constitution again to find out how old one must be to be eligible to hold the office of President and whether any U.S. residency requirements exist. If you search for the word "president," you find many occurrences of that word in the Constitution. If you search for "president" and "years," you again find many occurrences of both words in the Constitution, and they may not necessarily relate exactly to your search. If you use a proximity search, you can search for the word "president" within 20 words of "citizen" and "president" within 20 words of "age." With this search, you are more likely to get a hit on the first try. Figure 7.12 shows the search criteria entered on the screen. In the program shown, the proximity operator is the underscore character.

Figure 7.12
Search criteria for the proximity search.

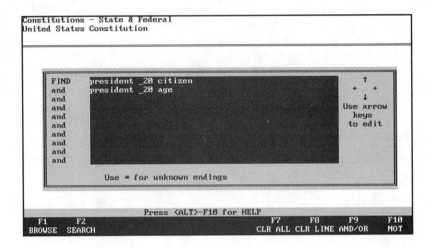

Your search was successful; you received only one hit by using this criteria (see fig. 7.13). The proximity operator is a useful search tool, although not all programs allow for proximity searches.

Figure 7.13
Successful proximity search.

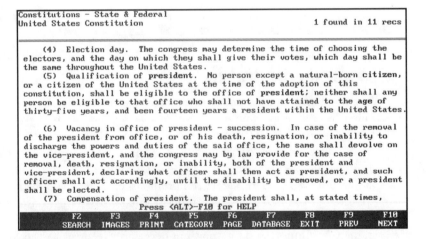

Combined Search Techniques

A combination of all these search techniques can give you the ability to find even the most remote information quickly and easily. Remember, though, that you may not be able to use every search method on every CD-ROM database. Most large full text databases offer the use of all search methods, but some do not. In the following example, assume that a,b,c,d,e,f,g, and h are words for which you want to search. If you combine all the search methods, you can represent a search as follows:

(A not _30 B) and _50 (C and D and E) or (F or (G and H))

This search translates like this: Show every occurrence of the word A where it is not within 30 words of the phrase B and is within 50 words of the words C and D and E, or is within 50 words of either F or both G and H.

You can see the power of combining the various search methods. Database developers realize that searches can become quite complicated and that you may need to reenter the search or refine it to get the desired results. Consequently, most CD-ROM databases keep the current criteria available in memory so that you can modify it accordingly as you refine the search. Many databases enable you to save your search criteria to disk and run or refine it at a later time. These databases also keep track of search histories so that you can see where you have been and what has succeeded and what has failed.

Using Links

Links enable you to retrieve data in a nonlinear way. While you search a database, you may come upon a word, phrase, or subject that might be enhanced by graphics, audio, or additional text, such as a definition or a related subject. Links enable you to explore information in a more natural way—it is the way people think and explore information, as opposed to the way machines do.

Linked Graphics

Many CD-ROM programs have graphics links in which a picture is associated with a particular record. This link is accomplished by embedding a pointer in the record that references another piece of data in the database; in this case, a graphic image.

Most CD-ROM databases access graphic images externally; that is, the graphic image is not embedded in the database, but is contained in a separate file, usually in a subdirectory on the CD-ROM.

Some CD-ROM databases, however, include the graphics within the database itself. Although the program shows the graphics on-screen, you cannot identify them as separate files on the CD-ROM or access them with other programs.

If you examine a CD-ROM disc that contains graphic images with XTree or a similar utility, you usually find a separate subdirectory that contains the graphic images. These images can be PCX, TIFF, BMP, or any of the many graphics formats supported by the PC. If you have a graphics viewing program, you can access these graphics separately with that program.

National Geographic's Mammals disc, for example, has many images, including video motion. Note that the camera icon enables you to view the graphics associated with this record. Figures 7.14 and 7.15 show the use of linked graphics.

Figure 7.14
Graphics
reference.

Figure 7.15
Referenced
graphic
displayed.

Linked Sound

Just as graphic images often are linked to a text record, sound also can be linked to a record. Three types of sound are currently used on CD-ROM: *Red Book Audio* (True CD audio), *Pulse Code Modulation* files (PCM), also called WAVE files that use the WAV extension, and *Musical Instrument Digital Interface* (MIDI) files, which usually have the MID extension. WAVE and MIDI files require that the user have a computer that meets the Multimedia PC (MPC) specification, so they are only used on discs that run under Microsoft Windows with Multimedia Extensions or Windows 3.1.

Non-Multimedia Windows discs that contain sound use Red Book Audio or non Red Book sound formats such as Real Sound (designated by the file extension .RS). Red Book Audio is placed on the CD-ROM by adding a CD Audio track or tracks to the disc. The sound is then accessed by the program and played through the audio jack of the drive.

Real Sound files are played through the PC's internal speaker. Since speaker placement on PCs is inconsistent, Real Sound files may be inaudible on many systems.

The MPC specification and these types of sound files are covered in detail in Chapter 12.

III

Practical Uses

Hypertext

Hypertext, or text linking, is another powerful feature included in many retrieval softwares. A hypertext link is similar to a graphics link; it refers or points to another piece of data. Unlike an external graphics link, however, the data pointed to is usually contained within the database. The link can refer to the definition of a word, the next occurrence of that word in the database, or a topic related to the word, words, or data currently being accessed. Figures 7.16 and 7.17 show a hypertext link and the related information pointed to by the link. In these figures, MediaBase Windows with the All About Cows database is being used. It contains just about everything you want to know about our bovine friends. A click on the link takes the user to the referenced material.

Figure 7.16
A hypertext link.

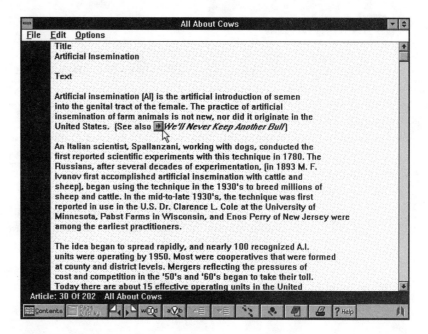

Figure 7.17
The related record accessed by clicking on the link.

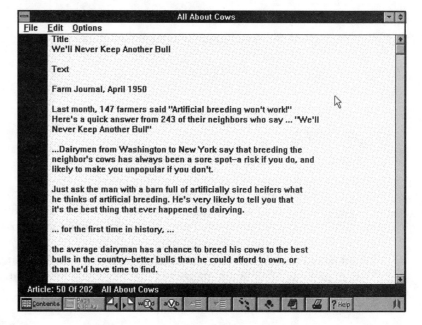

Summary

In this chapter, you learned that CD-ROM is a standardized medium in format, but that the retrieval softwares used with them are many and varied. You learned that retrieval softwares usually are chosen or written to meet the needs (or perceived needs) of the end user of a particular product. The eight basic types of CD-ROM discs, each with its own use, were discussed. You also learned about several methods of data retrieval and search methods. Most retrieval softwares have powerful search features that, with practice, enable you to pinpoint the information you need and access it in seconds. The capability to use hypertext and to associate graphics and sound, including true CD audio, with traditional text records also was discussed. All this is made possible by CD-ROM's large capacity and unique format.

In the next chapter you will examine examples of many of the popular CD-ROM titles available today.

CHAPTER

Types of Discs

The number of CD-ROM titles available today is staggering, and new titles are continuing to be released. This chapter provides an overview of some of the most popular discs on the market. Serious applications for professional researchers, such as MEDLINE from Dialog, to entertainment-oriented discs, such as PC GAMEROOM and The Book of Lists #3, are presented in this chapter.

Presented in each overview is the disc title, the publisher's name and phone number, the environment in which the disc operates, and a short description.

The best sources for CD-ROM title information are *CD-ROMs in Print*, *The CD-ROM Directory*, and *The CD-ROM of CD-ROMs*. The discs presented in this chapter are only a small sampling of the kinds of applications available on CD-ROM.

California Travel

Publisher: Ebook, Inc.

Environment: Windows

Description of Contents:

This disc contains a guided tour of California, with more than 1,000 full color photographs, restaurant recommendations, hotels, and museums. Includes maps.

Types of Data: Text, graphics

Ordering Information: 510-429-1331

Silicon Valley

The computer revolution affecting all of America has changed the face of San Jose and Silicon Valley, sixty miles south of San Francisco along the southern edge of San Francisco Bay.

Almaden Winery and Vinyards

Originally a bucolic ranching region, with a few pueblos and a Spanish mission in the 18th century, the valley developed in the 19th and early 20th centuries as the most important fruit-growing area in America. Prunes, plums, apricots, peaches, and cherries were shipped all over the country from here.

At the end of World War II a new industry emerged: electronics. San Jose began to grow, until the area is now the seventeenth-largest metropolitan region in the country. The county has one of the highest per-capita incomes in the United States. Computers, computer components, and other high-tech products, both civilian and military are the main items manufactured here.

III

Practical Uses

Picture Factory

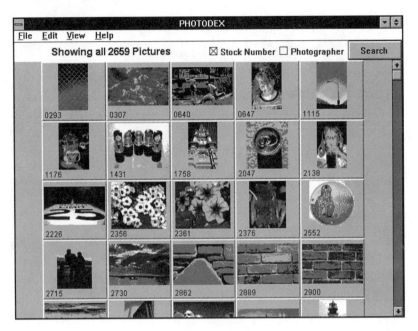

Publisher: PHOTODEX

Environment: Windows

Description of Contents:

This disc contains thousands of colorful photographs that are ready to export to other applications. Special search technology allows the user to quickly find the type of photograph required. The disc also contains thumbnails and full-screen views.

Types of Data: Text, graphics

Ordering Information: 800-377-4686

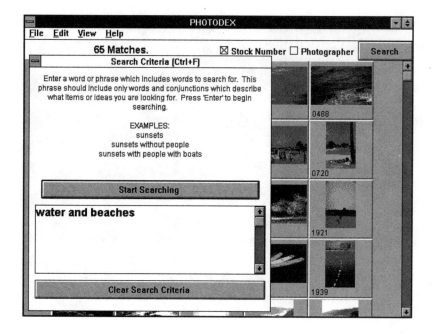

TestDrive

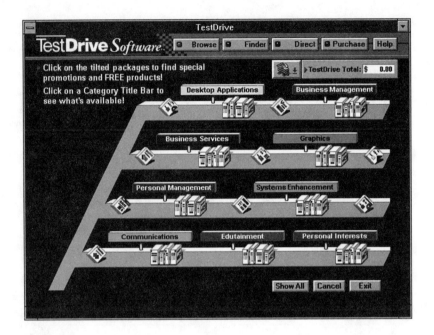

Publisher: TestDrive Corporation

Environment: Windows

Description of Contents:

This disc contains hundreds of program demonstrations and full working versions on one CD. Try a program and if you wish to purchase it, call the toll free number to receive the key number. The full program can then be installed directly from the CD.

Type of Data: Program

Ordering Information: 800-788-8055

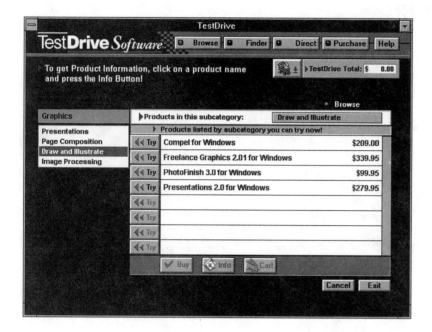

The Family Doctor, Windows, 3rd Edition

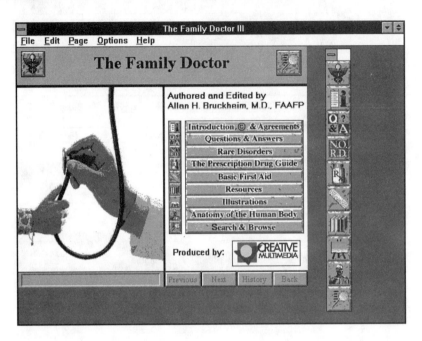

Publisher: Creative Multimedia Corporation

Environment: Windows

Description of Contents:

This disc is a comprehensive reference on general medical and health questions and concerns. The disc includes text, 300 full-color illustrations, animation, and a guide to more than 1,600 prescription drugs.

Types of Data: Text, graphics, animation

Ordering Information: 513-241-4351

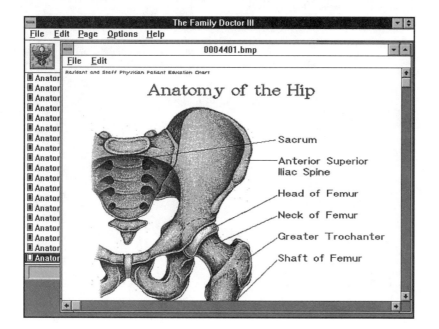

Monarch Notes

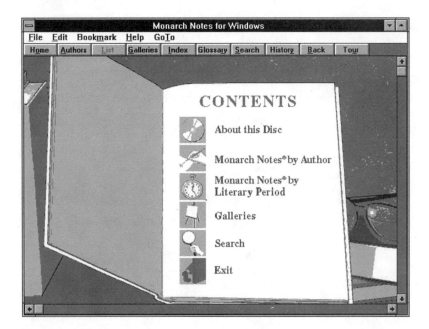

Publisher: Bureau Development

Environment: Windows

Description of Contents:

This disc contains the Complete Monarch Notes by Simon and Schuster on one CD-ROM. Included on the disc are video interviews with authors, animations of scenes, narrations of selected passages, and an author picture gallery.

Types of Data: Text, graphics, animation, video, audio

Ordering Information: 201-808-2700

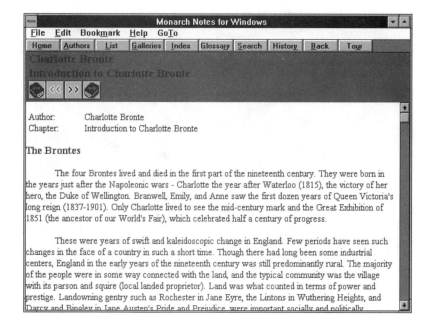

Author: Charlotte Bronte
Chapter: Introduction to Charlotte Bronte

The Brontes

The four Brontes lived and died in the first part of the nineteenth century. They were born in the years just after the Napoleonic wars - Charlotte the year after Waterloo (1815), the victory of her hero, the Duke of Wellington. Branwell, Emily, and Anne saw the first dozen years of Queen Victoria's long reign (1837-1901). Only Charlotte lived to see the mid-century mark and the Great Exhibition of 1851 (the ancestor of our World's Fair), which celebrated half a century of progress.

These were years of swift and kaleidoscopic change in England. Few periods have seen such changes in the face of a country in such a short time. Though there had long been some industrial centers, England in the early years of the nineteenth century was still predominantly rural. The majority of the people were in some way connected with the land, and the typical community was the village with its parson and squire (local landed proprietor). Land was what counted in terms of power and prestige. Landowning gentry such as Rochester in Jane Eyre, the Lintons in Wuthering Heights, and Darcy and Bingley in Jane Austen's Pride and Prejudice, were important socially and politically.

The CD-ROM of CD-ROMs

Publisher: Resource International Publishing

Environment: Windows

Description of Contents:

This disc contains a listing of available CD-ROMs with information on the publisher, price, content, platforms, and reviews.

Types of Data: Text, graphics

Ordering Information: 817-582-7373

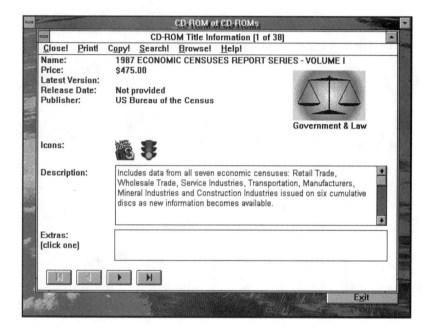

Sound Library Pro

Publisher: Wayzata Technology, Inc.

Environment: Windows, Mac

Description of Contents:

This disc contains a well-organized library of thousands of sound effects, with menus for easy location and access.

Types of Data: Text, graphics, audio

Ordering Information: 800-735-7321

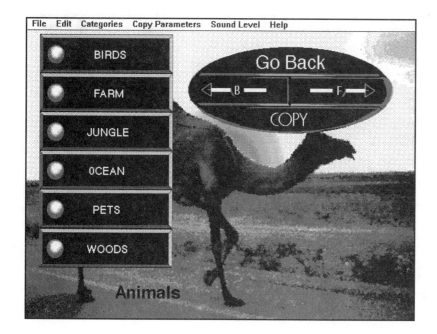

CD Fun House

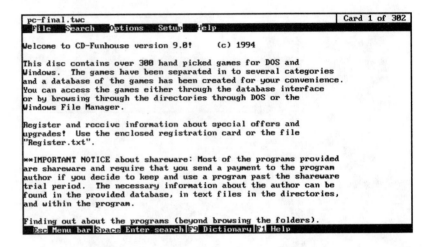

Publisher: Wayzata Technology, Inc.

Environment: Windows, Mac

Description of Contents:

This disc contains more than 1,000 games for all ages. Categories include Adventure, Arcade, Role Playing, Casino, Parlor, Sports, Space, and School.

Type of Data: Program

Ordering Information: 800-735-7321

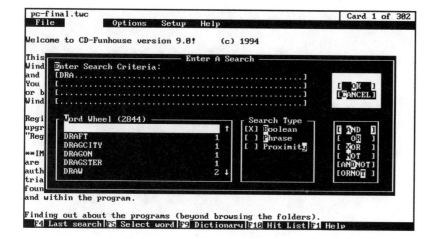

```
┌─────────────────────────────────────────────────────────┬──────────────────┐
│ pc-final.twc                                             │ Card 1 of 302    │
│ File            Options   Setup   Help                                      │
│ Welcome to CD-Funhouse version 9.0!      (c) 1994                           │
│ This┌─────────────────── Enter A Search ──────────────────────┐             │
│ Wind│ Enter Search Criteria:                                  │             │
│ and │ [DRA.................................................]   │             │
│ You │ [..................................................]  ┌──────────┐   │
│ or b│ [..................................................]  │ [  OK  ] │   │
│ Wind│ [..................................................]  │ [CANCEL] │   │
│     │                                                      └──────────┘   │
│ Regi│ ┌─Word Wheel (2844) ──────────────┐ ┌─Search Type ─┐ ┌──────────┐   │
│ upgr│ │                               ↑ │ │[X] Boolean   │ │[  AND  ] │   │
│ "Reg│ │ DRAFT                       1   │ │[ ] Phrase    │ │[  OR   ] │   │
│     │ │ DRAGCITY                    1   │ │[ ] Proximity │ │[  XOR  ] │   │
│ **IM│ │ DRAGON                      1   │ └──────────────┘ │[  NOT  ] │   │
│ are │ │ DRAGSTER                    1   │                  │[ANDNOT ] │   │
│ auth│ │ DRAW                        2 ↓ │                  │[ORNOT  ] │   │
│ tria│ └─────────────────────────────────┘                  └──────────┘   │
│ foun└─────────────────────────────────────────────────────────┘             │
│ and within the program.                                                     │
│                                                                             │
│ Finding out about the programs (beyond browsing the folders).               │
│ F4 Last search F5 Select word F9 Dictionary F10 Hit List F1 Help            │
└─────────────────────────────────────────────────────────────────────────────┘
```

III

Practical Uses

Loon Magic

Publisher: Wayzata Technology, Inc.

Environment: Windows, Mac

Description of Contents:

This disc contains a complete journey through the life of Loons, including hundreds of full-color photographs, sound, music, and video.

Types of Data: Text, audio, graphics

Ordering Information: 800-735-7321

AQUATIC TURF

"The remote, spruce-edged lake shown under the cold, bright moonlit spring night; a gray crust, the last remains of winter's ice, glittered along the lake's shore. Abruptly the silence was broken by loud wails, yodels, eerie cries and splashing of water. It was our first signal that the loons had arrived back from their winter sojourn in the south, ready for another season." -David Ewert, 1983

III

Practical Uses

Walkthroughs and Flybys

```
┌─────────────────────────────────────────────────────────────┐
│              Walkthroughs & Flybys CD Main Menu               │
├─────────────────────────────────────────────────────────────┤
│                                                               │
│          → 1 - Demos for the Sound Blaster                    │
│                                                               │
│            2 - Autodesk 3D Studio animations                  │
│                                                               │
│            3 - Demos created with GRASP                       │
│                                                               │
│            4 - Miscellaneous demos                            │
│                                                               │
│            5 - Credits and general information                │
│                                                               │
│            6 - Make a boot disk with this menu system installed│
│                                                               │
│            7 - Quit to DOS                                     │
│                                                               │
│                                                               │
│          17MB of phenomenal demos and scripts                 │
│                                                               │
│                                          Memory: 443 K        │
├─────────────────────────────────────────────────────────────┤
│                      Press H for Help                         │
└─────────────────────────────────────────────────────────────┘
```

Publisher: The Waite Group

Environment: DOS

Description of Contents:

This disc contains more than 500M of animations, Autodesk FLI files, and sound.

Types of Data: Graphics, animation, audio

Ordering Information: 800-368-9369

Amanda Stories

Publisher: The Voyager Company

Environment: Windows

Description of Contents:

This disc contains 10 animated children's stories by Amanda Goodenough. The disc features Inigo the Cat and Your Faithful Camel.

Types of Data: Graphics, animation, audio

Ordering Information: 800-446-2001

Microsoft Developer's Network

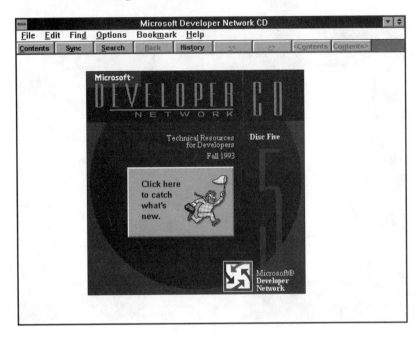

Publisher: Microsoft Corporation

Environment: Windows

Description of Contents:

This disc contains user manuals, source code, and other useful material for users of Microsoft programming languages.

Type of Data: Text

Ordering Information: 206-882-8080

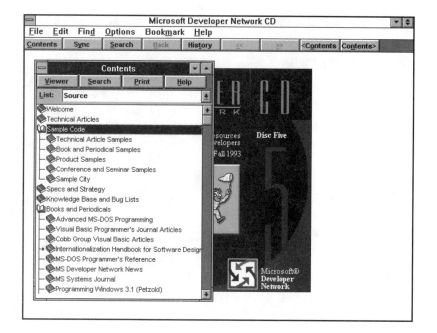

Twain's World

Publisher: Bureau of Electronic Publishing

Environment: Windows

Description of Contents:

This disc contains the full text of all Mark Twain's work, plus graphics and video.

Types of Data: Text, graphics, video

Ordering Information: 800-828-4766

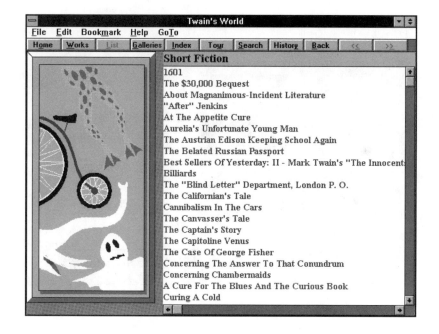

Short Fiction

1601
The $30,000 Bequest
About Magnanimous-Incident Literature
"After" Jenkins
At The Appetite Cure
Aurelia's Unfortunate Young Man
The Austrian Edison Keeping School Again
The Belated Russian Passport
Best Sellers Of Yesterday: II - Mark Twain's "The Innocent:
Billiards
The "Blind Letter" Department, London P. O.
The Californian's Tale
Cannibalism In The Cars
The Canvasser's Tale
The Captain's Story
The Capitoline Venus
The Case Of George Fisher
Concerning The Answer To That Conundrum
Concerning Chambermaids
A Cure For The Blues And The Curious Book
Curing A Cold

Electronic Library of Art

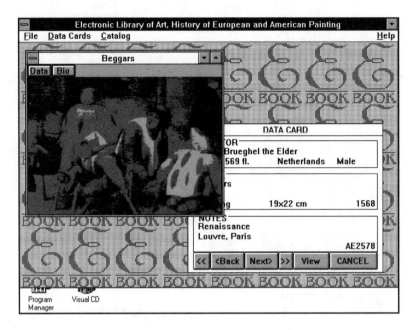

Publisher: Ebook, Inc.

Environment: Windows

Description of Contents:

This disc contains paintings, biographies, and other information on famous artists.

Types of Data: Text, graphics, audio

Ordering Information: 510-429-1331

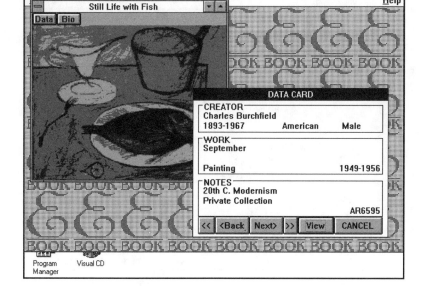

Street Atlas USA

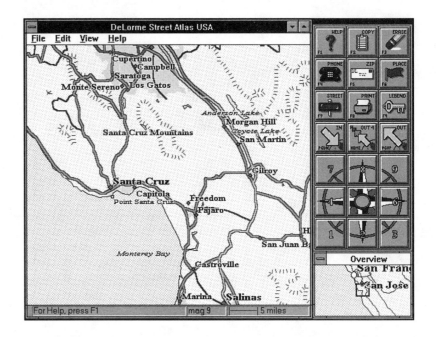

Publisher: DeLorme Mapping

Environment: Windows

Description of Contents:

This disc includes maps to street level of the entire United States, searchable by ZIP code or by phone number.

Type of Data: Vector Graphics

Ordering Information: 207-865-1234

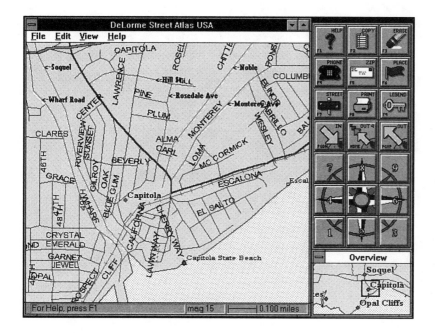

The CD-ROM Directory

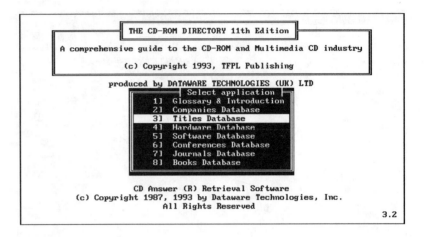

Publisher: TFPL Publishing

Environment: DOS

Description of Contents:

This disc contains a listing of titles, consultants, and manufacturers of CD-ROM products.

Type of Data: Text

Ordering Information: 202-296-6009

```
 F1:Help   F2:Full   F3:Search  F4:Actions   F5:Links   F9:Options   F10:Quit
=3.1.1=============================================Title List: 1 of 17
                                               ** - indicates demo/ad

Title                                   Publisher

Beyond the Wall of Stars                CMC - Creative Multimedia Corpora

Cancer 88                               CMC - Creative Multimedia Corpora

The Complete Works - Sherlock Holmes    CMC - Creative Multimedia Corpora

The Complete Works - William Shakespeare CMC - Creative Multimedia Corpora

The Family Doctor                       CMC - Creative Multimedia Corpora

India Tourism                           CMC - Creative Multimedia Corpora

International Wine Guide (EB)            CMC - Creative Multimedia Corpora


 ↑ ↓ PgUp PgDn, F2 or Enter to toggle to full, F3 to return to search
```

Visual CD

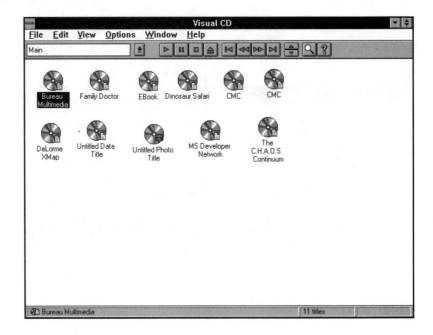

Publisher: Meridian Data

Environment: Windows

Description of Contents:

This disc contains an integrated environment for tracking and playing CD-ROMs and audio CDs. The disc also includes Photo CD images.

Types of Data: Program, Photo CD

Ordering Information: 408-438-3100

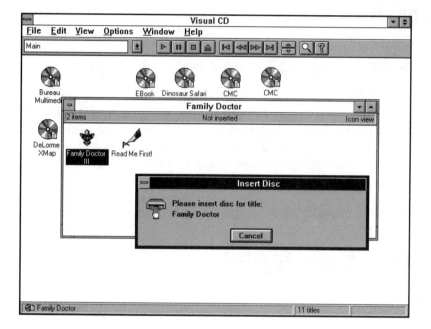

The Oxford English Dictionary on CD-ROM

Publisher: Tri-Star Publishing

Environment: DOS, Windows

Description of Contents:

This disc contains the entire original 12 volumes of the Oxford English Dictionary on a single CD-ROM disc. The searching menu is built on eight indexes that provide information on word definition, the history of words (etymology), and quotation references (by date, by author, by work, or by text of the quote).

Types of Data: Text, graphics

Ordering Information: 800-872-2828

The Master Search Bible

Publisher: Tri-Star Publishing

Environment: DOS

Description of Contents:

This disc is a complete Scripture reference library, which includes four Bible versions and ten reference works. Versions include the King James, New American Standard, New International Version, and Transliterated. The reference works include Greek/English and Hebrew/English dictionaries, Strong's Concordance, Wycliff Bible Commentary, and the Oxford Scofield Study Bible.

Types of Data: Text, graphics

Ordering Information: 800-29-BIBLE

American Business Phone Book

Publisher: American Business Information

Environment: DOS

Description of Contents:

This disc contains more than 10 million listings from more than 5,000 Yellow Page directories of United States and Canadian businesses. This disc enables you to search by company name, city, state, ZIP code, area code, or phone number.

Type of Data: Text

Ordering Information: 402-543-4595

Library of the Future Series, Second Edition

Publisher: World Library, Inc.

Environment: DOS, Windows

Description of Contents:

This disc contains more than 2,000 separate, complete, and unabridged pieces of literature, philosophy, history, religion, science, poetry, drama, and children's classics from more than 970 titles on one CD-ROM. You can search by author, title, word(s), phrase(s), era, country of origin, subject, and more. Features include on-screen tutorials, the capability to print part or entire works or save to disk, on-screen information on each author and title, split-screen comparison, more than 150 illustrations with index, Reader's Screen with automatic advance, Bookmark, and Notepad. This disc also offers mouse support.

Types of Data: Text, graphics

Ordering Information: 800-443-0238

III

Practical Uses

The New Grolier Multimedia Encyclopedia

Publisher: Grolier Electronic Publishing, Inc.

Environment: DOS, Windows MPC

Description of Contents:

All 21 volumes of the Academic American Encyclopedia are stored on this CD-ROM. Also included are 33,000 articles on science, world history, art, as well as thousands of pictures, more than 250 maps, audio, a timeline, and motion sequences. Features include Boolean logic operators, outlines, tables, fact boxes, links for cross referencing, and bibliographies.

Types of Data: Text, audio, graphics, motion sequences

Ordering Information: 800-356-5590

Novell Network Support Encyclopedia

Publisher: Novell, Inc.

Environment: DOS

Description of Contents:

This disc contains the full text of manuals, technical notes and bulletins, application notes, a buyer's guide, the NetWire Library, fixes, and downloadable files for Novell networking products.

Types of Data: Text, graphics

Ordering Information: 801-429-7000

World Factbook Navigator

Publisher: Wayzata Technology, Inc.

Environment: DOS, Windows

Description of Contents:

This disc includes maps and numerical data provided by the CIA about the people, government, economy, and geography of 247 countries, from Afghanistan to Zimbabwe. It also includes appendices on the United Nations, weights and measures, and abbreviations and descriptions of international organizations.

Types of Data: Text, graphics

Ordering Information: 218-326-0597

Microsoft Bookshelf

Publisher: Microsoft Corporation

Environment: DOS

Description of Contents:

This disc contains six popular reference volumes. Volumes include *The American Heritage Dictionary, The Concise Columbia Encyclopedia, Bartlett's Familiar Quotations, The Concise Columbia Dictionary of Quotations, Roget's Electronic Thesaurus,* and *The World Almanac and Book of Facts 1991.* Text can be cut and pasted into word-processing documents.

Type of Data: Text

Ordering Information: 206-882-8080

III

Practical Uses

TIME Magazine Compact Almanac 1991 Edition

Publisher: Time Warner Communications

Environment: DOS

Description of Contents:

This disc contains the full text of *Time* magazine from 1989 through April 1, 1991, with the Russian Revolution through September 9, 1991, plus major *Time* stories from the 1920s to the 1980s. Included on the disc are more than 200 still photos and 180 full-color charts. The almanac also includes full-color maps of the world, 400 tables from the U.S. Statistical Abstract, the Congressional Directory with fax and phone numbers, and basic documents of American history.

Types of Data: Text, graphics, audio, video

Ordering Information: 800-828-4766

Front Page News

Publisher: Wayzata Technology, Inc.

Environment: DOS

Description of Contents:

This disc contains the full text of more than 15 U.S and international-based wire services and news sources, including Comtex, United Press International, TASS, Chinese News Agency, Business Wire, French News Agency, Journal Graphics, Latin American News Agency, PR Newswire, OPEC, German News Agency, Market Consensus Surveys, News USA, and Reuters. Each disc covers a full year. Updates are published quarterly.

Type of Data: Text

Ordering Information: 800-735-7321

The Family Doctor

Publisher: Creative Multimedia Corporation

Environment: DOS

Description of Contents:

This disc is based on the work of Dr. Allen Bruckheim, physician and author of the Tribune Media's syndicated Family Doctor column. It contains easy-to-understand advice to nearly 2,000 of the most commonly asked health questions, plus 300 color illustrations, information on more than 1,600 prescription drugs, a glossary of more than 100 medical terms, and local and national resource listings.

Types of Data: Text, graphics

Ordering Information: 800-776-9277

U.S. History on CD-ROM

Publisher: Creative Multimedia Corporation

Environment: DOS

Description of Contents:

This disc contains the full text of 107 books relating to U.S. history, plus more than 1,000 photos, maps, and tables of historical events. Some of the books included are the *Watergate/Nixon Transcripts, America's Drug Habit, Iran-Contra Affair, Gettysburg, Exploring the West, Black Americans, Biology & The Bill of Rights,* and *Clash of Cultures.*

Types of Data: Text, graphics

Ordering Information: 800-776-9277

III

Practical Uses

Multimedia Audubon's Birds of America

Publisher: Creative Multimedia Corporation

Environment: DOS

Description of Contents:

This disc is an electronic reproduction of John James Audubon's 1840 portfolio of *Birds of America.* The disc includes fully indexed text and color plates with digital reproductions of bird calls.

Types of Data: Text, graphics, audio

Ordering Information: 800-776-9277

Multimedia Audubon's Mammals

Publisher: Creative Multimedia Corporation

Environment: DOS

Description of Contents:

This disc contains the complete text of the 1840 first edition "Octavo" set of John James Audubon's *Quadrupeds of North America,* with more than 150 full-color mammal lithographs, and mammal sounds from the Cornell Library of Natural Sounds.

Types of Data: Text, graphics, audio

Ordering Information: 800-766-9277

Shakespeare

Publisher: Creative Multimedia Corporation

Environment: DOS

Description of Contents:

This disc contains the complete works of Shakespeare—including the full text of plays, sonnets, and poems—in both American and Queen's English versions.

Type of Data: Text

Ordering Information: 800-766-9277

CD-ROMs in Print

Publisher: Meckler

Environment: DOS

Description of Contents:

This disc is an international guide to CD-ROMs, CD-I, CDTV, and electronic book products. It also includes information about information providers, publishers, distributors, and software producers for CD-ROM.

Type of Data: Text

Ordering Information: 800-226-6967

III

Practical Uses

Sherlock Holmes on Disc

Publisher: Creative Multimedia Corporation

Environment: DOS

Description of Contents:

This disc contains the complete text of Sherlock Holmes stories by Arthur Conan Doyle, with linoleum block print illustrations by Dr. George Wells, plus *The Medical Casebook of Arthur Conan Doyle* by Alvin E. Rodin and Jack D. Key and *Medical Poetry* by Dr. George S. Bascom.

Types of Data: Text, graphics

Ordering Information: 800-766-9277

Full Spectrum

Publisher: Alde Publishing

Environment: DOS

Description of Contents:

This disc contains approximately 12,000 images from Dover Publications Ready-to-Use and Quick Copy Art in PCX format. Categories include sports, circus, mythological creatures, hospital, house and real estate, and others.

Type of Data: Graphics

Ordering Information: 612-934-4239

Total Baseball

Publisher: Creative Multimedia Corporation

Environment: DOS

Description of Contents:

This disc contains more than 500 images of players, teams and ballparks, sound clips from baseball's most memorable moments, and more than 2,600 pages of text. Text includes statistics of more than 13,000 players; batting, pitching and fielding registers for all Major League players; MVP, Cy Young, Rookie of the Year and Hall of Fame Awards; full team rosters; and the top 100 all-time, lifetime, and single-season leaders in all categories.

Types of Data: Text, graphics, audio

Ordering Information: 800-766-9277

Font Fun House

Publisher: Wayzata Technology, Inc.

Environment: DOS

Description of Contents:

This disc contains more than 100 TrueType and PostScript screen and printer fonts for Windows and DOS.

Types of Data: Text, fonts

Ordering Information: 800-735-7321

III

Practical Uses

Nautilus Subscription Service

Publisher: Metatec/Discovery Systems

Environment: Windows

Description of Contents:

Nautilus is a multimedia "magazine" on CD-ROM. Discs include games, software demonstrations and reviews, shareware, multimedia applications, graphics and photo resources, audio tracks and music files. Subscription includes 12 issues per year.

Types of Data: Text, graphics, audio

Ordering Information: 614-961-6694

Lotus 1-2-3 Release 1.1 for Windows with Multimedia Smarthelp

Publisher: Lotus Development Corporation

Environment: Windows

Description of Contents:

This disc contains the complete version of Lotus 1-2-3 for Windows accompanied by online help and tutorials with text, sound, pictures, and animation. The complete text of all 1-2-3 manuals is included on this disc.

Types of Data: Text, graphics, audio, animation

Ordering Information: 800-554-5501

Compton's Family Encyclopedia

Publisher: Britannica Software, Inc.

Environment: DOS

Description of Contents:

This disc contains the full text of all 26 volumes of Compton's print encyclopedia, with more than 10 million words, 30,000 articles, 15,000 photographs, charts, maps, a world atlas, and 30 minutes of audio, plus the Merriam-Webster Dictionary.

Types of Data: Text, graphics, audio

Ordering Information: 312-347-7128

The New York Times on Disc

Publisher: UMI, Inc.

Environment: DOS

Description of Contents:

This disc contains the full text (in ASCII format) of articles published by *The New York Times* since 1990. The disc is updated monthly.

Type of Data: Text

Ordering Information: 800-521-0600

III

Practical Uses

Microsoft Bookshelf for Windows

Publisher: Microsoft Corporation, Multimedia Division

Environment: Windows MPC

Description of Contents:

This disc contains seven popular reference volumes. Volumes include *The American Heritage Dictionary, The Concise Columbia Encyclopedia, Bartlett's Familiar Quotations, The Concise Columbia Dictionary of Quotations, Roget's II: The New Thesaurus, The World Almanac and Book of Facts* , and the *Hammond Atlas of the World.* Microsoft Bookshelf for Windows is an illustrated, animated, talking reference library with word pronunciation, quotes, and music.

Types of Data: Text, graphics, audio, animation

Ordering Information: 206-882-8080

Book of Lists #3

Publisher: VT Productions

Environment: Windows

Description of Contents:

This disc contains entertaining lists of unusual people, places, and events in the fields of health, entertainment, politics, American history, sports, communications, science, space, and more. The disc includes drawings, pictures, and narration of selected subjects by author David Wallechinsky.

Types of Data: Text, graphics, audio

Ordering Information: 800-532-3766

GAMEROOM

Publisher: Digital Publishing Company, Inc.

Environment: DOS

Description of Contents:

This disc contains hundreds of games and shareware programs, graphics (GIF), and animation (FLI) files.

Types of Data: Text, graphics

Ordering Information: 800-279-6099

Macmillan Dictionary for Children

Publisher: Maxwell Electronic Publishing

Environment: Windows

Description of Contents:

This disc contains 12,000 entries, 1,000 illustrations, and 400 sound effects and pronunciations of words. This disc features "Zak," an animated character who shows how to get started and pops up occasionally throughout the application. This disc also includes word histories and language notes.

Types of Data: Text, graphics, sound

Ordering Information: 617-661-2955

Multimedia Beethoven—The Ninth Symphony

Publisher: Microsoft Corporation

Environments: Windows, MPC

Description of Contents:

This disc contains Beethoven's Ninth Symphony with study aids, musical analysis, historical perspective of Beethoven's world, a game, CD audio, and MIDI sound.

Types of Data: Text, graphics, sound

Ordering Information: 206-882-8080

III

Practical Uses

Dialog OnDisc MEDLINE: Clinical Collection

Publisher: Dialog Information Services

Environment: DOS

Description of Contents:

This disc contains five years of references and abstracts from 150 clinical medical journals from MEDLINE, plus citations to articles in the abridged Index Medicus and "Selected List of Books and Journals for the Small Medical Library" by Brandon & Hill.

Type of Data: Text

Ordering Information: 800-334-2564

Computer Select

Publisher: Ziff Communications Company

Environment: DOS

Description of Contents:

This disc contains the full text of more than 70 computer magazines and abstracts from more than 70,000 articles from other computer periodicals. Also included on this disc are hardware specifications for more than 70,000 hardware, software, and data communications products, 12,000 computer industry company profiles, and a 9,000-term glossary of computer terms. Each disc covers the previous 12 months.

Type of Data: Text

Ordering Information: 212-503-4400

Other CD-ROM Titles

The following list contains additional CD-ROM titles. With close to 6,000 titles available, space does not permit a more extensive listing. This list illustrates the variety of information available on CD-ROM.

Sources for CD-ROM Titles

Bureau of Electronic Publishing

141 New Road
Parsippany, NJ 07054
800-828-4766
201-808-2700
201-808-2676 (Fax)

CD-ROM, Inc.

1667 Cole Blvd., Suite 400
Golden, CO 80401
303-231-9373
303-231-9581 (Fax)

New Media Schoolhouse

Market Plaza Building
Box 390 Westchester Avenue
Pound Ridge, NY 10576
800-672-6002
914-764-0104 (Fax)

New Media Source

3830 Valley Centre Drive
San Diego, CA 92130-9834
800-344-2621
619-793-4823 (Fax)

Peter J. Phethean Ltd.

1640 E. Brookdale Avenue
La Habra, CA 90631
714-990-5524
714-990-0137 (Fax)

Softec Plus

1200 East River Road
Tuscon, AZ 85718
800-779-1991
602-882-4930

III

Practical Uses

Updata CD-ROM
1736 Westwood Blvd.
Los Angeles, CA 90024
800-882-2844
602-888-4930

Selected CD-ROM Titles

AIDS CD-ROM
Maxwell Electronic Publishing

AIDS Information and Education Worldwide
EBSCO Publishing

Aircraft Encyclopedia
Quanta Press

About Cows
Quanta Press

ADA Buffet
ALDE Publishing

ADA Whitesands
ALDE Publishing

Advanced Math Workshop
Top Class Technology

Agri/Stats I
Hopkins Technology

Aloha Hawaii
Motherlode, Inc.

Amazing Moby, The
ALDE Publishing

American Business Phone Book

American Business Information

American Family Physician

Creative Multimedia Corporation

American Medical Directory, The

American Medical Association

Annals of Internal Medicine CD-ROM

Maxwell Electronic Publishing

Atlanta Journal and Constitution on CD-ROM

UMI

Atlas Pack

Software Toolworks, Inc.

Aviation Compendium

Flightline Electronic Publishing

Banking Library

IHS Regulatory Products, Inc.

Bible Library

Ellis Enterprises, Inc.

BiblioMed

Healthcare Information Services, Inc.

BiblioMed Cardiology Series

Healthcare Information Services

Biological Abstracts on Compact Disc

SilverPlatter Information, Inc.

Biomedical Engineering Citation Index

Institute for Scientific Information

Biotechnology Citation Index

Institute for Scientific Information

Book Review Index

H.W. Wilson Company

Books in Print Plus

Bowker Electronic Publishing

Books in Print with Book Reviews Plus

Bowker Electronic Publishing

Books Out of Print Plus

Bowker Electronic Publishing

Business Lists on Disc

American Business Information

Business Yellow Pages of America

Innotech, Inc.

C CD-ROM

ALDE Publishing

Canadian Encyclopedia

Reteaco, Inc.

Cancer on Disc 1988

Creative Multimedia Corporation

CANCER-CD

SilverPlatter Information, Inc.

Career Opportunities

Quanta Press

CASEBASE-The Arkansas Report

Law Office Information Systems

CASEBASE-The Connecticut Report

Law Office Information Systems

CASEBASE-The Rhode Island Report

Law Office Information Systems

CD-ROM Developer's Lab

Software Mart, Inc.

CD Gamepack

Software Toolworks

CD-ROM Sampler

Discovery Systems

CD-ROM Sourcedisc

Linda Helgerson Associates

CD-ROM Directory 1991

UniDisc

CD-ROMs in Print

Meckler

CDWord Interactive Biblical Library

Moody Press

Chemistry Citation Index

Institute for Scientific Information

III

Practical Uses

Chicago Tribune Ondisc

UMI

Chicano Database on CD-ROM

Chicano Studies Library, University of California, Berkeley

Children's Reference Plus

Bowker Electronic Publishing

Christian Science Monitor Ondisc

UMI

CIA World Factbook

Quanta Press

Classic Art

G&G Designs

Classic Book Collection

World Library

Clip Art 3-D

NEC Information Technologies

Coate's Art Review-Impressionism

Quanta Press, Inc.

Code of Federal Regulations

CD Book Publishers

College Handbook

Maxwell Electronic Publishing

ColorBytes Mini Sampler

ColorBytes, Inc.

Compton's Multimedia Encyclopedia

Britannica Software, Inc.

Computer Products Database

GML Corporation

Computer Select

Computer Library

Computing Archive

ACM CD-ROM Publications

Comstock Desktop Photography

Comstock

Comstock Desktop Photography CD-ROM: Volume I

Comstock

Comstock Desktop Photography CD-ROM: Volume II

Comstock

Comstock Desktop Photography CD-ROM: Volume III

Comstock

Constitution Papers

Johnston & Company

Consumer Information

Quanta Press

Consumers Reference Disc

National Information Services Corporation

Consumer Reports on CD-ROM

National Information Services Corporation

III

Practical Uses

CorelDRAW! 2.01 on CD-ROM

Corel

Corporations

Standard and Poor

County and City Data Book 1988

US Bureau of the Census

Countries of the World

Bureau of Electronic Publishing

Cross-Cultural CD

SilverPlatter Information, Inc.

Defender of the Crown

Faxon Company

DIALOG OnDisc HEALTHCARE PRODUCT COMPARISON SYSTEM

Dialog Information Services, Inc.

DIALOG onDisc MEDLINE

Dialog Information Services, Inc.

DIALOG OnDisc MEDLINE CLINICAL COLLECTION

Dialog Information Services, Inc.

DiscLit-American Authors

OCLC

DiscLit-British Authors

OCLC

DRUGDEX

Micromedex, Inc.

Eastern Europe Business Database

American Directory Corporation

EMERGINDEX

Micromedex, Inc.

Enviro/Energyline Abstracts Plus

Bowker Electronic Publishing

Excerpta Medica CD: Drugs and Pharmacology

SilverPlatter Information, Inc.

Excerpta Medica CD: Gastroenterology

SilverPlatter Information, Inc.

Excerpta Medica CD: Immunology and AIDS

SilverPlatter Information, Inc.

Exerpta Medica CD: Neurosciences

SilverPlatter Information, Inc.

Excerpta Medica CD: Psychiatry

SilverPlatter Information, Inc.

Facts on File World News Digest CD-ROM 1980-1989

Facts on File

Family Doctor

Creative Multimedia Corporation

FDA on CD-ROM

FD, Inc.

FindIt Webster with Pronunciation

Innotech, Inc.

III

Practical Uses

Food Analyst

Hopkins Technology

Food Analyst Plus

Hopkins Technology

Front Page News 1990

Wayzata Technology, Inc.

Geophysics of North America

National Geophysical Data Center

Ghost Tracks

Falcon Scan

Great Cities of the World: Volume 1

InterOptica Publishing

Great Cities of the World: Volume 2

InterOptica Publishing

Greatest Books Collection

World Library

Guiness Disc of Records 1990

Faxon Company

Harrap's Multilingual CD-ROM Dictionary Database

Harrap Publishing Group

Hazard Awareness Health and Safety Library

ON LINE Computer

History of the World

Bureau of Electronic Publishing

Index to Legal Periodicals

The H.W. Wilson Company

International Graphics Library

Educorp

Image Gallery

NEC Information Technologies

Index to U.S. Government Periodicals

H.W. Wilson Company

International Encyclopedia of Education

Pergamon Press Ltd.

Jane's All the World's Aircraft, 1989-1990

Jane's Information Group

Jane's Armour and Artillery, 1989-1990

Jane's Information Group

Jane's Armoured Fighting Vehicle Systems, 1989-1990

Jane's Information Group

Jane's Avionics

Jane's Information Group

Jane's Battlefield Surveillance

Jane's Information Group

Jane's Fighting Ships, 1990-1991

Jane's Information Group

Jane's Infantry Weapons

Jane's Information Group

Jane's Land-based Air Defense

Jane's Information Group

Jane's Military Communications

Jane's Information Group

III

Practical Uses

Jane's Military Logistics

Jane's Information Group

Jane's Radar & Electronic Warfare Systems

Jane's Information Group

Journal of the American Medical Association

Creative Multimedia Corporation

Languages of the World

NTC Publishing Group

LegalTrac on InfoTrac

Information Access Company

Library of the Future Series, First Edition

World Library, Inc.

Library Reference Plus

Bowker Electronic Publishing

Lotus One Source: CD/Banking

Lotus Development Corporation

Magazine Article Summaries

EBSCO Electronic Information (EEI)

Magazine Index Plus

Information Access Company

Magazine Rack

Ziff Communications Company

Mammals: A Multimedia Encyclopedia

National Geographic Society

Mark Encyclopedia of Polymer Science and Engineering

John Wiley & Sons, Inc.

MasterSearch Bible

Tri-Star Publishing

Materials Science Citation Index

Institute for Scientific Information

Medical Devices on CD-ROM

FD, Inc.

MEDLINE on Silver Platter

SilverPlatter Information, Inc.

Microcomputer Index

Learned Information, Inc.

Microlog-Canadian Research Index

Micromedia Limited

Microsoft Programmer's Library

Microsoft Multimedia Division

Microsoft Stat Pack

Microsoft Multimedia Division

Middle East Diary

Wayzata Technology, Inc.

Minnesota Statutes 1988, 1989, 1990

Minnesota State Reviser of Statutes Office

Montana Statutes

Innotech, Inc.

Multi-Bible

Innotech, Inc.

National Portrait Gallery

Abt Books, Inc.

National Register of Historic Places
Wayzata Technologies, Inc.

Neuroscience Citation Index
Institute for Scientific Information

New England Journal of Medicine
Maxwell Electronic Publishing

New Mexico Law on Disc
The Micnie Company

NIF Drugs and Crime Library
Abt Books, Inc.

North American Indians
Wayzata Technology

Officer's Bookcase
Quanta Press

Online Hotline News Service CD-ROM
Information Intelligence, Inc.

Oxford English Dictionary
Tri-Star Publishing

Oxford Textbook of Medicine
Oxford Electronic Publishing

Patent Images
MicroPatent

PC Blue
ALDE Publishing

PC Globe
PC Globe, Inc.

Pediatric Infectious Disease Journal: 1985-1989

Creative Multimedia Corporation

Pediatrics in Review/Redbook: 1985-1990

Creative Multimedia Corporation

Pediatrics on Disc: 1983-1990

Creative Multimedia Corporation

Pesticides Disc

Pergamon Press

Peterson's College Database

SilverPlatter Information, Inc.

PhoneDisc USA

PhoneDisc USA Corporation

Photo Gallery

NEC Information Technologies

Physician's Data Query

Cambridge Scientific Abstracts

Physician's Desk Reference

Medical Economics Company

POISINDEX

Micromedex, Inc.

Pro Phone—Business + one

New Media Publishing

Professional Photography Collection

Discimagery

Programmer's ROM

Quanta Press

Publique Arts

Quanta Press

RBBS in a Box

Quanta Press

Reader's Guide Abstracts

H.W. Wilson Company

Reference Library

Software Toolworks

San Francisco Chronicle Ondisc

UMI

Scenic and Architecture

CD-ROM Galleries

Scenic and Castles

CD-ROM Galleries

Search Master Business Commercial Library

Matthew Bender & Company, Inc.

Search Master California Library

Matthew Bender & Company, Inc.

Search Master Collier's Bankruptcy Library

Matthew Bender & Company, Inc.

Search Master Federal Library

Matthew Bender & Company, Inc.

Search Master Intellectual Property Library

Matthew Bender & Company, Inc.

Search Master New York Library

Matthew Bender & Company, Inc.

Search Master Personal Injury Library

Matthew Bender & Company, Inc.

Search Master Tax Library

Matthew Bender & Company, Inc.

Search Master Texas Library

Matthew Bender & Company, Inc.

Science Helper K-8

PC-SIG, Inc.

Seals of the U.S. Federal Government

Quanta Press, Inc.

Select Demos

Computer Library

Shareware Carousel

ALDE Publishing

Shareware Gold

Quanta Press

Shareware Grab Bag

ALDE Publishing

SIRS CD-ROM

Social Issues Resources Series, Inc.

Social Sciences Citation Index

Institute for Scientific Information

SOCIOfile CD

Sociological Abstracts, Inc.

Software CD

Information Sources, Inc.

Software Du Jour

ALDE Publishing

Software Jukebox

Selectware Technologies, Inc.

Spectrum Clip Art

ALDE Publishing

Sporting News Baseball Guide and Register

Quanta Press

Super Blue

ALDE Publishing

Support on Site

Computer Library

Supreme Court on Disc

HyperLaw

Supermap Hong Kong

Space-Time Research

Terrorist Group Profiles

Quanta Press, Inc.

Toronto Star on CD-ROM

Southam Electronic Publishing

TypeGallery LJ

NEC Information Technologies

U.S. Atlas

Software Toolworks

U.S. History on CD-ROM

Bureau of Electronic Publishing

U.S. Presidents

Wayzata Technology, Inc.

USA Factbook

Quanta Press

USA Wars—Civil War

Quanta Press

USA Wars—Korea

Quanta Press

USA Wars—Vietnam

Quanta Press

Virginia Law on Disc

The Michie Company

Voter Lists on Compact Disc

Aristotle Industries

West CD-ROM Delaware Corporation Law Library

West Publishing Company

West CD-ROM Federal Securities Library

West Publishing Company

West CD-ROM Federal Tax Library

West Publishing Company

West CD-ROM Government Contracts Library

West Publishing Company

III

Practical Uses

Wheeler Quick Art
Quanta Press

Wildlife & Fish Worldwide
NISC

Wall Street Journal Ondisc
UMI

Washington Post Ondisc
UMI

Wild Places
Aris Entertainment

Women—Partners in Development
CD Resources Inc.

Word Cruncher Disc
Electronic Text Corporation

World Atlas
Software Toolworks

World Energy CD-ROM
National Information Services Corporation

World Research Database
National Information Services Corporation

World View
Aris Entertainment

World WeatherDisc
WeatherDisc Associates, Inc.

Worldscope Profiles
Wright Investors' Service

Selected Multimedia Titles

The following multimedia titles are available on CD-ROM. They may require an MPC-compatible PC, but they all include some form of audio as well as graphics; some discs also include video and animation.

Airwave Adventure: Murder Makes Strange Deadfellows

Tiger Media

Airwave Adventure: The Case of the Cautious Condor

Tiger Media

AmandaStories: Interactive Stories for Children

Voyager Company

American Visa

Applied Optical Media Corporation

Animation Works Interactive

Gold Disk, Inc.

Annabel's Dream of Ancient Egypt

Texas Caviar

Battle Chess MPC

Interplay Productions

Berlitz Think and Talk Series (French, German, Italian, Spanish)

HyperGlot Software Company

Beyond the Wall of Stars

Creative Multimedia Corporation

Billboard History of Rock and Roll

Compton's NewMedia

Birds of North America

Applied Optical Media Corporation

Book of Lists #3

VT Productions

Book of MIDI

Opcode Systems, Inc.

Buzz Aldrin's Race Into Space

Interplay Productions

Chaos Continuum

Creative Multimedia Corporation

Chessmaster 3000

Software Toolworks

CIA World Tour

Bureau of Electronic Publishing

Compton's Multimedia Encyclopedia for Windows

Compton's New Media

Corel ArtShow '91 CD-ROM

Corel Systems Corporation

Countries of the World Encyclopedia

Bureau of Electronic Publishing

Desert Storm—The War in the Persian Gulf

Warner New Media

DigiSound Audio Library

Presentation Graphics Group

Dinosaur Safari

Creative Multimedia Corporation

Doctor's Book of Home Remedies

Compton's New Media

Dvorak on Typing

Interplay Productions

Electronic Library of Art

Ebook, Inc.

Encore

Passport Designs, Inc.

Future Wars

Interplay Productions

Great Cities of the World—Volume 1

InterOptica Publishing Limited

Great Cities of the World—Volume 2

InterOptica Publishing Limited

Great Literature, Classic Edition

Bureau of Electronic Publishing

Guiness Multimedia Disc of Records 1991

Compton's New Media

Headline Harry and the Great Paper Race

Davidson & Associates

HyperClips for Windows

HyperMedia Group

Introductory Games in Spanish and Introductory Games in French

Syracuse Language Systems

Jones in the Fast Lane

Sierra Online

III

Practical Uses

Just Grandma and Me

Broderbund Software

KnowledgePro

Knowledge Garden, Inc.

Learn to Speak Spanish

HyperGlot Software Company

LINKS

Access Software, Inc.

Living Books

Broderbund Software

Magic Death—Virtual Murder 2

Creative Multimedia Corporation

Mammals: A Multimedia Encyclopedia

National Geographic Publishing

Mantis: XFS700 Experimental Space Fighter

Paragon Software

Martian Memorandum

Access Software

Master Tracks Pro

Passport Designs, Inc.

Media Music

Passport Designs, Inc.

Mediasource

Applied Optical Media Corporation

Microsoft Works for Windows

Microsoft Corporation

Midisoft Studio for Windows

Midisoft Corporation

Mixed-Up Mother Goose

Sierra Online

Monarch Notes

Bureau Development

Monologue

First Byte

Multimedia Audubon's Mammals

Creative Multimedia Corporation

Multimedia Beethoven: The Ninth Symphony

Microsoft Corporation

Multimedia Birds of America

Creative Multimedia Corporation

Multimedia Explorer

Autodesk, Inc.

Multimedia World Fact Book

Bureau Development

MusicBytes

Prosonus

New Russia and Her Republics

InterOptica Publishing Limited

Orient

InterOptica Publishing Limited

Our House

Context Systems, Inc.

Oxford English Dictionary, 2nd Edition

Oxford University Press

Parenting—Prenatal to Preschool

Creative Multimedia Corporation

PC Magazine Select Demos

Computer Library

Presidents: It All Started with George

National Geographic Society

Roger Ebert's Movie Home Companion

Quanta Press

Sherlock Holmes Consulting Detective

Icom Simulations

Software Toolworks Multimedia Encyclopedia

Software Toolworks

Star Trek: 25th Anniversary Game

Interplay Productions

Supertoons

Wayzata Technology, Inc.

Time Table of Arts and Entertainment

Compton's NewMedia

Time Table of Business, Politics, and Media

Compton's NewMedia

Treehouse

Broderbund Software

Trax

Passport Designs, Inc.

U.S. Atlas

Software Toolworks

U.S. History on CD-ROM

Bureau Development

USA Wars: Civil War

Quanta Press

USA Wars: Korea

Quanta Press

Virtual Worlds

Wayzata Technology

Vital Signs: The Good Health Resource

Texas Caviar

Wave for Windows

Turtle Beach Systems

Where in the World is Carmen Sandiego?

Broderbund

Who Killed Sam Rupert?

Creative Multimedia Corporation

Word Munchers

Minnesota Educational Computer Corp.

World Atlas Multimedia 3.0

Software Toolworks

Zoo Keeper

Davidson & Associates

III

Practical Uses

Selected CD-I Titles

The following CD-I titles are available. They require a Philips or Magnavox CD-I player; some require a Full Motion Video (FMV) cartridge.

CD-I titles are available from Philips Media Electronic Publishing, 800-824-2567.

Digital Video—Feature Films

Apocalypse Now
Black Rain
Fatal Attraction
The Firm
The Hunt for Red October
Indecent Proposal
Naked Gun 2 1/2
Patriot Games
Posse
Sliver
Star Trek VI: The Undiscovered Country
Top Gun
White Christmas

Digital Video—Music*

An Evening with Bon Jovi
Andrew Lloyd Webber: The Premier Collection
Billy Ray Cyrus: Live
Bryan Adams: Waking Up the Neighbors
The Cream of Eric Clapton
Sting: Ten Summoner's Tales

Requires Digital Video Cartridge

Sports

A Great Day at the Races
ABC Sports Presents: Power Hitter
ABC Sports Presents: The Palm Springs Open
Caesar's World of Boxing
Caesar's World of Gambling
International Tennis Open
NFL Trivia Challenge
Video Speedway

Games

Alice in Wonderland
Alien Gate
Backgammon
Battleship
CD Shoot
Connect Four
Dark Castle
Defender of the Crown
Escape from CyberCity
Jigsaw
Laser Lords
Link: The Faces of Evil
Lords of the Rising Sun
Mystic Midway: Rest in Pieces
Pinball
Sargon Chess
The Seventh Guest
Tetris
Text Tiles
Voyeur
Zelda: The Wand of Gamelon
Zombie Dinos from Planet Zeltoid

Children's

Beauty and the Beast
The Berenstain Bears On Their Own
The Best of Baby Songs
Brer Rabbit and the Wonderful Tar Baby
Cartoon Jukebox
Children's Musical Theatre
The Dark Fables of Aesop
David and Goliath
Draw 50
The Emperor's New Clothes
Girl's Club
Hanna-Barbera's Cartoon Carnival
How the Rhinoceros Got His Skin
How the Camel Got His Hump
Little Monster at School

III

Practical Uses

More Dark Fables From Aesop
Moses: Bound for the Promised Land
Moses: The Exodus
Noah's Ark
Paint School I and II
Pecos Bill
Pegasus
Richard Scarry's Best Neighborhood, Ever!
Sandy's Circus Adventures
Shari Lewis: Lamb Chop's Play-Along Action Songs
Stickybear Reading
Story Machine: Magic Tales
Story Machine: Star Dreams
The Story of Jonah
The Story of Samson
Tell Me Why I and II
A Visit to Sesame Street: Numbers
The Wacky World of Miniature Golf

Music

Classical Jukebox
Cool Oldies Jukebox
Earth Rhythms
Gershwin Connection
Gifts to Behold
Golden Oldies Jukebox
James Brown: Non-Stop Hit Machine
Jazz Giants
Louis Armstrong: An American Songbook
Luciano Pavarotti: O Sole Mio
Mozart: A Musical Biography
Prelude
Rembrandt: His Art and the Music of His Era
Todd Rundgren: No World Order
You Sing Christmas Favorites

Special Interest

ACT College Search
Amparo Museum
Anne Williams Presents: The Foods of France
Art of the Czars: St. Petersburg and the Treasures of the Classical Guitar
Compton's Interactive Encyclopedia
Dutch Masters of the Seventeenth Century
The Flowers of Robert Mapplethorpe
The French Impressionists
Gardening by Choice: Flowers and Foliage
Harvest of the Sun: Vincent Van Gogh
Hermitage
Jazz Guitar
A National Parks Tour
Playboy: Complete Massage
Rand McNally's America: United States Atlas
Renaissance Gallery
Rhythm Maker
Rock Guitar
Shark Alert
The Smithsonian Presents: The Riches of Coins
The Smithsonian Presents Stamps: Windows on the World
Time-Life Astrology
Time-Life Photography
Treasures of the Smithsonian
World Of Impressionism

III

Practical U

9

CHAPTER

Scenarios

This chapter illustrates the way in which CD-ROM technology is being used by companies today to distribute information, increase productivity, enhance creativity, lower costs, and make business decisions. You will learn about real companies that use CD-ROM in their operations, as well as how different departments within any company can use CD-ROM to accomplish specific tasks. You will also learn why information becomes more accessible and useful when it is delivered in CD-ROM format.

Using CD-ROM in the Medical Field

When Dr. Patrick Roney was hired by Swedish Hospital in 1988 to deal with physicians' needs, he also acquired responsibility for the computer services department. He was a visionary who saw the potential computers had for hospital applications, such as information access to billing and patient histories, communications between departments and individuals, and what he called a "library without walls." This last concept was what led Swedish Hospital to install a LAN and add a dedicated CD-ROM server. Dr. Roney envisioned a central source for electronically delivered information that would be available on every computer workstation in the facility.

According to Carl Weber, head of the Computer Services department at Swedish, the hospital now has 16 networked CD-ROM drives that contain 12 applications. These applications are available to any of 300 workstations on the network. The network connects computers in the main building, as well as computers in an annex three blocks away. They also provide remote access, via modem, from hospitals in downtown Denver, Vail, Breckenridge, Steamboat Springs, Aspen, and Cheyenne, Wyoming, as well as to doctors who need to do research at home. The CD-ROM applications alone average between 1,000 and 1,500 accesses per month. Ten percent of the usage of the applications is from remote dial-in users.

The CD-ROM applications on the network include SilverPlatter's Medline, Microsoft Bookshelf, PDR (Physician's Desk Reference), Micromedex, CINAHL (Cumulative Index on Nursing and Allied Health Literature), and Scientific American Medicine. Doctors use Medline, which contains information provided by the National Library of Medicine, to do research for papers, discussions, and presentations. They use the Physician's Desk Reference to look up the most current information on drugs, their dosages, and contraindications.

Nurses, however, are the ones who benefit the most from having this vital information at their fingertips. According to Kathy Tamulewicz, registered nurse and liaison between the nursing staff and the Computer Services department, after a patient is admitted into the emergency room or into Pediatrics, the nurses use Micromedex to compute dosages of "core" drugs according to a patient's age and weight, then record them on the patient's medical chart. Core drugs are the ones that must be administered without delay should the patient experience an arrest of any function, such as breathing or heartbeat. Before Micromedex was available, these calculations had to be done by hand, which was a laborious and time-consuming process.

Micromedex also enables nurses to print out drug information sheets for patients to take home with them. Before Micromedex was available, this information was often handwritten. The emergency room staff also uses Micromedex for instant access to treatment information for injuries. Nurses use Scientific American Medicine to learn about specific diseases. CINAHL is used for research papers, presentations, and continuing education.

Tamulewicz says that the benefits derived from using CD-ROM rather than print media include the availability of more information on more types of drugs and diseases, ease of use, faster and more efficient calculations of dosages, and more up-to-date information. Printed publications that contain the same information are updated annually, but most of the CD-ROM discs are updated quarterly. Another consideration is the elimination of much of the paper copies used to distribute this information. Instead of sharing printed copies of this information, the nurses can access networked CD-ROM applications electronically and read it from the screen.

Swedish Hospital now stores its patient records on a mainframe computer with a 10-gigabyte capacity. Mr. Weber says that he is considering the possibility of storing some of this archival information on CD-Recordable discs to free space on the mainframe. He looks forward to the day when the paper copies of all the hospital's records, which require enormous amounts of storage space, can be stored on CD-ROM discs as images of the actual documents.

Using CD-ROM in Government

The United States Government must compile and distribute vast quantities of information for all of its agencies. This information includes, but is not limited to, information about every part (from a resistor to an entire helicopter) that is stocked, stored, and issued by the U.S. Government—about 12 million different parts. Included with this information are part descriptions, part numbers, National Stock Numbers (NSN), manufacturers, ordering information, shipping specifications, prices, and CAGE (Commercial and Government Entity) codes for every manufacturer.

In 1982, this information took up about three gigabytes of storage space. At that time, the information was distributed on microfiche and in print form as eight different publications. As you can imagine, the amount of information alone was sufficient to make distributing and using it a logistical nightmare. The government began to look for a more efficient way to distribute this data. At first, officials were told that it could not be done.

The government kept looking, however, and by the mid 1980s, the Department of Defense was working on a project called the "paperless ship." Much of the weight carried by Navy ships is in the form of paper contained in filing cabinets. The Navy tried to find other ways to store the information; one of the ways was to use CD-ROM. The Department of Defense decided to try CD-ROM to store their logistical information on land as well as at sea.

In 1991, the contract for the project of collecting, indexing, storing, and distributing this data on CD-ROM was awarded to Optical Publishing, Inc. (now OPTIMUS Corporation) of Fort Collins, Colorado. OPTIMUS, working to the government's specifications, designed a customized indexing-and-retrieval system specifically to meet the needs of the government agencies who needed to use this information, and developed a product called Federal Logistics Data on CD-ROM, or FED LOG.

The Defense Logistics Service Center in Battle Creek, Michigan, collects information from the Army, Navy, and Air Force every month. This data is recorded to 50 9-track tapes that hold 91.6 megabytes each of data. These tapes are then shipped to OPTIMUS and allowed to sit for 24 hours to acclimatize (data on magnetic tape is susceptible to temperature changes). OPTIMUS then loads the tapes on an IBM mainframe computer and uses special indexing-and-compression techniques to reduce the size of the data to 1.96 gigabytes.

After the data has been indexed and compressed, OPTIMUS software builds an image of the data on the mainframe as it will appear on CD-ROM. At this point, the data is verified by an automatic testing procedure for at least 24 hours. After the testing, OPTIMUS ships the compressed, indexed, premastered, and tested data to a mastering facility to be mass-produced on CD-ROM. The entire process, from the data's arrival to its departure for the mastering facility, takes about 12 days.

FED LOG is used by the Army, Navy, Air Force, NASA, Veteran's Administration, FAA, NATO countries, and other military services and civil agencies to order parts that are stocked by the U.S. Government.

Today, the information has grown to more than 5 gigabytes. If it were still being distributed on microfiche, at a reduction of 48-to-1 over paper, this stack of microfiche sheets would be over a foot high, or over 3,000 sheets. Not only is that much microfiche difficult to mail and store, but it also is difficult to use.

If you wanted to look up a part, for example, you had to look on one set of microfiche for the part number. Then you had to cross-reference that part number by

using another set of microfiche to find the National Stock Number (NSN). To find out the cost of the part and how to order it, you looked at yet another set of microfiche; to see a description of the part, you looked at still another set of microfiche. This process had to be repeated for each part. To make things even more interesting, the different microfiche publications were updated according to different schedules; the information, therefore, was not always compatible.

According to Greg Lewis at the Defense Logistics Services Center, OPTIMUS's FED LOG on CD-ROM provides government agencies with a way to find information in one place about all the parts stocked by the government. Users can search for parts by part number, NSN, supplier, manufacturer, name, description, CAGE code, or any other field. It is even possible to search by partial name or partial number.

OPTIMUS's customized interface cross-references all the separate databases so that one search pass results in all the needed information. A special batch-mode feature enables users to enter part numbers in a batch file, walk away as the computer processes the search, and then collect the data later. Another feature, called the External Systems File Interface, allows the resulting data to be output to a file on a hard disk or floppy disk, to a tape, or to a printer. The output also can be tailored to include specific fields in any order.

FED LOG is distributed on a set of four compact discs. The set is updated every month. Each month, 22,000 four-disc sets are shipped. Lewis says that the cost of publishing this information on CD-ROM is about two-thirds the cost of using microfiche. The cost of distribution alone is one-third the cost for the microfiche and print versions, even though it is now updated monthly rather than annually or quarterly. The productivity increase over microfiche is conservatively estimated at eight-to-one. Although FED LOG is available only to government agencies, it is a stunning example of the suitability of CD-ROM for storing and distributing formerly unmanageable amounts of data.

Using CD-ROM in a Typical Business

Bill Henry, Inc. is a fictional company invented for the purpose of demonstrating the way in which any company can use CD-ROM technology to enhance creativity, boost productivity, stay competitive, and increase efficiency. All the departments at Bill Henry—including marketing, art, administration, finance, and computer services—use CD-ROM applications.

III

Practical Uses

The Marketing Department

The marketing department uses information provided by the Bureau of the Census and Supermap to identify and target potential markets. Suppose, for example, that Bill Henry, Inc. knows that the people most likely to buy its product are college students. By using the Census Bureau information and Supermap, marketing personnel can find the geographic locations in which higher-than-average concentrations of students live. Local advertising can be purchased in those regions to reach the potential market.

To reach this market with direct mailings, marketing uses PhoneDisc USA and the American Business Phone Book on CD-ROM. These discs contain the names and telephone numbers of most individuals and businesses in the United States.

To stay abreast of developments and trends in the business world, the marketing staff uses *The Wall Street Journal, Time* magazine, and *Front Page News.* All these publications are currently available on CD-ROM. Instead of searching stacks of old issues of magazines and newspapers for articles on their target market, staffers simply insert the appropriate disc, type in a keyword or phrase, such as "college student," and let the computer and CD-ROM drive identify and display every article in which the word or phrase appears.

The Art Department

The art department works closely with the marketing department to create product sheets and advertising artwork. The artists use CorelDRAW!, which is distributed on a CD-ROM disc, to create artwork. The artists use Font Fun House to import eye-catching fonts that appeal to their young customers. They also can use the clip art that is included on the CorelDRAW! disc or on the NEC Clip Art 3D disc to add pizzazz to their artwork. The artists can create a polished, professional look by incorporating photographs from the Comstock Desktop Photography disc.

The art department also can create multimedia presentations that include graphics, sound, text, and animation by using Authorware, a multimedia authoring program that is distributed on CD-ROM. Nautilus, a monthly multimedia "magazine" on CD-ROM, helps the artists keep up to date on the developments in multimedia and provides copyright-free graphics and sound files that the artists can use in their multimedia projects.

The Administrative Support Staff

The administrative support staff is responsible for writing letters, distributing memos, and finding the right answer or the correct background information. The

staff uses Microsoft Bookshelf, which includes a dictionary, thesaurus, world atlas, almanac, encyclopedia, and two books of quotations on one CD-ROM disc. For more in-depth information, they can consult the Oxford English Dictionary, Grolier's Encyclopedia, and the Reference Library. The Reference Library includes a dictionary and thesaurus, the New York Public Library Desk Reference, the 20th Century History Guide, and more than 800 business forms.

Tip

Languages of the World is an indispensable application for dealing with international distributors. It contains 18 different bilingual dictionaries for 12 languages, which enable you to translate a word not only from English to Finnish, but from German to Chinese.

The Financial Department

The chief financial officer of Bill Henry uses Standard & Poor's CD-ROM, which contains detailed information on 4,000 companies on the New York, American, and Canadian stock exchanges. The officer also uses Lotus Onesource: CD/ Corporate, which has information on privately held companies, to keep track of the competition. When the company was first starting out, the CFO used Microsoft's Small Business Consultant to help make decisions. This CD-ROM contains more than 220 publications from the Small Business Administration, from other government agencies, and from one of the country's leading accounting firms. In addition, it costs less than half of what the print versions cost.

Because Bill Henry, Inc. relies heavily on temporary help in the finance department, Lotus 1-2-3 with Multimedia Smarthelp is helpful for training and refreshing the skills of the temporary workers. This CD-ROM contains the complete version of Lotus 1-2-3 for Windows, accompanied by text, sound, pictures, and animation to help users learn 1-2-3 on the job.

The Computer Services Department

The computer services department of Bill Henry, Inc. is responsible for ensuring that the data processing equipment used by all departments is functioning efficiently and meeting the needs of employees. The analysts use Computer Select, which contains the full text of over 70 computer magazines and periodicals, article summaries of over 100 more, and a 9,000-term computer glossary, to research products and new developments in the computer industry. SOS (Support On Site) is another CD-ROM application by the providers of Computer Select that contains technical support documentation for many popular hardware and software products.

III

Practical Uses

To run the company's Novell LAN efficiently, the computer services department uses the Novell NetWare Encyclopedia on CD-ROM as a reference. This disc contains the contents of seven Novell NetWare manuals, as well as technical notes, diagrams, files, patches, fixes, and product information.

Because Bill Henry, Inc. has networked its CD-ROM drives, all discs are available to all users at all times and are subject to any security limitations that the network administrator decides to impose.

The computer services department also is responsible for evaluating, recommending, and installing software for the company. The staff uses a CD-ROM disc from InfoNow Corporation that contains demos of programs. These demos help staffers decide which programs to buy. After they make a purchasing decision, the analysts can call the disc's publisher, and a software key number enables them to access and install that software from the same CD-ROM disc. Analysts also have a disc called Zip++ that compares their mailing address database to a list of every mailing address in the United States and automatically corrects any errors.

Although Bill Henry, Inc. is a fictional company, all the CD-ROM products mentioned in this scenario are real. They are a small sample of the more than 6,000 applications that are available on CD-ROM.

Summary

This chapter has shown you examples of the ways in which real companies use CD-ROM technology that is available today to accomplish specific goals. If you did not find an application mentioned in this chapter that you think would be useful to you, that does not mean that such an application does not exist. This chapter has barely scratched the surface, and more CD-ROM titles are being produced every day. If the data you want to use is not yet available on CD-ROM, you can produce your own application. The next chapter explains the process of publishing your own CD-ROM disc.

CHAPTER 10

How to Produce a CD-ROM

When CD-ROM technology was first introduced, many people considered CD-ROM production a mysterious, expensive, and time-consuming procedure that should be left to the experts. This thinking has changed dramatically since the early days of the technology. Today, companies and individuals can produce a simple CD-ROM quickly and at a reasonable cost.

This chapter answers the most common questions regarding CD-ROM production. Specifically, this chapter answers the following questions:

✔ Why manufacture a CD-ROM?

✔ When is CD-ROM the appropriate medium for publishing?

✔ How much does it cost to produce a CD-ROM?

✔ How do you produce a CD-ROM?

Why Manufacture a CD-ROM?

The vast storage capacity of CD-ROM, the low cost of CD-ROM drives, and the standards that are in place for the media, all combine to make CD-ROM the ideal way to distribute large amounts of information at a low cost. CD-ROM also is a cost-effective way to distribute, publish, or gain access to information that you or your company works with on a regular basis.

If your company, for example, has a large collection of data that it presently publishes in print form and distributes, it should consider publishing that information on CD-ROM. Suppose, for example, that your company now publishes a technical training manual that includes graphics and text. If you distributed this information on CD-ROM, you could enhance the manual with sound and video clips to explain complicated procedures in detail. You could index the text completely so that the reader can quickly find the exact reference needed. This manual could be shared over a network, rather than passed from one person to another. Because no person could remove or write on pages from the manual, the manual would stay intact. If needed, pages could be printed. The cost of producing and distributing the information on disc rather than in print is considerably less than printing several copies of the manual.

CD-ROM's versatility also makes it an excellent medium for marketing and sales presentations. You can include all the elements of a lecture with a slide show and music on one small disc. This disc can be played on a portable computer with a CD-ROM drive.

CD-ROM is a universal medium, and the economics are compelling. The factor that drives CD-ROM growth is the amount of digital data in the world. Digital data is doubling every three years with no end in sight.

With the advent of multimedia, another compelling reason to consider publishing on CD-ROM is apparent. The capability to present information enhanced by sound and graphics in a single self-contained package opens up new possibilities for electronic publications in marketing, education, training, and entertainment. CD-ROM offers a way to combine these elements that no other publishing or information distribution medium offers.

What Data Is Appropriate for CD-ROM?

If you are considering CD-ROM production, keep this general rule in mind: data is data. The only differences between data stored on a hard disk and data stored on a CD-ROM disc are the manner in which the data is arranged and the fact that, after committed to CD-ROM, the data cannot be changed. Your data must be in a static

form, which means that it needs no further changes. You can make changes only by updating the data and producing a new disc.

Storing Static Data

Static data is ideal for distribution on CD-ROM because once the CD-ROM is produced, updates are not necessary. A good example of static data is a collection of historical documents or a collection of classical literature. After you store information such as this on a disc, you never need to update the disc. You can replicate the disc once, and if sufficient discs are produced for the market, only stamping is ever required. If you need to produce more discs, you can submit the original premaster tape or one of the CD-ROM discs to the mastering facility as input for the second production run.

Many mastering facilities retain the original master discs for the same purpose. Discs of this type benefit both the publisher and the consumer. The publisher does not have to be concerned with constant updates of the material; therefore, the disc can be sold at a reasonable price. As long as the disc contains the raw information only and no commentary, historical perspectives, or references to other dynamic material, no changes are necessary. The only updates may be to add improved search software or to fix program bugs.

Updating CD-ROM Discs

In today's world, however, information is rarely static. Frequent updates make useful information more expensive to acquire and produce on disc. Yet some of the most useful and powerful CD-ROM applications are those that are updated regularly.

Update frequency is determined by the nature of the data. Information that changes regularly, however, may be suited for CD-ROM storage. CD-ROMs that are updated monthly or even weekly are very common. Many people specifically choose CD-ROM as the distribution medium for dynamic data because of its low production and shipping cost and the stability of the medium.

If the data you want to store is prone to change, you must evaluate your willingness to update the CD-ROM. Updating the disc means future costs for a new CD-ROM that contains the new information. If you are hesitant to commit to updating the data, other means of storing your information may be better suited to your task.

III

Practical Uses

How Much Does It Cost?

The cost of producing a CD-ROM title depends on many factors. The actual cost of physically replicating a CD-ROM disc by mass production (500 or more copies) is about $1.50 per disc. This figure assumes that the information has been through the processes that make it ready to be transferred to disc. Each element of the development cycle is examined in more detail later in this chapter.

Previously, a small stamping of discs (one to 25) was rather expensive. With the introduction of one-off CD-ROM writers from companies such as Sony, JVC, Ricoh and Philips, the cost of producing a small quantity of CD-ROMs has decreased. You can, for example, purchase your own desktop disc mastering system for around $3,800. If you take the data through the production process, you can have a single CD-ROM cut by a service bureau for as little as $99. Mastering facilities also offer special rates (near $500) for one to ten prototype discs.

Mastering costs have been stable for the last four years and are unlikely to go much lower.

Barring a shortage of raw materials, mastering costs are unlikely to go any higher. Mastering costs have been stable for the last four years and are unlikely to drop by more than 10 percent.

In the past, a CD-ROM project was likely to cost from $50,000 to $500,000. Hardware and software costs alone could run over $100,000. CD-ROM technology was limited to Fortune 500 companies and governmental agencies because the process required expensive, powerful, dedicated hardware, and a highly technical staff.

Fortunately for CD-ROM consumers, things have changed. If you already have the programs or indexed data that you want to place on CD-ROM, producing a single CD-ROM disc can cost as little as $99. Replicating 100 discs can cost as little as $1,500.

Keep in mind that mastering costs do not include your development time and expense. Depending on the project, even development costs can be kept to a minimum. The development process usually is the most expensive cost you incur in producing a CD-ROM. As with other technologies, such as television, hand-held calculators, and microcomputers, the cost of development has decreased.

The demand for affordable CD-ROM publishing prompted the CD-ROM industry to find better and cheaper ways to make CD-ROM available to a wider market.

Because you can farm out parts of the process to service bureaus, you no longer need thousands of dollars of equipment. The software necessary for development is executed by a personal computer, rather than a mainframe, and the variety of retrieval software available offers a wide range of prices and features for any budget or application. Today, small businesses and individuals can produce CD-ROMs on their desktops.

How Do You Produce a CD-ROM?

In the past, the CD-ROM production process was a mystery. It seems as if a special magic was necessary to produce a CD-ROM disc. With the tools that are available today, however, you can complete the process with most any data. In most cases, if you can run the data on your hard disk, you can produce it on CD-ROM.

If just this simple rule applies, why does so much confusion exist about CD-ROM production? The answer becomes apparent when you separate the various parts of the CD-ROM production process. The final steps in the production process require special hardware, software, or special expertise that previously has been available only to a limited few. If you break down the CD-ROM development cycle into the various processes, however, the project seems less intimidating.

Table 10.1 summarizes the processes that are involved in producing a CD-ROM.

Table 10.1
CD-ROM Development and Production Processes

Process	Purpose
Data acquisition	Assembling the information that is placed on CD-ROM
Rights acquisition	Acquiring the permission to use the information
Software acquisition	Choosing an indexing and retrieval program that is suitable for your data
Data conversion	Altering the data to a format that can be handled by the indexing and retrieval software
Indexing	Using the indexing and authoring software to catalog the data for searching and linking to audio and graphics

continues

Table 10.1, Continued
CD-ROM Development and Production Processes

Process	Purpose
Premastering	Putting the data in CD-ROM format while it still resides on a hard disk
Testing	Simulating the CD-ROM environment so that the application's operation can be tested and optimized before committing it to a final premastered image to send to a mastering facility
Mastering	Producing the glass master and steel stamper for replicating CD-ROM discs

Figure 10.1 illustrates the process from data preparation through delivery of discs. If you are going to produce a CD-ROM title, you or the service bureau are responsible for data preparation and premastering. The rest of the process is done by the mastering facility.

Figure 10.1
Data preparation through disc delivery.

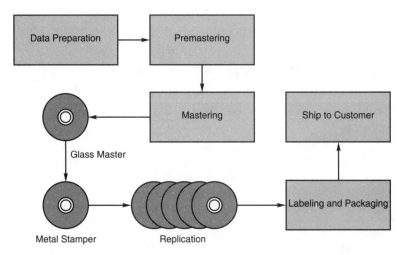

Data Acquisition and Analysis

If you own the data that you intend to publish, this step is not a concern. If the data belongs to another person or organization, however, you must acquire not only the data, but the rights to use the data. This process is called *data acquisition*. In some cases, this process involves considerable time and effort in contract negotiations. Royalties, copyright issues, exclusive and non-exclusive licenses, and other matters can take much time to discuss and finalize.

Many discs produced today contain information compiled by government agencies of the United States. This information often is available to anyone for no cost or for a modest fee. State government information may or may not be as easily available.

Often data analysis is performed after the data is acquired. Much to the surprise of the potential CD-ROM publisher, the data is not in the required format. Data analysis should take place during the data acquisition stage. As you negotiate rights to the data, make sure that you see samples of the data as it will be delivered to you. Your contract should include a backup plan for you in case the data is not delivered in the promised format.

You can get data in many different formats, all of which you must transfer to a large hard disk for the conversion and indexing processes. Figure 10.2 shows several media formats that are commonly used to transfer data.

III

Practical Uses

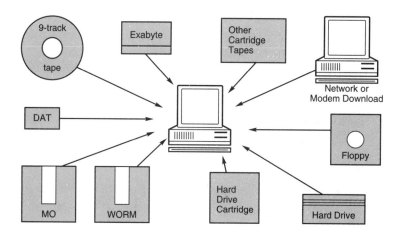

Figure 10.2
Media formats
for data transfer.

Text

If the data you intend to use is now on paper, the information must be put into an electronic format—generally a word processing document. The two methods that you commonly use to convert text on paper to a word processing document are scanning by an Optical Character Recognition (OCR) package and keyboarding.

OCR and keyboarding are expensive propositions, and neither is 100 percent accurate. If a service bureau promises you a 99.5 percent accuracy rate, you must consider what effect this accuracy rate can have on your project. Consider that a standard typewritten page contains about 2,000 characters. With an accuracy rate of 99.5 percent, each page would contain 10 misspelled characters (2,000 – 1,990 = 10). This error rate could translate to 10 words per page for which the user cannot successfully search. If the words that cannot be searched happen to be important words, an accuracy rate of 99.5 percent does not look quite as attractive.

If the material is especially sensitive to accuracy, such as legal materials, medical materials, or financial data, the only way to ensure an accurate transition from paper to electronic format is to proofread the material against an original copy. This step can be time-consuming and costly. If you can avoid converting text from paper to electronic format, do so. In many cases, such as out-of-print books, the original typesetting tapes or disks may still exist. Frequently, you can convert this information to the format you need without the problems associated with paper to electronic conversion.

You can convert text files from one word processing format to another by using either the functions built in to many word processors or by using a dedicated word processor conversion program. Programs such as R Doc X from Advanced Computer Innovations and Software Bridge from Systems Compatibility enable you to make these conversions. Data conversion services that specialize in converting one word processor format to another also can be of help. These services often can convert between hundreds of different formats.

Graphics

You can use almost any graphics format on CD-ROM. You are limited only by the retrieval software that you use. The retrieval software must be able to display the graphics format that you want to use. The most common graphics formats are PCX (PC Paintbrush, Windows Paintbrush), TIF (Tagged Image File Format), and BMP (Windows Bitmap).

You can convert most graphics formats successfully to these common formats. Many graphics conversion software packages are available. These packages include HiJaak and HiJaak PS from Inset Systems, Graphics Workshop from Alchemy Mindworks, and Envision It! from Envisions.

As an example, the following graphics formats can be converted by HiJaak:

ATT	ATT Group 4
LFF	AMIGA ILBM
DXF	AutoCAD
CAL	CALS Raster
GIF	CompuServe Graphics Interchange Format
DBX	DataBeam
CUT	Dr. Halo
IMG	GEM Image
PCC	HP LaserJet
PGL	HP Plotter
IGF	Inset Systems
PIX	Inset Systems
KFX	Kofax Group 4
PIC	Lotus
WMF	Windows Metafile
MAC	MacPaint
PCT	Macintosh PICT
CGM	Computer Graphics Metafile
MSP	Microsoft Paintbrush
PCX	PC Paintbrush
TIF	Tagged Image Format
TGA	Truevision Targa
GED	Wicat
BMP	Windows/OS/2 Bitmap

III

Practical Uses

WPG	WordPerfect Graphics
DIB	Device Independent Bitmap (Same as BMP)

Hijaak PS also can convert EPS (Encapsulated PostScript) files to more than 30 different file formats.

Many word processors also include graphics conversion features. Check your word processor's manual to see whether you already have the tools for the graphics conversion that you need. Programs such as Windows Paintbrush and CorelDRAW! also can convert graphics files to different formats, although they may not do batch processing. The use of these programs may be limited to small numbers of graphics.

Generally, the quality of the scanned image is only as good as the quality of the material you are scanning.

If the data you acquire includes photographs, line drawings, or charts and graphs, scanning these images usually results in a good quality image. Although the equipment used to scan the images may slightly improve the final scan, the quality of the scanned image is generally only as good as the quality of the material you are scanning.

See Appendix B for a list of CD-ROM disc catalogs and titles.

Although stock photographs may be copyrighted and require a usage fee, you can find collections of copyright-free clip art and photographs available on CD-ROM disc that require no fees for unlimited use. Comstock Desktop Photography, Full Spectrum (clip art), and PhotoDisc are just a few examples of these collections. More collections are available.

In certain cases, you may want or need to manipulate your images in various ways, or you may need to create your graphics. Programs such as Aldus Photstyler, Image-In-Color Professional, CorelDRAW!, and Publisher's Paintbrush from ZSoft work well. Remember that Window's PC Paintbrush is adequate for simple image manipulation.

For more information on Red Book audio, see Chapters 2 and 12.

Sound

If you are planning a multimedia disc that includes sound, you must decide how you want the sound presented. You can place sound on a CD-ROM as Red Book audio, PCM (.WAV) files, or as MIDI files. The format you choose depends greatly on the final results that you want. Each of these formats, for example, provide different output quality and use different amounts of space. Red Book audio, for instance, uses over 10M per minute of sound. You must select a format based on how much space you have allotted to sound while balancing the output quality you need.

Certain sound demands, such as converting audio from one format to another or recording narration, require special hardware and software. Keep in mind that music is subject to copyright laws and, in many cases, can be used only by permission. For information about music copyrights and licensing, contact BMI (Broadcast Music Incorporated) or ASCAP (American Society of Composers, Authors, and Publishers). Copyright-free music and sound effects are available on compact disc, such as MEDIAsounds, Mediasource, and Digisound.

You can capture Red Book audio sound on your PC by using a DAL (Digital Audio Labs) or other sound capture board. If you need extremely high quality music or sound, consider using the service of a recording studio or sound lab. If you have doubts, check with the mastering facility to see what type of input is required. You can capture MIDI sound from a musical instrument on your PC by using a synthesizer interfaced to a sound card with MIDI capabilities.

Figure 10.3 illustrates the various ways you can capture data for a CD-ROM project.

III

Practical Uses

Figure 10.3
Data capture.

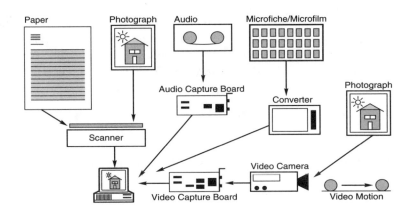

Search and Retrieval Software

Choosing search and retrieval software is the most important step in the process of producing a CD-ROM. If the software you choose cannot deal properly with the data types that you intend to put on the disc, your project comes to a quick halt. Search and retrieval software is available from many different vendors and in a wide range of prices and features.

See Chapter 7 for a discussion of the nine general types of discs.

The software you choose depends on the type of disc you want to produce. If you plan to produce a program, clip art, or typeface disc, for example, you may need no retrieval software. If you plan to produce a disc that contains shareware, you can organize the programs into subdirectories according to function. Each subdirectory can contain a READ.ME file that lists the programs in each subdirectory and their function.

Some shareware discs contain archived files. The use of a compression utility, such as PKZIP, enables you to store much more than 680M of programs on a disc. The best type of compression utility enables you to view the contents of a file before decompression. If you have to

decompress an entire subdirectory just to find one program, you can get frustrated. Check that all the software on the shareware disc is, in fact, shareware and that the license agreement of each program allows you to distribute the program.

You can construct a clip art disc in much the same way you construct a shareware disc. Many clip art discs include an image viewer that enables you to view an image before the image is downloaded to your hard disk for use in another program.

You also can produce archive discs without search and retrieval software. Because the material contained on archive discs is data produced by other programs, your users are expected to have a copy of the appropriate program on their hard disk.

Index and data-only discs frequently are produced without search and retrieval software because, as with archive discs, the user is expected to have available the software that created the indexes or software that reads the indexed data. Check the license agreement of the software that indexed the file or with the software manufacturer to verify that you can distribute the information in an indexed form.

Full text, fielded data, and multimedia applications all require that you include a search and retrieval software program on your CD-ROM.

In the past, many CD-ROM producers provided their retrieval software on floppy disks that accompanied the CD-ROM. The modern practice is to place the retrieval software and an installation or setup program on the CD-ROM itself. This makes installation simple and saves the cost and trouble of producing and shipping a floppy disk with each CD-ROM. In certain circumstances, such as a disc that is completely full with data, providing the retrieval and installation software on floppy disk may still be necessary.

Full Text Retrieval Software

You have a choice of many commercially-available, full text search and retrieval software programs for CD-ROM. Often you can choose more than one way to arrange your data with these packages. If possible, look at other similar applications produced with the search and retrieval package you are considering. This step ensures that the package you select will work with your data.

Most software companies are happy to provide you with a demonstration package that highlights its software's features. For a reasonable price, some companies will index a small amount of your data and produce a prototype. If you run this sample on your hard disk, you can test the software's interaction with your data.

As you select a search and retrieval package, keep space limitations in mind. Contact the company that produces the package in which you are interested and ask about the software's typical indexing overhead. If you have 600M of data, for example, the remaining 80M available on your CD-ROM disc may not be sufficient to hold the program-created indexes. In that case, consider a package that can *span discs*. If the package can span discs, it can keep track of what piece of information is on which disc when your data is spread over two or more discs.

Additionally, make sure that the software you choose allows the search strategies your prospective users may require. If proximity searching is a requirement, make sure that the software has that function. If the database will be used to generate reports, make sure that the software has a reporting capability or can export marked records to a file. In this way, users can manipulate the information in other software packages to generate reports. If the same search criteria may be used repeatedly, the software needs to enable users to save, edit, and re-execute search criteria.

Fielded Data Retrieval Software

If your data is *fielded data*—data that can be broken up into separate small parts or fields—consider using an indexing software that is specifically made for fielded data. Many full text retrieval software packages handle both full text and fielded data. If you have substantial amounts of fielded data, however, a software made specifically for this type of data gives you the best performance results. If your users need to search for keywords, do numeric comparisons, and search for items such as < $2000.00 or > 500 ml, fielded data-only software is a necessity.

Multimedia Software

If you plan a multimedia application, consider which elements of the multimedia (or multiformat) world you want to include. For a full-blown multimedia application, you need software that enables you to link to Red Book audio, MIDI files, PCM (.WAV) files, graphics, animation and video motion files.

Graphics are of two general types: raster and vector. A *raster* image is a bit map, or a complete picture represented by individual dots or pixels such as a scanned

document or video image. A *vector* image is a mathematical representation of an object, usually a set of line end points that relies on algorithms in software or hardware to draw the image in real time when given the end points alone. A vector image takes up less space than an equivalent raster image, but often the desired image resolution requires a raster graphic image.

The three types of audio (MIDI, PCM, and Red Book) require different types of hardware for playback. Red Book audio, or true CD audio, can be played on speakers or headphones attached to the audio jack on your CD-ROM drive. MIDI and PCM files require special hardware and software that is capable of playing these sound formats, such as the Sound Blaster Pro or ProAudio Spectrum sound cards.

Many companies have spent millions of dollars developing CD-ROM search software. Strive to take advantage of that research.

Writing Search and Retrieval Software

Producing your own search and retrieval software can be a huge undertaking and is not recommended unless no software is available that can deal properly with your data. If your data has unique search, display, or output requirements that are not addressed by search software currently on the market, talk to the search software companies about those requirements.

Many software developers can supply, for an additional charge, an Application Programmer's Interface (API), which enables you to customize the software to meet your particular needs. Developers also can tailor their software to meet your requirements. If you do decide to produce your own software, be aware that you not only must deal with the CD-ROM development cycle, but also with the software development cycle.

Data Conversion

After you decide on the type of CD-ROM you want to produce, collect the materials you want to include, and select a search and retrieval package, you can begin the data conversion. *Data conversion* is the process of converting the included materials' raw input into the formats required by the search and retrieval software you chose. You may have text files in WordPerfect format, but your indexing software requires that the text be in ASCII format with paragraph markers. Perhaps you have graphics files in PCX format, for example, but your indexing software requires BMP files. Fortunately, translators are available for data conversion.

You can convert most word processing formats to ASCII format from within the word processing program. You usually can convert graphics formats also. Alternatively, you can use one of the many graphics conversion software packages that are available.

If you have many images that you want to crop or scale, plan on allocating much time to complete this part of the project. Depending on the images, you may be able to convert them in batches, but each image may need individual attention.

Data Indexing

In a perfect world, data indexing would be an automatic procedure in which you tell the program which files to index, and then the program performs the task. Although most programs can index your data unattended, one-pass indexing requires that you have all formatting codes in place. Unfortunately, perfectly formatted data is unusual; therefore, attended indexing sessions are the norm.

The amount of time you set aside for this step varies depending on the amount of data you are including on your disc, the speed at which the program indexes, and other program-related factors. Indexing speeds vary; some programs can index up to 50M per hour on a 486 computer. Another time factor is the reaction of your software to incorrectly formatted data. Various indexing software reacts differently to improperly placed or missing codes. The reaction can vary from complete program lockup to very clear error messages and reports as to what is amiss or to failure to provide any error message at all.

Unless you prepared your data perfectly, your first few passes through the indexing software can either fail or produce unacceptable results. Depending on what the program expects to see as formatting codes, one misplaced or missing code can throw the whole process into confusion. This problem is not necessarily a shortcoming of the software, but is a necessary evil that rears its head whenever you are working with large amounts of data. Within 300,000 pages of text, for example, you are bound to find a missing or misplaced formatting code no matter how careful you were as you formatted the data.

Premastering

After your database is running on your hard disk, you must take the data and put it into the ISO 9660 format before the mastering facility can place the data on CD-ROM. This step requires that you use a premastering system or premastering software. The costs for these systems and software vary widely. Most mastering facilities can do premastering for you at an extra cost, but they prefer that you send an ISO image to them on tape or other transfer media.

 The mastering facility is not responsible for testing your application.

If you want the mastering facility to do the premastering, you have no assurance that the transition from hard disk to CD-ROM disc will not adversely affect your data. The mastering facility is not responsible for testing your application. It is responsible only for mastering the disc in ISO 9660 format. If your application contains mistakes or problems, they are forever etched in polycarbonate, along with the rest of the data. You end up with a shipment of thousands of carefully labeled and packaged coasters. (A *coaster* is a term used for a bad disc. It is useful for putting your coffee mug on, but of little else.)

Performing your own ISO formatting and testing, therefore, is your best bet. If you cannot do your own formatting, have a one-off disc cut by a service bureau or mastering facility. Test your product thoroughly, especially if this is your first CD-ROM project.

 Making an ISO image is a straightforward procedure if you have the appropriate software. ISO formatting software is available from several sources and ranges in cost from $300 to $3,000. The less powerful, inexpensive ISO formatting software simply converts the data into the ISO 9660 format from a DOS file structure. The more expensive software includes such features as simulation, optimization, and data manipulation. It also affords greater versatility in the layout of the physical structure of the disc.

III

Practical Uses

Simulation and Optimization

Simulation and optimization are helpful features offered by some indexing and CD-ROM formatting and development systems. *Simulation* is the process of simulating the CD-ROM environment as closely as possible on a hard drive. Essentially, simulation slows the access speed of the retrieval software to more closely approximate the retrieval time the user obtains when accessing data at 250–500ms, as compared to the 10–28ms access of the hard disk on which the program is stored. This slowdown is done by introducing processor wait states, or by actually mirroring the sector structure of a CD-ROM on a hard disk, which slows the performance of the program.

Simulation also renders the data read-only so that any functions that require the capability to write to the disc can be rewritten or eliminated. For many applications, simulation is important. What appears to be blazing retrieval speeds and apparent instantaneous graphic refresh rates during development on a hard disk, may turn out to be agonizingly slow performance on CD-ROM.

Optimization is the process of physically arranging the files on a disc for optimum performance. Some optimization software enables the developer to choose the location on the disc of files based on their access frequency. Other packages merely determine, based on the structure of the database, the placement of files to achieve fastest performance for the application.

Because of the manner in which CD-ROM drives retrieve information from a disc, the location of files on a CD-ROM disc becomes an important factor in the performance of an application. Files near the beginning of the disc can be accessed much more quickly than files at the outer edge. Related files should be placed close together to decrease seek time. Installation files, which may be used only once, should be placed at the end of the other data. The optimization process should be part of the development of every CD-ROM application. Many CD-ROM development software include optimization programs that can rearrange files so that the most frequently accessed files are located near the beginning of the disc.

Testing

If the premastering software that you are using simply converts data from DOS to ISO 9660 format, it creates an image file that can reside on a hard disk or be transferred to tape or other transportable media. The image file cannot be accessed by using DOS commands. In this case, the data cannot be manipulated further, and the next step is to master the data to disc.

Other software enables you to access the image file as if it was already a CD-ROM disc. In this case, the data can be tested and optimized. The CD-ROM environment can be simulated so that you can make any final changes that you find necessary for optimum performance. After you make the changes, the data can again be placed in ISO 9660 format, tested, and sent to the mastering facility.

Testing is an important step in the CD-ROM development process because once a disc is replicated, bug fixes or other changes are expensive. An entire replication run is worthless if the product was not properly tested and problems appear after the stamping is finished.

Most mastering facilities and service bureaus can make a one-off disc for you for as little as $99. This test disc enables you to test the real product and have several people use the disc. If you plan to do a large project, several test discs and a round of beta testing is appropriate.

Problems that may not be apparent to the developer show themselves quickly when a novice tests the disc. Include the installation program on the disc and have several people install it. Their comments help ensure your end users get a product that installs smoothly, runs efficiently, and gets the intended job done with a minimum of trouble. Figure 10.4 shows the process of data conversion, indexing, testing, ISO formatting, simulation, and optimization.

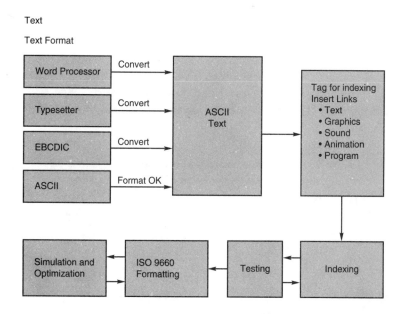

Figure 10.4
The CD-ROM production process through the premastering stage.

Mastering

After you premaster an image on tape or other media, you are ready to send it off for disc replication. Mastering facilities charge a mastering fee of around $1,400 plus $1.50 to $1.80 per disc. A two-color label and a jewel case are usually included in this price, although you must supply the artwork for the label. Artwork is usually required a week or more before the data. Make sure, therefore, that you contact the mastering facility and ask about its policies beforehand.

How Do You Use a Service Bureau?

If you want to produce a CD-ROM, but still are unsure that you want to take all of the responsibility yourself, consider using a CD-ROM service bureau. A CD-ROM service bureau can help you with the process by providing everything from initial consultations that get you started doing the project yourself to complete CD-ROM development services.

Because service bureaus have experience in all phases of the CD-ROM development process and can see potential pitfalls in proposed projects, these companies can offer you much help. A service bureau can analyze the data that you intend to put on a CD-ROM, perform data conversion, including scanning and OCR, image scanning, scaling, cropping, image capture, data preparation, and SGML (Standard Generalized Markup Language) tagging, indexing, simulation, optimization, testing, and premastering. A service bureau also can advise you about current replication prices and practices.

Before you decide on which service bureau to use, ask for references and a list of titles they have produced. Contact former clients. A good service bureau is happy to provide you with references of satisfied customers.

Most service bureaus work with between one and three retrieval software packages. Limiting the number of retrieval packages has several advantages for the service bureau. First, indexing software is complex. Companies may find it difficult to know or to afford many different indexing packages. Second, many service bureaus are a division or a partner of the producer of the software.

Be cautious if the service bureau recommends one particular retrieval software, especially if it is a dealer for that software. Do not use a search software that is inappropriate. Look for alternatives. Look for a company that can acquire the appropriate software or can recommend another company that can meet your needs.

Summary

CD-ROM development can be a frustrating job at times. You learned in this chapter, however, that with the right planning, the frustration can be eliminated and the results can be satisfying and profitable.

This chapter discussed some of the considerations you must look at before you manufacture a CD-ROM disc. Also discussed in this chapter was the cost you can expect to pay to produce a disc. You examined situations in which placing information on CD-ROM is the appropriate method of storage.

This chapter described the process that you must follow to produce a CD-ROM disc. You learned that the development process contains eight steps. These steps include data acquisition, rights acquisition, software acquisition, data conversion, indexing, premastering, testing, and mastering.

In Part IV, you learn about the future of CD-ROM technology.

Part IV

The Future

The Future of CD-ROM Technology

The future of CD-ROM is not hard to predict. CD-ROM was first commissioned in 1984 as a commercial product; by 1988, its file formatting had become an international standard under ISO 9660. This early international acceptance put it above the crowd of laser video discs and floppy disks that are still searching for international interoperability. The years 1988 to 1993 were the gestation period for CD-ROM.

CD-ROM is a universal medium—the economics of CD-ROM are compelling. The source of CD-ROM growth (as well as the computer industry, in general) is the amount of digital data available, which is doubling every three years with no end in sight.

A Growing Industry

In only five years, CD-ROM has moved from an "interesting technology" to an "industry." The CD-ROM industry continues to grow for several reasons. CD-ROM is strategically placed as the primary data distribution medium at the dawn of the information age. This chapter includes predictions from some of the CD-ROM industry's leading experts.

Quest for Knowledge

Driving the computer industry is a worldwide hunger for knowledge combined with information overload. Complicating the problem of the quest for knowledge is the inefficiency of our own human input devices (eyes and ears) to quickly assimilate this data by traditional means. Reading requires the filtering of too much rhetoric between facts. Researching back issues of journals or multiple volume sets of data in book form is an art that requires too much time and labor for the modern world. Information science working with electronic data storage/ retrieval machines is the art of the 21st century.

Search engines once used only by high-level intelligence agencies are now standard research tools used in industry, commerce, and education. Relational threads can be formed between data to make gross assumptions, and from these assumptions knowledge is gained.

The addition of digital graphics and sound to database systems has enhanced our applications beyond the technology of five years ago. The past practice of simple facsimile capture from paper documents and storage of the image in electronic file cabinets for ease of printing is no longer considered modern. Conversion of documents into electronic text provides global searching of content. The capability to collect and string pieces of information together from this electronic well of data is a standard technique in today's information systems. Value has been added to electronic mapping by linking remote sensing, census, and demographic data. For the first time, dynamic spatial visualization of complex issues can be used as an aid to understanding our human problems.

The addition of digital graphics and sound to database systems has enhanced our applications beyond the technology of five years ago.

The mapping segment of our digital revolution has created a seven-billion-dollar industry in four short years. This industry is called GIS (Geographic Information Systems) and is being used by entities from the National Parks Service to McDonald's restaurants. Many new industries and scores of old ones share GIS's one major problem: they have the capability to generate huge data files (500+ megabytes) that are hard to store and retrieve, let alone distribute to their user base. CD-ROM is the solution to these problems.

Marketing Segments

The CD-ROM industry has matured to its current position through a long and painful period of application development in which real revenues consistently lagged behind the predictions of market analysts. Today, with over 5,000 commercially available applications on the world market, CD-ROM is beginning to fulfill its early promise.

The demise of a separately defined CD-ROM industry is imminent as the use of CDs as a storage and distribution medium melts into the mainstream of the computer and consumer electronics industries. Soon, talking about the CD-ROM industry will be as silly as discussing the floppy disk industry. Instead, applications of CD technology will be defined in terms of market segments, such as Library Information Products, General Reference, Education, or Electronic Entertainment. The use of CDs to deliver content to these markets will become as routine as the use of CDs in today's music industry. The delivery platforms will vary from computer workstations to video game systems to hand-held information appliances.

The new "multimedia" technologies, such as CD-I, whose birthplace and nursery has been the CD-ROM industry, will have an impact in the education and entertainment markets. Digital video technologies will see their most important application in the telecommunications industry in a wide range of new applications including personalized television programming, multimedia e-mail, video telecommunications, and interactive "tele-entertainment." The FCC's recent decision in favor of allowing transmission of video information over the nation's telephone network clears the way for full implementation of these applications. The "information superhighway" is, after all, only a pipeline for information. The obvious choice for storing the information that goes through the pipeline is CD-ROM.

IV
The Future

As CD-ROM leaves the realm of the specialist and enters the mainstream as the delivery medium of choice, the dream of the CD-ROM industry will at last be realized. But the future lies in many different market segments, some of which existed long before the birth of CD-ROM.

The Future of Hardware and Software

As technology continues to improve, CD-ROM drives will become faster and more economical. The Red Book specification, from which all other compact disc specifications are derived, calls for data to be read from the disc at a constant speed of 75 sectors per second, and this rate of speed has been carried over to the Yellow Book (CD-ROM) and Green Book. A new kind of CD-ROM drive on the market bends this rule, however. This new drive still reads Red Book audio data at the specified 75 sectors per second (so that music does not sound like the Chipmunks). But for CD-ROM data other than Red Book audio, the new drive reads at 150 sectors per second. This boosts the data transfer rate up to 300K per second—twice that of other, single-speed CD-ROM drives. Many CD-ROM drive manufacturers now offer double- and triple-spin drives, and quadruple-spin is not far in the future.

CD-ROM Drives

Drives also will become more versatile. One manufacturer has already integrated a digital video processor into a CD-ROM drive. Sound boards also could be integrated into CD-ROM drives, making it that much easier to upgrade an existing computer to a multimedia machine. Also on the horizon are multi-function drives capable of reading (and writing) all of the compact disc standards.

The price of CD-ROM drives will be $100 retail by 1995, and all computers will be equipped with a CD-ROM drive. Software and data will be available on CD-ROM that cannot be obtained on floppy disks, and CD-ROM discs will be less expensive.

In addition, CD-R also will be inexpensive; it may become the floppy disk of the last half of the 1990s. Mini-Disc (MD) may come to be recognized as the "mini" CD media. The MD-ROM media will be manufactured the same way as existing CD-ROM discs. For reading, you can expect the SCSI command set to be the same as for CD-ROM. This also means that ISO 9660 and ECMA 168 (the new CD-ROM and CD-R standard) will work with this media.

Sony will deliver Mini-Disc for computers in 1994. It will support two types of media: MD-ROM and MD-MO. MD-ROM will be 150M read-only media produced on existing CD production equipment and cost $1 each to replicate. MD-MO will be 150M read/write media costing between $10 and $20 per disk. This new media may replace floppy disk drives in computers by 1997. You can also expect multi-function drives, which will handle CD-ROM, MD-ROM, and MD-MO, to be available by 1997. These multifunction drives will be the preferred drive for desktop and network computers; single-function drives will be used in Notebook and Palm computers. Both CD and MD will coexist and use the same file system;

CDs have a greater capacity and a large installed base. The greater capacity of CD also is necessary to deliver the large amounts of information needed for multimedia titles that use full motion video.

The Future of CD-ROM Discs

As the installed base of CD-ROM drives becomes larger, the variety and scope of applications will grow proportionally. Developers have barely scratched the surface of the information that would benefit from being published on CD-ROM, and traditional print publishers are increasingly exploring the possibilities of expanding their markets by offering books on disc as well as on paper.

Hundreds of thousands of current print publications could be transferred to CD-ROM, enhancing their value by allowing nonlinear access to the data. And hundreds of thousands of other potential CD-ROM applications exist in the multimedia field. Traditional publications that did not lend themselves well to CD-ROM transfer because pictures were an integral part of the publication now can be successful multimedia applications. These publications are even richer than the print version because sound and motion can be added. Artists, writers, musicians, and others can use CD-ROM and multimedia as their creative medium. Original works can be created and never exist on paper at all. Current digital data in all formats can be combined to produce useful reference, educational, and entertainment works.

Hundreds of thousands of current print publications could be transferred to CD-ROM, enhancing their value by allowing nonlinear access to the data.

As multimedia fueled the development of double-, triple-, and quad-spin drives, Video CD will give rise to a demand for double-, triple-, and quad-capacity discs. In order to hold a full-length movie compressed in MPEG 1, the capacity of a CD-ROM must be doubled. This has already been demonstrated by Nimbus and by ODC, manufacturers of CD-ROM mastering equipment, who increased the "track pitch," or the number of tracks per inch, of a standard compact disc. Within two years, we will very likely see a new standard announced that will allow up to four times as much data (2.7 gigabytes) to be stored on a compact disc. When combined with faster drives, this makes compact disc an even more attractive medium for storing video data. We may soon be renting and buying movies on CD—and they will never have to be rewound.

IV

The Future

Retrieval Software

CD-ROM retrieval software continues to evolve. As it does, better user interfaces and more powerful search methods will appear. Full text applications will be enhanced by the addition of audio recordings of the text. A standard data format that allows the same data to be accessed by different search and retrieval engines across all three major platforms—Macintosh, DOS-based, and UNIX-based—is now offered by several software vendors.

Producing CD-ROMs

CD-ROM production will become as commonplace as desktop publishing. More data already in electronic format means less data conversion and scanning from print. Affordable desktop CD-ROM production tools, both hardware and software, will make electronic publishing on CD-ROM an option available to small businesses as well as Fortune 500 companies. Like the small print shop, or copy shop, expect to see more CD-ROM one-off shops where you can take your data to have it indexed, formatted, optimized, and transferred to CD-ROM in a matter of hours. Someday soon, CD-R services will be as ubiquitous as fax services.

CD-ROM, as a logical extension of electronic publishing, will continue to expand. Instead of a 10 to 20 year lifespan for CD-ROM, start thinking about a 50 to 100 year horizon. Add to that the decreasing cost of starting a CD-ROM publishing effort.

Five years ago, for instance, a CD-ROM recording system cost over $100,000. Now they cost as little as $4,000. Extrapolating this cost for two or three years will take the industry into the era of the "personal CD-ROM recorder." Combine price with appendability via CD-Recordable, and you usher in the age of "personal imaging systems." With extremely low-cost CD-ROM recorders and low-cost media, an individual can easily contemplate using CD-ROM as the vehicle for personal imaging.

Current CD write-once media costs around $20. Within two years, media costs will be under $10. At a cost of $10 for 680M, the cost per megabyte equals about one and a half cents.

You will find it less expensive on a cost-per-megabyte basis to store information on CD-ROM than on floppy disks.

Developing Multimedia

If CD-ROM developers have not scratched the surface, then the full potential of multimedia is not even a twinkle in the eye of multimedia developers. While the multimedia applications of today may inspire and thrill computer users with sound and pictures, they will certainly appear crude when compared to future applications—even those that will be available just a year from now. For example, remember "Pong?" It was the first video game most of us ever saw. If you have visited a video arcade lately, however, you have some idea of what can be accomplished when you combine technology and imagination.

Besides economics, two more reasons that CD-ROM will continue to grow are multimedia and the percentage of PCs that will be equipped with CD-ROM drives. Every computer manufacturer is developing multimedia application software to meet the perceived need to utilize an interactive audio-video approach for training, education, and point-of-sale applications. Likewise, all computer manufacturers have independently chosen CD-ROM as the medium of choice to distribute software and technical manuals. Many computer manufacturers now include a CD-ROM disc with each computer that contains a catalog of full working copies of software programs. The programs can be evaluated from demos on the disc, and purchased from the vendor by phone. The vendor supplies a software code or "key" that allows the software to be installed from the disc. Paper documentation for the product can then be delivered by mail. These computer manufacturers and software vendors see CD-ROM as a way to simultaneously reduce internal information distribution costs and tap new markets.

Note also that the largest computer manufacturer, IBM, has begun construction of its own in-house pressing facility. This type of "self-contained mastering facility" has been made possible by companies that package pressing facility components installable in-house. More of these are sure to appear as large corporations discover the extreme competitive advantage inherent in CD-ROM publishing.

No end is in sight for CD-ROM growth. Because of its universal acceptance and its economics, CD-ROM will continue to expand well beyond the year 2000.

CD-ROM is now, and will be, the only technology that can provide the economical answer to storage/retrieval and distribution of digital data. It will be eased out as a technology in the next 25 years by Electron Trapping Optical Memory (ETOM), direct satellite reception/transmission, and fiber-optic linking of the office, home, and school. Segments of the CD-ROM industry will migrate unscathed to the new technologies. These segments include the following areas:

IV

The Future

- ✔ data provision
- ✔ human interface
- ✔ editing
- ✔ fulfillment
- ✔ data conversion
- ✔ menuing
- ✔ authoring
- ✔ distribution
- ✔ data capture
- ✔ illustrating
- ✔ permissions
- ✔ billing
- ✔ animating
- ✔ publishing
- ✔ software development

The information-handling tools have developed faster than the delivery platforms. Hypertext, interactivity, graphical user interface (GUI), and multimedia are key technologies of the Information Age. These have passed the development stages and are ready for production. In the "works in progress" stage are the areas of consistent interface and cross-platform authoring. In the "coming soon" category is a user base of computer hardware using compatible or adaptable operating systems. Now the only consistency among hardware manufacturers, software developers, and data providers is the agreement that CD-ROM is unexcelled as a data storage and distribution medium.

The technical capabilities that CD-ROM has provided to our desktop will turn out to be essential to the development of the technologies that will replace it.

The industry has matured during the last five years. Much weight is now given to standards, interoperability, and downward compatibility. The drive of the future

will be made with faster transfer rates, higher capacities, and internal audio and video digital signal processing. Some will offer multiple-session writing. Yet with all these innovations, a new drive of the '90s will still read your first-purchased discs of the late '80s.

The market to watch in the next five years is the "home" area where the consumer faces a decision clouded by many standards. Multimedia PC (MPC), Macintosh, CD-I (Philips), Photo CD (Kodak), Sega Mega CD (Sega), Super NES CD (Nintendo), 3DO, and TurboGrafix CD (NEC) are all lined up for the race. The bell has sounded, the gate is up, and some will share in the big prize of the market share. Only one will receive the first prize—domination.

Domination in the home market will provide sufficient user base numbers to attract "major" software development and information publishing. This will lead to the creation of a massive title library and cause a reverse migration of "home" hardware into schools, libraries, and businesses. The information revolution will depend on software and content to drive the hardware. It will ride on the back of CD-ROM technology no matter who wins the race for home dominance.

Summary

Look around! CD-ROM hardware and software are already found in "the mall" at Babbage's, Electronic Boutique, and B. Dalton's. Tomorrow they will be found in used bookstores, the library shelf of a middle school, your children's study desk, and your family room.

You can look forward to a single box that is the center of digital-to-analog translation for every business, school, and home. It will play our movies, provide 3-D simulations for greater understanding of lessons, produce holographic environments, and alternate realities. It will be a vicarious teleport to the Earth's past and the galaxy's future, and it will all revolve around this silver platter we know as the compact disc.

IV

The Future

CHAPTER

CD-ROM and Multimedia

C D-ROM has become an integral part of the multimedia phenomenon and specification because of its large storage capacity, large installed drive base, low drive prices, and capability to play true CD audio sound—a capability unavailable in hard drives, WORM (Write-Once-Read-Many) drives, or magneto optical (MO) drives.

Many early CD-ROMs were, in fact, multimedia applications in that they contained not only text, but also graphics and sometimes Red Book audio. An application does not have to comply with MPC (Multimedia PC Marketing Council) specifications to be considered a legitimate multimedia application. A popular multimedia application that is not MPC-compatible is *Audubon's Birds of America* by CMC Research. This disc contains text, 256-color images, and birdcalls in Red Book audio. The popularity of this type of disc is reflected in the fact that almost three years after its introduction, it is still among the best-selling CD-ROM titles. For more information on the MPC standard, see "Developing Multimedia Standards" in this chapter.

Defining Multimedia

Multimedia is a much-used and misunderstood term. Multimedia means different things to different people. To many marketing departments, it is a term attached to anything at all, used in hopes of increasing sales. Indeed, as *PC Magazine* recently noted in a cover story on multimedia, one manufacturer was touting a disk carrying case with pockets for both 5 1/4-inch and 3 1/2-inch disks as a "multimedia" diskette case. This claim may be true to the term, perhaps, but unlikely to fulfill the promise that multimedia holds for the future of desktop computing. To the average PC user it may mean nothing at all, wrapped up as it is in shameless marketing hype. In the near future, when the hype dies down and developers are left to develop products for a broad base of PCs equipped with low-cost audio and video hardware, it will mean rich applications with seamless integration of text, graphics, sound, animation, and full-motion video.

In the broadest sense, multimedia means an application that includes information in more than one format. The multimedia field can be narrowed somewhat by limiting the discussion to multimedia as it pertains to CD-ROM titles intended for the IBM PC and compatibles.

Developing Multimedia Standards

The key to multimedia, as well as CD-ROM, is a standard that assures users and developers that applications developed to that standard will run on machines conforming to the same standard. The standard for multimedia was set by vendors who joined together to form the Multimedia PC Marketing Council. This marketing group, made up of Microsoft Corporation and a growing number of hardware manufacturers, defined a minimum configuration for a PC to be multimedia compliant.

The basic requirements include a PC, a CD-ROM drive, an audio board, speakers or headphones, and Microsoft Windows with Multimedia Extensions or Windows 3.1. A computer equipped with these components is capable of playing any multimedia CD-ROM bearing the MPC logo. The MPC Council licenses the MPC logo to hardware companies manufacturing hardware that meet the MPC standard, and to software companies that produce applications that make use of the hardware. The MPC Council has recently released the MPC2 specification. See table 12.1 for a comparison between the original MPC specification and MPC2.

Table 12.1
Comparison of the MPC and MPC2 Specifications

	MPC Level 1	MPC Level 2
RAM	2MB	4MB
Processor	386SX 16MHz	486SX 25MHz
Hard Drive	30MB	160MB
CD-ROM Drive	150KB/sec sustained transfer rate, maximum average seek time < 1 sec	300KB/sec sustained transfer rate, maximum average seek time of < 400 ms, XA Ready, Multisession capable
Sound	8-bit digital, 8-note synthesizer, MIDI playback	16-bit digital, 8-note synthesizer, MIDI playback
Video	640 × 480, 16 colors	640 × 480, 65,536 colors
Ports	MIDI, I/O, joystick	MIDI, I/O, joystick
Recommended		
RAM		8MB
CD-ROM	64K buffer on drive	64K buffer on drive
Sound		CD-ROM XA audio capability, support for IMA ADPCM
Video		640 × 480, 256 colors, must deliver 1.2 megpixels per second with 40% of CPU bandwidth

Note Note that Microsoft has incorporated all of the multimedia features of Windows 3.0 with Multimedia Extensions 1.0 into Windows 3.1. Although the Screen Saver, Joystick, and Display utilities do not come with Windows 3.1, they are not necessary to run MPC applications.

The PC

The minimum MPC Level 1 configuration is as follows:

- ✔ 80386SX or higher processor
- ✔ 2M of RAM
- ✔ 30M hard disk
- ✔ VGA display, 16 colors
- ✔ Two-button mouse
- ✔ 101-key keyboard

The minimum MPC Level 2 configuration is as follows:

- ✔ 80486SX or higher processor
- ✔ 4M of RAM
- ✔ 160M hard disk
- ✔ VGA display, 256 colors
- ✔ Two-button mouse
- ✔ 101-key keyboard

The Processor

A 386SX or higher PC is required because the MPC standard relies heavily on Microsoft Windows. A 286 machine is just not sufficient to run Windows productively. Fortunately, 386SX prices are falling lower and lower; this will also soon be the case for machines based on the 486SX and 486DX processors. Competition to Intel from AMD, Cyrix, and Chips and Technologies (with others waiting in the wings) will make these more powerful machines affordable to the average PC user. Processing power and speed are necessary for Windows to perform in such a way that multimedia applications can live up to their potential. This is not to say that the minimum configuration is not workable. Multimedia applications can be resource intensive, and the more resources available for an application, the better it will run. As noted above, the MPC2 specification requires a 486SX or better processor.

Memory Requirements

The 2M RAM minimum also is related to Microsoft Windows and is not a necessary requirement of the other MPC components. Windows requires large amounts of

memory to run efficiently. Once again, although 2M works, more is better. The MPC2 specification requires a minimum of 4M of RAM.

Hard Drive

The MPC specification calls for a minimum of a 30M hard drive; but realistically, 80M or more is necessary if you want to load several Windows applications onto the hard drive. If you intend to create your own sound and graphics files, 120M is a better minimum. The MPC2 specification is more realistic on hard drive size, requiring a minimum capacity of 160M.

Display

A VGA display is necessary because many multimedia applications rely heavily on color graphics. Many applications contain both 16- and 256-color images; the images displayed are determined by the user's hardware. Some applications require 256-color capability. The MPC2 specification requires 256 displayable colors out of a palette of 65,536 colors.

Input Devices

Input devices are requirements that need not be stated because most 386 and above systems come with 101-key keyboards, and most mice have two buttons. Although you can run Windows without a mouse, it is not recommended because many of the "point and click" features that make Windows easy to use are unavailable or extremely awkward to use without a mouse.

The CD-ROM Drive

For MPC Level 1, the CD-ROM drive must meet the following requirements:

1. CD-DA (Digital Audio) outputs
2. Minimum sustained 150K per second data transfer rate without consuming more than 40 percent of CPU bandwidth
3. Maximum seek time of less than one second

For MPC Level 2, the CD-ROM drive must meet the following requirements:

1. CD-DA (Digital Audio) outputs
2. Minimum sustained 300K per second data transfer rate without consuming more than 40 percent of CPU bandwidth

IV

The Future

3. Maximum seek time of less than 400ms

4. CD-ROM XA ready, multisession compatible

The CD-ROM drive criteria are specific, but most modern drives meet these requirements. *CD-DA outputs* are the audio jacks on the CD-ROM drive. Because some multimedia discs use Red Book audio, the digital audio output is required. The sustained data transfer rate of 150K per second is necessary for smooth animation and speedy access. To better handle video sequences, the MPC2 specification requires a double-speed (300K per second) CD-ROM drive. Seek time is the time it takes the read head to reach the data on the disc after a request has been issued to the drive. The MPC2 requirement of less than 450ms seek time is more realistic for today's CD-ROM drives.

The maximum seek time required by MPC1 of less than one second is somewhat puzzling because most drives today have a seek time of half that or less. This part of the specification may be an attempt to boost the market by enabling manufacturers to sell multimedia machines at lower prices; a few of the lowest-priced drives do in fact have seek times approaching one second.

The Sound Board

For MPC Level 1, the sound board must meet the following requirements:

✔ 8-bit DAC linear PCM sampling, 22.05 and 11.025 kHz rate, DMA/FIFO with interrupt

✔ 8-bit ADC, linear PCM sampling, 11.025 kHz rate, microphone level input

✔ Music synthesizer

✔ On-board analog audio-mixing capabilities

✔ MIDI I/O port

✔ Joystick port

For MPC Level 2, the sound board must meet the following requirements:

✔ 16-bit DAC linear PCM sampling, 44.1, 22.05 and 11.025 kHz rate, DMA/FIFO with interrupt

✔ 16-bit ADC, linear PCM sampling, 44.1. 22.05 11.025 kHz rate, microphone-level input

✔ Music synthesizer

✔ On-board analog audio-mixing capabilities

✔ MIDI I/O port

✔ Joystick port

MPC-compatible sound boards solve the disc space problem inherent in adding sound to an application, and provide developers with great flexibility in deciding what type of sound is appropriate in what situation.

MPC-compatible sound boards support Pulse Code Modulation (PCM) sound as well as Musical Instrument Digital Interface (MIDI) sound. These sound formats provide a great savings in disc space, although they do somewhat reduce sound quality. Remember, however, that a simple narration does not need to be CD audio quality. Narration can be presented with 8-bit sound at 11.025 kHz with fine results.

CD Audio

Sound, an important part of many multimedia applications, traditionally had to be implemented in CD-ROM applications by using standard CD audio tracks on the CD-ROM and playing the appropriate sections at the appropriate times. Many sound clips can be recorded, placed on a CD audio track, and then referenced by their location on the disc—that is, by minutes and seconds.

A program may make a call to play track 2 from 28:02:15 to 29:31:12 upon the happening of a certain event (for example, user input, display of a particular graphic, or program startup). This works fine, and the quality of the sound is excellent, but stereo CD audio takes about 10M of disc space per minute of sound. Developers were forced to choose between sound and not much data, or data and not much sound. Red Book Audio, the highest quality of digitized audio available (44.1 kHz and 16-bit sampling), can be played on systems that include a CD-ROM drive equipped with an audio jack for speakers or headphones. The *DAC* (digital-to-analog converter) for the CD audio standard is built into the drive.

Waveform Audio

Waveform audio is a form of digital audio that can be stored, manipulated, and played back from a hard disk. Waveform audio files also can be stored on CD-ROM. The standard sampling frequencies used for digital sound other than Red Book audio are 22.05 kHz and 11.025 kHz. However, 16-bit sound boards can

IV

The Future

sample sound at 44.1 kHz. Bits-per-sample can be reduced to 8, or 256 possible values; and *monaural,* or single-channel sound, can be substituted for stereo sound. Each of these reductions in fidelity cuts in half the space required to store the sound. Sound can be recorded and played back in these formats by sound boards, such as the Sound Blaster or ProAudio Spectrum, and others that have been developed to the multimedia specification.

Waveform audio can be played on a system that includes a sound board with a Digital to Analog Converter (DAC) that can interpret different fidelity audio signals. The source of the sound can be either the CD-ROM disc or the hard disk. The speakers or headphones are plugged into the sound board rather than the CD-ROM audio jack, and the rear audio jack on the CD-ROM drive is plugged into the audio board to pass Red Book audio through to the audio output on the board.

Musical Instrument Digital Interface (MIDI)

Musical Instrument Digital Interface (MIDI) sound is an excellent way to present music with great space savings over both Red Book audio and PCM files. MIDI files contain digital descriptions of music in the form of commands for the sequence of notes, the timing of the notes, and the instrument designations. Music is created from a preset "palette" of sounds that can be incorporated into the audio card. Two minutes of MIDI sound can be contained in a file the same size as that which holds two seconds of PCM sound. MIDI audio is a representation of sound that can be interpreted by an audio board with MIDI capability. MIDI sound files also can be stored on either the CD-ROM or the hard disk, and speakers or headphones can be plugged into the audio board.

Headphones or Speakers

Headphones or speakers are required for sound output, and many options are available. Portable stereo headphones work fine and are inexpensive. Many manufacturers offer amplified speakers; the cost and quality of these components varies. In addition, you can use any stereo system to play the sound. All you need is a cable that converts the sound card output jack to the type of input jacks (usually RCA) that you have on your stereo system. Small speakers intended for use with a Walkman stereo cost only around $20 and work sufficiently.

Software Requirements

The MPC standard relies on Microsoft Windows as its base program and MS-DOS as its operating system. The following Windows versions are required:

1. Microsoft Windows Graphical Environment Version 3.0 or later, with Windows 3.1 or Microsoft Windows Multimedia Extensions Version 1.0 or later

2. MS-DOS or PC DOS operating system Version 3.1 or later

3. MS-DOS CD-ROM Extensions Version 2.2 or later and a MSCDEX driver that implements extended audio APIs

Microsoft Windows with Multimedia Extensions and Windows 3.1

Microsoft's Multimedia Windows looks and acts the same as Windows 3.0, but includes additional software in the form of device drivers that allow applications to use multimedia hardware, such as sound boards and CD-ROM drives. Windows 3.1 has the Multimedia Extensions built-in, and has replaced Windows 3.0 with Multimedia Extensions.

Several utilities are included in Multimedia Windows that enable you to configure and control the sound board and other multimedia devices. A discussion of these utilities follows.

The Control Panel in Multimedia Windows contains six new icons for the utilities that enable you to control the multimedia devices (see fig. 12.1). These utilities include the following:

- ✔ Sound—Enables you to add sounds to certain program events
- ✔ MIDI Mapper—Enables you to edit or change MIDI setups
- ✔ Drivers—Installs and configures device drivers to support audio and video hardware
- ✔ Joystick—Enables joystick calibration
- ✔ Screen Saver—Enables you to change your video mode without running Setup
- ✔ Video—Enables you to change your video mode without running Setup

The Joystick, Screen Saver, and Video utilities are not included with Windows 3.1.

IV

The Future

Figure 12.1
The Multimedia
Windows 3.0
Control Panel.

Sound Utility

The Sound utility enables you to assign prerecorded or original waveform sounds to play in conjunction with certain events, such as startup, warnings, alarm clock reminders, and so on. Macintosh users are familiar with this capability. The Sound utility makes this capability available on the PC. Now you can hear the sound of a door opening or an engine starting up as Windows loads. Your warning beep can be "Uh-oh," and your shutdown sound when you exit Windows can be your own voice saying "I'll be back." Figure 12.2 shows the new Sound utility.

Figure 12.2
The Multimedia
Windows and
Windows 3.1
Sound utility.

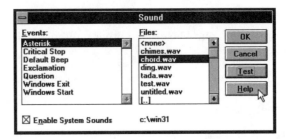

MIDI Mapper

If you have a synthesizer connected to your sound board, you can use the MIDI Mapper to select setups for sound devices and to edit key maps, channel maps, and patch maps. The MIDI Mapper screens are shown in figures 12.3 and 12.4. You only need to edit these maps if Windows does not support your synthesizer.

Consult your Windows documentation or the manual for your synthesizer for more information on the MIDI Mapper.

Figure 12.3
The Multimedia Windows MIDI Mapper screen.

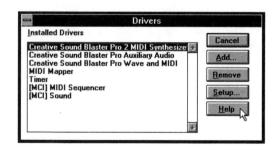

Figure 12.4
The Multimedia Windows MIDI Setup screen.

Drivers

The Drivers utility enables you to install, remove, and configure drivers for your sound board or other audio or video devices that you can add to your computer. Figures 12.5 and 12.6 show the Drivers screens.

Figure 12.5
The Initial Drivers screen.

IV

The Future

Figure 12.6
The Add Drivers
screen.

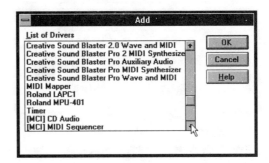

Although the following utilities are not multimedia specific, they are included with Multimedia Windows. The Joystick utility enables you to test and calibrate the joystick, if you have one attached. This screen is shown in figure 12.7.

The Screen Saver utility enables you to choose from several screen saver patterns, and to configure various elements of the chosen pattern. Figure 12.8 shows the Screen Saver utility.

Figure 12.7
The Joystick
utility dialog
box.

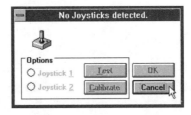

Figure 12.8
The Screen
Saver utility
dialog box.

The Video utility enables you to change your video setup without running the Windows Setup program. The Video utility is shown in figure 12.9.

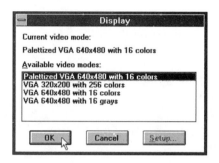

Figure 12.9
The Video Display utility dialog box.

In addition to these supplementary utilities in the Control Panel, Multimedia Windows includes the Sound Recorder, Media Player, and Music Box.

Sound Recorder

Sound Recorder is found in the Accessories window. It enables you to attach a microphone or line-input device to your sound board and record waveform audio files, which you can then speed up, slow down, add echo, reverse, or paste into other recordings. These files can be anything from your own voice, to sound effects, to music. Figure 12.10 shows the Sound Recorder.

Figure 12.10
The Sound Recorder.

Media Player

The Media Player, also installed initially in the Accessories window, plays either MIDI, Red Book Audio, or Waveform files. It also plays from other hardware devices, such as laser video discs, if the correct hardware and drivers are installed. Any device that has drivers written to the Media Control Interface (MCI) standard can presumably be attached to the MPC. The Media Player will also play Microsoft Video for Windows files and Quicktime for Windows files.

At this time, full-motion video is not widely used on CD-ROM multimedia titles. Additional hardware or software is required to compress the video, and several proposed standards are being considered. Microsoft has released Video for Windows and Apple's entry is Quicktime for Windows. Both are interesting implementations of software-only video compression but at 15 frames per second the picture quality leaves much to be desired. Figure 12.11 shows the Media Player.

Figure 12.11
The Media Player in Multimedia Windows and Windows 3.1.

Sound Mixer

A Sound Mixer utility comes with the sound board you have. This utility is not a Windows utility and, therefore, may be specific to your particular sound board. Sound Mixer enables you to create an audio file by mixing sound from several sources, such as a microphone, synthesizer, or CD audio input. You can adjust sampling rates as well as overall output, and send the files to the Sound Recorder or any other recording software. The Creative Labs Sound Mixer is shown in figure 12.12.

Figure 12.12
The Creative Labs Sound Mixer.

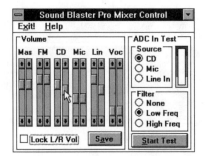

MIDI Jukebox

Some sound boards come with a MIDI jukebox that enables you to cue up MIDI files and play them. This capability is not provided by Multimedia Windows or Windows 3.1, although you can play single MIDI files from the Media Player. Figure 12.13 shows the Creative Labs MIDI JukeBox.

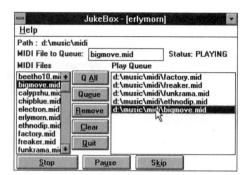

Figure 12.13
The Creative Labs
MIDI JukeBox.

Music Box

The Music Box enables you to play CD audio discs and to enter the name of the disc and the names of the tracks. This information is saved to a file so that when you insert a disc, the Music Box identifies the disc and brings up the associated playlist. You can choose which tracks to play by creating a playlist, or you can play the disc in shuffle mode. Unlike the Media Player and the Sound Recorder, no interruption of sound occurs when other programs that require heavy hard disk access are run. Because the CD audio sound is played from the disc, the disc continues playing even after you exit Windows if you do not stop it manually. The Music Box is shown in figure 12.14, and the Playlist screen is shown in figure 12.15.

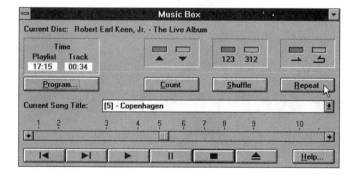

Figure 12.14
The Multimedia
Windows Music
Box.

You can play CD audio sound, MIDI sound, and Waveform audio simultaneously with interesting results.

IV

The Future

Figure 12.15
The Music Box
Playlist.

Music Box - Program Playlist

Disc Title: Robert Earl Keen, Jr. - The Live Album

Tracks:

[1] - I Wanna Know
[2] - The Front Porch Song
[3] - Goin' Down in Style
[4] - If I Were King
[5] - Copenhagen

Playlist:

[1] - I Wanna Know
[2] - The Front Porch Song
[3] - Goin' Down in Style
[4] - If I Were King
[5] - Copenhagen

Edit...   Select All   Add>>   Remove   Deselect All

Save Info   Restore Info   OK   Cancel   Help...

Examining IBM's Ultimedia

IBM also offers a multimedia PC, but does not adhere to or endorse the MPC
standard. Instead, IBM has developed a personal computer called Ultimedia that
includes a CD-ROM drive that supports CD-ROM XA (Extended Architecture) as
well as DVI (Digital Video Interactive). The system also includes a 16-bit audio
sampling sound board without MIDI (as compared to 8-bit with MIDI, the minimum configuration for MPC sound cards), XGA graphics (IBM proprietary), and
the OS/2 operating system in addition to DOS and Microsoft Windows. This
implementation of multimedia has its own advantages and disadvantages. By
setting its own standard, IBM sets itself apart from the MPC standard, and does not
guarantee that any MPC title will play on the Ultimedia system—though most of
them should. Also, Ultimedia is only available on a PS/2 system with microchannel
architecture; the Ultimedia PC is more expensive than other off-the-shelf multimedia PCs. On the other hand, the CD-ROM XA and DVI capabilities put the
Ultimedia system a step ahead of MPC systems.

Making Your System MPC Ready

If you want a system that conforms to the MPC specification, you have three
choices: buy a new, preconfigured MPC off the shelf, buy an upgrade kit, or buy
individual components and assemble your own MPC. Because new models,
upgrade kits, and individual products appear every day, the most up-to-date
sources of information on manufacturers, features, and prices are computer
magazines, such as *New Media Magazine*, *CD-ROM World*, *CD-ROM Today*, and
Multimedia World.

Off-the-Shelf Systems

If you have an older system with a 286 processor and a monochrome, CGA, or EGA monitor, you may be ready to purchase a new system anyway. In this case, it may be a good idea to buy a preconfigured multimedia PC with the VGA display, CD-ROM, and sound board built-in, and Windows 3.1 included. Some manufacturers also include some CD-ROM titles and speakers to get you started. This method is the easiest, but not the cheapest, way to enter the realm of multimedia computing.

Upgrade Kits

If you already have a 386SX or better PC with a VGA display, 2M of memory, and DOS 3.1 or later, several upgrade kits are available that include everything you need, from a CD-ROM drive and audio board to speakers, microphone, and multimedia CD-ROM titles. These kits are well within the technical abilities of anyone with a little patience, as they involve installing the sound board and the CD-ROM drive.

Individual Components

If you already have a personal computer with either a sound board or a CD-ROM drive, all that remains to make your system multimedia-compatible is the addition of the missing component and Multimedia Windows or Windows 3.1. For a sound board to carry the MPC logo, it must be packaged with the other elements of an MPC upgrade kit, such as a CD-ROM drive. However, a sound board without the logo can be labeled "MPC-compatible" and works just as well. By the same token, a CD-ROM drive need not carry the MPC logo to be MPC-compatible—it only needs to meet the specifications.

Summary

Multimedia is destined to change the way we use computers. Even ordinary, workaday applications such as spreadsheets, word processors, and e-mail will soon be enhanced with multimedia. At this time, the widespread use of multimedia is facing the standard chicken-and-egg dilemma: without a large user base of multimedia computers, developers are hesitant to invest resources in multimedia applications; without compelling applications, users are hesitant to invest in multimedia computers. The MPC Council is trying to solve this problem by establishing a standard of minimum hardware and software requirements for compatibility.

Although IBM has created a competing standard, it also offers developers programs and classes to help create more Ultimedia applications. On the software side, Microsoft Windows with Multimedia Extensions and Windows 3.1 provide a standard platform to create and play back multimedia applications. Their open-ended design ensures that new multimedia hardware, such as video cameras, digital gloves, and items that have not even been invented yet, can be seamlessly integrated. Software that makes use of the features of Multimedia Windows and Windows 3.1 will place multimedia applications development in the mainstream.

This chapter discussed CD-ROM and multimedia, introducing you to the MPC standard. You learned what hardware, memory requirements, CD-ROM drive specifications, and sound board functions and specifications you must have. This chapter also compared the MPC specifications to IBM's Ultimedia standard.

In the next chapter, you are introduced to some of the latest developments in CD-ROM technology. You will learn about complementary CD technologies, which include CD-ROM XA, CD-I, Video CD, and Kodak's Photo CD.

Explaining Compact Disc Standards

Compact disc technology is one of the fastest growing and changing areas of the computer industry. In addition to CD-ROM and CD audio, many other exciting possibilities exist. Some of these alternative formats for compact disc have been around for years, others have just recently become available, and even more are being developed.

Because of their versatility, adaptability, and capacity, compact discs are likely to be the data delivery medium for the home entertainment and computer systems of the future. This chapter discusses a few alternative formats and implementations of the compact disc.

As you have learned in previous chapters, the CD audio disc is defined by the Red Book standard. The Yellow Book standard, which is based on the Red Book standard, defines CD-ROM discs. Although these two types of compact disc are the most common, they are just two of the standards that define compact discs: Green Book, which defines CD-I, and Orange Book, which defines CD-R and CD-MO, are two other notable types. In addition, the most recently announced standard is the White Book, which contains elements of all the other standards and defines CD Karaoke and Video CD.

For the newcomer to the world of CD-ROM, and even for those who have been a part of it for years, it can be difficult to keep these standards straight. They overlap in places and borrow capabilities from each other—a disc may even be recorded in more than one standard.

In the near future, some of these types of discs will become the common in-home entertainment systems. For example, CD-I has been called the logical successor to the VCR, and video CD creates exciting possibilities in the delivery of full-length motion pictures. This chapter explores compact disc formats and related technologies.

CD-DA (Compact Disc-Digital Audio): Red Book

Red Book, or CD-DA (Compact Disc-Digital Audio) was defined by Sony and Philips in 1980; all other standards are based on the Red Book specification for digital audio. Audio CDs are recorded by converting analog audio signals into digital samples at the rate of 44.1 kHz (44,100 samples per second). Each sample is assigned a value in a range of 65,536 possible values (16 bits). The samples are converted to binary code and placed on the CD as a series of pits and lands arranged in a spiral. This is a simplification of the process, which also includes subcode channels, index points, and limited error correction. Because the purpose of the CD audio disc is only to play audio data in a stream—that is, from the beginning of a song straight through to the end—the Red Book specification is simple, elegant, and entirely sufficient. The most important aspect of the Red Book standard is that it is a standard—all CD-DA discs will play on all CD-DA players, as well as on all of the players designed to play discs recorded in successive standards.

CD+G (Compact Disc + Graphics)

When developers designed the Red Book specification, they had the foresight to include space for graphics information to be stored on the compact disc along with audio. Graphics information is recorded in the control-byte area of each audio sector. Each control byte includes 8 bits, named P, Q, R, S, T, U, V, and W. Each letter represents a subcode channel. The P and Q subcode channels contain information about the data's location on a track, as well as the time elapsed from the beginning of the disc and the beginning of the track. Most audio CD players use this information to display the music-playing time.

Subcode channels R through W are available for 6 bits of user information. On most CD audio discs, these subcodes are recorded as zeros; some discs on the market, however, contain graphical data. This data might be lyrics, liner notes, or pictures related to the music. Because this user-data space is limited (each disc can hold about 20M of graphics), and because the information must be collected from thousands of blocks of data to form an image (it could take up to seven seconds to collect enough data for one image), this compact disc format is rarely used. Because the graphics themselves are low-resolution, they are not likely to hold the interest of an audience accustomed to music videos.

Most audio CD players ignore the presence of graphics, and the graphics do not affect the playback of the audio. Discs that do take advantage of this capability are *Compact Disc + Graphics (CD+G)* discs. You can only display CD+G disc graphics by using a CD-I player, JVC's special audio CD player, or NEC's Turbo Grafix with a CD accessory unit.

The special encoding techniques necessary to record CD+G discs are owned by Sony and Philips and are available only to their licensees. The CD+G format was the industry's first attempt at multimedia. Although it has not been a huge success, it has led indirectly to the creation of CD-I and other multimedia specifications.

CD-3

CD-3 discs are identical to compact discs as far as content and standards are concerned, but they are only 8cm (3 inches) in diameter. These discs hold about 20 minutes of music or 180M of information. CD-3 discs are sometimes called "CD Singles." You can play a CD-3 disc in the same player as regular-size CDs by inserting it into an adapter. Portable CD Audio players, Sony's Data Discman, and Sony's portable CD-ROM XA player all play CD-3 discs. CD-3 audio discs and CD-3 CD-ROM discs are already available, as are CD-3 recordable discs.

CDI-Ready Discs

CDI-ready discs are standard audio discs with some extra features. The discs play CD audio on a normal CD audio player, but the special features can only be accessed by using a CD-I player.

The Red Book specification defines index points in each track that instruct the CD audio player to skip to specific points in the track. Usually, the track only uses index points 0 and 1. Index 0 marks the beginning of a track; index 1 marks the beginning of the music in a track. Between these points are two or three seconds of silence—about 12 blank sectors.

An audio CD player skips the first two-second gap between index 0 and index 1 at the beginning of the disc and starts playing the music on the first track. It plays the remaining gaps—one for each track (song) on the disc—between each track. You can extend the length of this gap to at least three minutes (182 seconds) and place CD-I data in this area. The data could include lyrics, liner notes, biographical information about the performer, or graphics. Although a CD audio player plays only the music, a CD-I player also reads the CD-I–ready disc's information in the pregap and displays it on screen.

The player displays this information in one of two ways. The information pertinent to each track might be loaded into the CD-I player's memory before the audio starts to play. The information then appears while the music plays from the disc. Lyrics or graphics related to the song, for example, might appear on the screen. Alternatively, the disc also can be read in the standard CD-I method, playing interleaved audio and visual information from the data in the pregap. An example of this method might include audio and video data of an interview with the performer.

CD-ROM (Compact Disc-Read Only Memory): Yellow Book

You learned in earlier chapters that CD-ROM is defined by a set of standards called the Yellow Book. Yellow Book is an extension of Red Book that was specifically designed to store text and program data, as well as audio and other types of data. Two basic types of data reside on a compact disc: audio and visual data, which degrade gracefully; and text and computer data, which do not. Graceful degradation means that the data is not rendered inaccurate or unusable by uncorrected errors. A missing byte of information will not make much difference in audio or visual data. A one-bit error in text or computer information, however, could change a letter of text or crash a program.

Mixed Mode Discs: Mode 1 and Mode 2

A mixed mode disc is a CD-ROM disc that contains tracks having both Red Book audio and Yellow Book data. The Yellow Book specification defines two data structures: Mode 1 and Mode 2. The mode byte, which is included in the header field of a CD-ROM sector (Chapter 2), describes the type of data contained in the data field. Mode 1 denotes CD-ROM data with EDC/ECC (2,048 bytes of user

data) and is used to store text and program data. Mode 2 indicates CD-ROM without EDC/ECC (2,336 bytes of user data) and is used to store Red Book audio.

The trade-off of extra error correction for user data space allows more audio data to be stored. Each track on a disc can be designated as either Mode 1 or Mode 2, containing sectors of only one type of data. Mixed mode discs, which are described in Chapter 4, contain both Mode 1 and Mode 2 tracks, but the first track is always Mode 1. CD-ROM discs are recorded in Yellow Book, Mode 1 and may contain audio tracks recorded in Mode 2.

MPC Discs

MPC (Multimedia Personal Computer) is the standard for multimedia, set by vendors who joined together to form the Multimedia PC Marketing Council. This is a marketing group made up of Microsoft and a growing number of hardware manufacturers that have defined a minimum configuration for a PC or an application to be `multimedia` compliant. The basic requirements include a PC, CD-ROM drive, audio adapter card, speakers or headphones, and Microsoft Windows with Multimedia Extensions or Windows 3.1. A computer equipped with these components is capable of playing any multimedia Yellow Book CD-ROM bearing the MPC logo. The MPC Marketing Council licenses the MPC logo to hardware companies that manufacture hardware meeting the MPC standard, and to software companies that produce applications that will play on the hardware.

MPC discs are Yellow Book CD-ROM applications that include files that require the multimedia capabilities of Windows. The big difference between MPC titles and "regular" CD-ROM titles is the addition of audio, which is recorded in "waveform" PCM (Pulse Code Modulation) format, a form of lower-quality CD-audio sound that takes less disc space to store than Red Book audio. Instead of sampling at a rate of 44.1 kHz, waveform audio is recorded at 22.5 or 11.025 kHz, and the possible range of values assigned to the samples can be either 16 bits or 8 bits. Each of these reductions in quality of sound reduces the space required to store the sound by half.

Comparing CD-I and CD-ROM XA

Just as CD-ROM is an extension of CD audio, CD-I and CD-ROM XA are extensions of CD-ROM. When Philips and Sony announced the first two compact disc specifications (Red Book for CD audio and Yellow Book for CD-ROM), they were aware of the potential variety of data formats—text, sound, graphics, video, and animation—that might be stored on a compact disc. The companies also realized that the variety of delivery platforms, such as video displays, operating systems, and audio cards, made it impossible to ensure that every computer system could access every multiformat disc. Universal accessibility was largely responsible for the enormous success of the CD-audio disc and player. In an effort to achieve this level of compatibility for multimedia titles, they announced the CD-I, or *Green Book*, specification in February 1986. The CD-ROM XA specification, which is an extension of Yellow Book with some of the features of Green Book, was announced in 1989.

The Green Book specification for Compact Disc Interactive (CD-I) describes an entire hardware and software system, a variety of special compression methods for audio and visual data, and a method of interleaving audio, video, and textual data. These audio compression and data interleaving methods are also used in CD-ROM XA. Before you learn about the differences between CD-I and CD-ROM XA, it may be helpful to learn the ways in which they are alike. Concepts that are common to CD-I and CD-ROM XA are data interleaving, interactive capabilities, and ADPCM audio.

Data Interleaving: Form One and Form Two

As explained in the section on mixed mode discs, a Yellow Book CD-ROM disc's text/program data and audio data reside on the disc as separate elements (see fig. 13.1). Red Book audio and CD-ROM data must be recorded on different tracks. You can play sounds while text or graphics appear on the screen by loading the image first and then playing the sound, or by playing Red Book audio from the CD-ROM disc while accessing data (text or graphics) that the application program has transferred from the disc to the hard drive. You cannot play sound and other data (animation, graphics, or text) from a CD-ROM disc simultaneously. The optical head must read alternately from the audio track and data track, resulting in a delay while the optical head finds the appropriate spot on the audio track.

Figure 13.1
Graphics and audio from a standard CD-ROM.

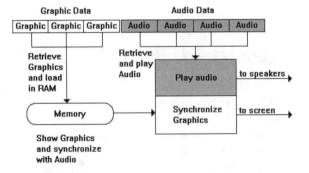

CD-ROM Multimedia Disc (Yellow Book)

For the Green Book specification, Yellow Book Mode 2 is further defined into Form 1 and Form 2. A Form 1 sector (2,048 bytes of user data, plus EDC/ECC) is nearly identical to a Mode 1 sector, and Form 2 (2,328 bytes of user data, no EDC/ECC) corresponds to Mode 2. The eight-byte difference between a Mode 2 sector and a Mode 2, Form 2 sector is used to store the information that identifies the contents of the sector as audio/video and text/program data. However, these two kinds of sectors can be combined in a single Mode 2 track by alternately recording frames of each kind of data.

This interleaving allows a seamless presentation of audio/video and text/program data, with error correction applied where needed. It is possible, for example, to show a person speaking with the sound of his voice perfectly synchronized, or to display animation or video with simultaneous narration. The hardware that controls the CD-ROM XA drive and the CD-I player separates the elements of the data stream so that the audio is decompressed and sent to the speakers as the computer data, video, and graphics are sent to the computer or to the TV screen. CD-I, CD-ROM XA, and Video CD discs (see section on the White Book specification) are all recorded in Mode 2.

Interactive Media

CD-I and CD-ROM XA can be *interactive*, which means that instead of simply watching or listening to the contents of a disc chronologically, you can actively choose your own "path" through the application. You might, for instance, see an image on the screen with three doors. Choosing one of the doors starts a script related to whatever is behind that door. You are then presented with an image of a room in which each object is related to another script, and so on. You choose items by using a remote control on a CD-I player or by using a keyboard or mouse on a PC equipped with a CD-ROM XA drive.

Because of the unique nature of the interleaved, interactive data, creating multimedia CD-ROM XA and CD-I applications calls for skills in script writing, sound engineering, video editing, and post-production authoring, as well as a knowledge of the personal computer and basic programming.

ADPCM Audio

Another difference between CD-I, CD-ROM XA, and CD-ROM is the type of sound that the disc contains. Multimedia and mixed mode CD-ROM discs can include true CD audio (Red Book), PCM, and MIDI sound files, whereas CD-I and CD-ROM XA discs use a special condensed transcription of sound called *Applied*

Differential Pulse Code Modulation (ADPCM). ADPCM audio records the differences between successive digital samples instead of the full values of the samples. ADPCM sound requires a minimum amount of storage space—as little as one-sixteenth of the space required for Red Book audio. The CD-I standard defines three levels of ADPCM: Hi-Fi, Mid-Fi, and Speech (see fig. 13.2). Red Book audio can be recorded on CD-I and CD-ROM XA discs, but it cannot be *interleaved,* or read simultaneously, with the text and graphics as ADPCM sound can. Red Book audio must reside in a CD audio (Mode 2) track.

Figure 13.2

CD-I audio format table.

Level	Encoding	Sampling	Channels	1 second of sound	Playing time
CD Audio	PCM	44.1 kHz	1 stereo	171.1 kilobytes	1 hour
"A" Hi-Fi	ADPCM	37.8 kHz	2 stereo	85.1 kilobytes	2 hours
			4 mono	42.5 kilobytes	4 hours
"B" Mid-Fi	ADPCM	37.8 kHz	4 stereo	42.5 kilobytes	4 hours
			8 mono	21.3 kilobytes	8 hours
"C" Speech	ADPCM	18.9 kHz	8 stereo	21.3 kilobytes	8 hours
			16 mono	10.6 kilobytes	16 hours

As you learned in Chapter 12, you can reduce audio storage space requirements by lowering the sampling rate, reducing the number of bits per sample, or by decreasing the number of channels. Each reduction, however, decreases both the quality of the sound and the space required to contain it. The highest level of ADPCM audio (Hi-Fi) is about the same quality as high-end FM stereo sound.

CD-I (Compact Disc Interactive): Green Book

The *Compact Disc Interactive (CD-I)* standard defines a complete hardware and software system, including a CPU, operating system, memory, controllers for video display and audio output, and a variety of special audio and visual data compression methods (see fig. 13.3). A CD-I system does not include a floppy disk or hard drive—only a CD-I disc player, a ROM-based operating system, and the necessary hardware to control a video-display and audio system. A CD-I disc contains the application as well as the information the application accesses.

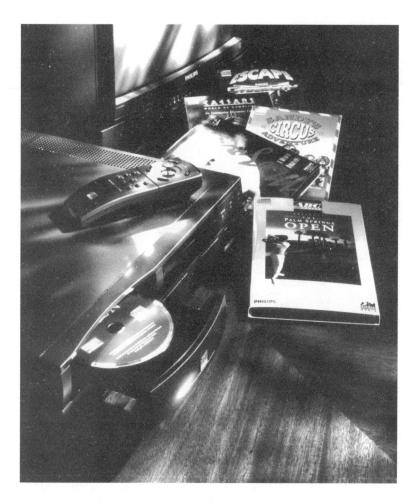

Figure 13.3
Philips CD-I
player.

The hardware standard is already defined; incorporating the application with the information therefore ensures that any CD-I disc player can play any CD-I disc. CD-I technology is targeted to the consumer market and designed to interface with televisions and stereo systems. Many consider CD-I the logical successor to the VCR. A $200 component called an *FMV (Full Motion Video) cartridge* can be installed to add VHS quality and full-screen, full-motion video capabilities to existing CD-I players. CD-I discs that contain up to 74 minutes of compressed video and audio are now available.

CD-I is becoming a popular platform for use in kiosks, in the classroom, and for the delivery of training programs to those who are unfamiliar with—or who dislike—computers. However, because CD-I discs contain the application software

IV

The Future

as well as the information to be accessed, and because the operating system of the CD-I player (OS/9) is CD-I-specific, it is not possible to play CD-I discs on other platforms. CD-I players are capable of playing standard CD audio, CD+G, CDI-Ready, CD-Bridge, Photo CD, and Video CD discs. Figure 13.4 shows CD-I's relationship to CD audio and CD-ROM.

Figure 13.4

CD-I's relationship to CD audio and CD-ROM.

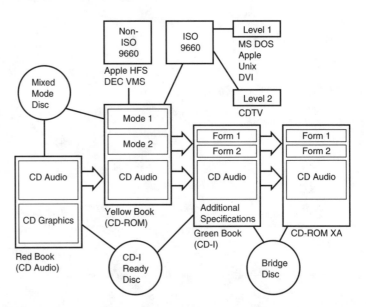

CD-ROM XA (CD-ROM Extended Architecture)

CD-ROM Extended Architecture (CD-ROM XA) is a multimedia extension of CD-ROM. This technology borrows from the CD-I specification, but it defines only audio and image formats and the interleaving of data and audio. It does not define the hardware platform or the operating system of its player. Like CD-ROM, but unlike CD-I, CD-ROM XA theoretically runs on any platform with the correct software and hardware interface. CD-ROM XA discs can play on a personal computer that includes an XA drive and controller card (some CD-ROM drives can play XA when controlled by an XA card) and a VGA or Super VGA monitor. Sony, Microsoft, and Philips jointly announced the CD-ROM XA standard in December 1989.

The latest MPC specification, MPC II, includes a CD-ROM XA-ready drive, as well as an upgraded CPU and other enhancements. (See Chapter 12 for a complete definition of MPC II.) Industry forecasters predict these specifications will be

upgraded in the future to include full-motion video playback as described later in this chapter. The multimedia PC is still a computer, however, and can perform other functions besides playing multimedia CD-ROMs. The CD-I player, on the other hand, conforms to a strict implementation, including operating-system, audio, and video standards, and is only intended to play CD-I, CD audio, CD+G, and Photo CD discs.

CD-ROM XA drives and controller cards are currently available from many manufacturers. Although CD-ROM XA drives will play Photo CD discs, some of the drives labeled "Photo CD Capable" support only Mode 2, Form 1 discs, and are not fully CD-ROM XA-capable drives.

CD-I/CD-ROM XA Bridge Disc

A CD-ROM XA disc may contain the same kinds of information as a CD-I disc, and it may even appear to be the same. In fact, CD-I and CD-ROM XA discs are interchangeable if they are recorded to both the CD-ROM XA and CD-I standards and if the disc contains an application that is playable by the CD-I operating system. This format is called a *CD Bridge* disc. A Photo CD disc is an example of a CD Bridge disc because you can play it on a CD-I player or on a computer equipped with a CD-ROM XA drive.

Photo CD

Photo CD is Kodak's proprietary implementation of CD-ROM, CD-ROM XA, CD-I, and CD-R standards. Photo CD technology was announced by Kodak in September 1990. A *Photo CD* disc stores digitized 35mm photographs on compact discs. In addition to having your 35mm film processed as prints, negatives, and slides, you now can take your film to a Photo CD developer and have the pictures placed on a write-once compact disc. You can have a 24-exposure roll of film placed on disc for about $25. You later can add additional photos until the disc is full. Each disc can hold about 100 images, or four rolls of 24 exposures. The disc comes packaged in a jewel case with an "index print" of each image that is recorded on the disc. The compact disc medium provides the same advantages to storing photographs as it does to text: security, longevity, and accessibility.

IV

The Future

You can display these images by using a Kodak Photo CD player, a CD-I player, or CD-ROM XA drive attached to a personal computer with Photo CD Access software.

Figure 13.5 pictures a Kodak Photo CD player. Images can be enlarged, cropped, panned, rotated, and programmed to display in a user-specified sequence. Because they are digitized, you can convert the pictures to other, non-proprietary formats for use in other computer applications. Kodak has announced software that enables you to incorporate text, graphics, and sound on a Photo CD. Photo CD players also will play standard audio CDs. Photo CD media is recorded in Mode 2, Form 1.

Figure 13.5
Kodak Photo
CD player.

Video CD (Compact Disc Video):
White Book

The White Book specification for Video CD, which was announced by JVC and Philips in July 1993, is a special implementation of CD-ROM XA designed to store MPEG 1 video. MPEG stands for Motion Picture Experts Group, which is a joint committee of the International Standards Organization and the International Electrochemical Commission. The White Book specification defines a Mode 2, Form 2 disc that can contain up to 74 minutes of VHS-quality, full-screen, full-motion video. Video CD can be played on a personal computer with a

CD-ROM XA drive and an add-in MPEG video card, a CD-I player with an FMV cartridge, or on a number of players soon to be available from several electronics manufacturers.

The problems with storing video data on compact discs are twofold: there is a large amount of data and the rate of output is slow. One second of uncompressed VHS-quality video would require 5M of storage space. A 680M compact disc could contain about 2 minutes of video. Using a single-speed drive, whose rate of output is 150K bytes per second, it would take over an hour to show 2 minutes of uncompressed video. Obviously, the data must be compressed for storage, then decompressed for real-time display. MPEG 1 uses various techniques to compress video data by a factor as high as 200:1.

Because MPEG is an international standard, any manufacturer can make hardware capable of recording, compressing, and playing MPEG video. Because it is not limited to any one platform, MPEG video can also be recorded and played back from Red Book and Yellow Book CDs, given the necessary hardware and interface. MPEG can be used by any CD-ROM publisher to include video clips in multimedia applications. The rates of video and audio compression can be varied according to the application.

As a home entertainment medium, Video CD offers many advantages over video-tape: discs are compact, durable, and inexpensive, while videotape can be damaged by excessive play, can stretch and break, and must be rewound after each use. Although the capacity of current types of CDs limits the length of the video to 74 minutes, within two years you can expect a new standard that will increase capacity by a factor of three or four.

Compatibility

With all of these different formats and operating systems, the question of which works successfully with another becomes very important. In the future, a single multifunction compact disc drive may be developed that will be able to read all of the formats. For now, figure 13.6 is a compatibility matrix that demonstrates which formats are playable by which delivery systems.

Figure 13.6
Most systems cannot play all formats.

Media Format or Content	Delivery System								
	CD-DA	CD-ROM* 1	2	3	CD-ROM XA*	CD-I	CDTV	Photo CD	CD-WO*
CD-DA	Y	Y	Y	Y	Y	Y	Y	Y	Y
CD-ROM Mode 1	N	Y	Y	Y	N	N	N	N	Y
CDTV	N	N	N	N	N	N	Y	N	Y
CD-ROM Mode 2	N	N	Y	Y	Y	N	N	N	Y
XA	N	N	?	?	Y	Y	N	N	Y
CD-I	Y**	N	N	N	Y	Y	N	N	Y
Photo CD	N	N	Y	Y	Y	Y	N	Y	Y
CD-WO 1	N	N	N	N	N	N	N	N	Y
CD-WO 2	N	N	N	Y	N	N	N	N	Y
CD-WO 3	Y	Y	Y	Y	Y	Y	Y	Y	Y
CD-WO 4	N	N	Y	Y	N	N	N	Y	Y

* Controlled by a DOS PC
** CD-I Ready Discs only
CD-ROM 1-3:
1 Current generation
2 Next generation (soon)
3 Multifunction (future)

CD-WO 1-4:
1 Unrecorded, blank disc
2 Partially recorded disc (no lead-in or lead-out)
3 Finalized disc (one lead-in and lead-out)
4 Multisession or hybrid disc (multiple lead-ins and lead-outs)

Summary

This chapter explored the different ways that you can use compact discs to store and disseminate information. Compact discs are a versatile medium, and the possible uses of this technology are many. One or more of the technologies described in this chapter may soon appear as part of your home entertainment center or in your place of business.

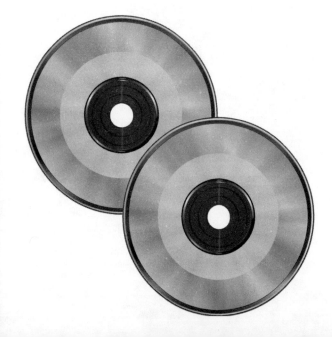

14 CHAPTER

CD-Recordable Technology

CD-R (Compact Disc-Recordable) technology allows companies and individuals to create single, unique compact discs on the desktop. CD-R uses special media, incorporating a layer of organic dye and a very thin layer of gold on a pre-grooved polycarbonate disc. The dye polymer, when exposed to a cutting laser beam in a desktop CD-R recorder, reacts with the polycarbonate to form a bump; this bump can later be read by the laser in a CD-ROM or CD audio drive, just as a pit is read on a regular mass-produced compact disc.

Five years ago, a CD-R system cost over $100,000 and was available from only one company. Three years ago, a system cost $28,000, obtainable from only two vendors. Today, the hardware alone is available for under $3,000, and systems are available from a dozen different companies, including Philips, JVC, Yamaha, Sony, and Ricoh (see figs. 14.1-14.4). A recent survey predicts that the installed base of CD-R units will increase from 42,000 in 1993 to 180,000 in 1994, and to 775,000 in 1995. By 1996, the installed base of CD-R units will reach 1 million worldwide.

Figure 14.1
Sony CD-R
Drive.

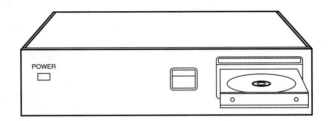

Figure 14.2
Philips CD-R
Drive.

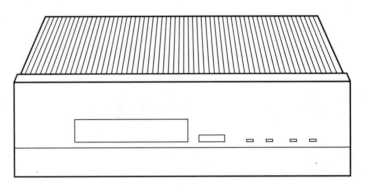

Figure 14.3
JVC CD-R Drive.

CD-R was once used almost exclusively by companies on the cutting edge of CD audio and CD-ROM publishing to create prototype discs for testing prior to committing audio and data to thousands of mass-produced discs. It is now being used as an archival, backup, and distribution medium as well as a replacement for paper, magnetic tape, microfiche, and on-line distribution of data. CD-R service bureaus, which offer the service of placing their customer's data on disc, have sprung up in every part of the country—a well-known nationwide video rental franchise has even announced plans to offer their customers the on-site service of creating CD-R discs containing games, music, software, and video.

Figure 14.4
Yamaha CD-R
Drive.

Understanding Compact Disc-Recordable (CD-R) Technology

The *Compact Disc-Recordable (CD-R)* disc is a special exception to the "read-only" nature of the compact disc. Although most compact discs are mass-produced, you can create unique "one-off" discs in a desktop environment by writing to specially treated discs with a laser recorder. These systems are used to produce small quantities of discs for prototypes, information distribution, and archival storage. The information contained on them can be in CD-ROM, CD audio, CD-I, CD-ROM XA, or any compact disc format. Developers have proposed a new media standard that will allow you to append CD-R discs—this proposal will soon result in a new ISO format.

IV

The Future

First Generation

The earliest of these recording systems was created by Meridian Data in 1989, using a Yamaha recording unit— its cost at this time was about $100,000. Sony developed a laser recorder/encoder in 1991 and offered it for about $28,000. These first systems, or *cutters*, could only write to blank Recordable discs. Like mass-produced CDs, discs produced by the first generation systems had to be written all at one time. They could not be added to, and they were not as robust as mass-produced compact discs. In addition, these systems could only write to discs, not read them. If the data to be written exceeded the disc capacity (usually about 625M), the data would write off the edge of the disc.

Second Generation

The second generation of CD-R drives is now available from Philips, Sony, JVC, Ricoh, and Yamaha for $4,000 to $8,000 (see figs. 14.1-14.4). Most of these drives have read and write capabilities, which allow them to append data to a special disc. The advantage of this method is that systems using the Recordable CD as an archival medium no longer must collect the archived data on a magnetic disk or tape until the amount collected fills a disc. In addition, media is not wasted because discs are produced at less than full capacity. Instead, users can update the disc as frequently as needed until the disc is full. The recordable discs come in three sizes, capable of holding 18, 63, or 74 minutes of audio sound or data. Because the CD-R can read as well as write, the blank discs are time-stamped to tell the WO drive the size of the disc it is recording. If the data to be recorded exceeds the size of the disc, the CD-R unit does not write to it.

Media

The discs written by CD-R drives are very distinctive. Unlike the usual mass-produced discs, which are usually silver on the data side and labeled on the other side, a CD-R disc is green on the recordable side and gold on the other. The green color is produced by a layer of special organic dye that is sensitive to the laser light. When the cutting laser beam focuses on the dye, the dye reacts with the polycarbonate by melting and forming a bump. The gold color is a layer of pure gold, which reflects the laser light better than aluminum when the disc is read.

CD-R Physical Standard

The standard for the CD-R media is defined in the Orange Book, Part II. This standard defines the media only, not the drives used to record or play it. Therefore the CD-R drives that use the media may or may not be able to read or append the

disc. The media itself can be in any of four states: a blank disc that is pregrooved and time-stamped, a partially recorded disc, a *finalized* or *fixed* disc, and a multisession disc. Currently, only finalized discs are readable in current drives, but they can be recorded using any of the standards described in Chapter 13.

CD-R Logical Standard

As of this writing, CD-Recordable drives can append data according to the CD-I Bridge disc specification or according to other proprietary logical formats. The situation is similar to the early days of CD-ROM—there is no one single universal logical format for CD-R appendability.

As with CD-ROM, industry leaders have formed a committee to create a standard for file organization of the Orange Book media. This group is called the Frankfurt Group, named after their initial meeting place in Germany. Their proposal for CD-R appendability is called the Frankfurt Proposal. The ECMA (European Computer Manufacturers Association) has examined and accepted this proposal, and submitted it to the International Standards Organization for consideration as the international standard. ISO approval is expected by Fall 1994. This standard, referred to in this book as *ECMA 168*, might eventually replace ISO 9660 because it is more flexible—for example, the directory information required to support UNIX is included, as well as support for ISO 10646 (a new standard that supports all the character sets of the world). This standard also can be extended to support future file systems.

Appendability

Currently, the Frankfurt Group's proposal allows both ISO 9660 and ECMA 168 tracks on the same disc. ISO 9660 format requires that the *volume descriptor*, which contains information about the contents of the disc, be located at sector 16 of the first track. To be accessible, the location of all files and directories on the disc must be included in the path and directory tables in sector 16. Because the contents included in sector 16 must be known in advance, and this sector can only be written once, it is impossible to append information to a writable disc recorded in ISO 9660 format.

ECMA 168 standard, on the other hand, allows volume descriptors to be located at sector 16 of any track on the disc. A CD-R drive, writing to a disc which is to be recorded in several sessions, leaves track 1 blank. Tracks are recorded using ECMA 168, and each track contains a volume descriptor at sector 16. When the disc is full, track 1 is recorded using both ECMA 168 and ISO 9660 so that the disc is compatible with both standards. This multiple-session disc contains information about all

IV

The Future

the files and directories in all the tracks found on the disc in sector 16 (of the first track). A CD-R drive, therefore, must have the capability to read the disc, as well as write to it, so that it can append data to a partially recorded disc, and so that track 1 can include the information from all the tracks on the disc.

In the future, CD-ROM discs used for archival information will also take advantage of the multisession format. The next generation of CD-ROM drives will probably be able to read these discs as well—only minimal modifications must be made to existing drive designs. Partially recorded discs, however, require more fundamental changes—the drives that can read these discs might not be available until sometime next year. A new version of Microsoft Extensions for the PC will be needed to take full advantage of the ECMA 168 standard.

Examining Implementations of CD-Recordable

Below are product descriptions from three companies who have developed CD-Recordable-based systems to augment and enhance their product line.

Data/Ware Development's Enterprise Authoring System

Data/Ware Development, Inc., in San Diego, CA, has developed the Enterprise Authoring System as a viable alternative to off-line distribution of data (see fig. 14.5). Using this system, data that was previously output from mainframe to print and microfiche systems for immediate—in some cases, overnight—distribution, can now be distributed on CD-ROMs. Data/Ware's system was developed for the IBM mainframe platform and takes advantage of the processing power and speed of the native mainframe environment for indexing and authoring the data.

The data, which has been converted from EBCDIC to ASCII, indexed, and ISO-formatted on the mainframe, is sent via a direct channel connection from a mainframe computer to a SCSI-based CD-Writer System (consisting of a high-capacity hard drive attached to a CD-Recordable drive). The hard drive emulates a standard 3480 tape cartridge subsystem. The interim step of writing the data to a hard drive ensures that the data will flow uninterrupted to the CD-Recordable device. With four CD-Recordable devices, this system is capable of producing 64 unique CDs in one 8-hour shift, or the equivalent of 28,000 fiche.

Many banking institutions currently output statements nightly to microfiche. For

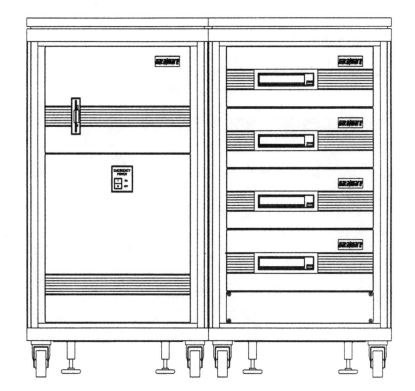

Figure 14.5
EAS Control Unit
and CD Cabinet.

larger banks, a single night's output of statement data could be a 70-inch stack of six inch by four inch fiche. A set of the statement data on microfiche is sent to each bank branch, where it is accessed, one user at a time, on a microfiche reader. Individual fiche can easily be misfiled or lost. By using CD-Recordable media instead, this same data can be produced and distributed at a fraction of the cost of microfiche, with the added advantage that the data is indexed and easily retrievable. The data can be accessed by multiple simultaneous users in a networked PC environment with CD-ROM access.

Meridian Data's NETSCRIBE

Meridian Data, Inc., in Scotts Valley, CA, is a pioneer in CD-ROM publishing and networking systems. In 1986, the Meridian Data CD Publisher was the state of the art in CD-ROM development. In 1989, Meridian created the CD Professional, which incorporated the Yamaha CD-Write Once device. Until the advent of Sony's first generation CD-Recordable drive in 1991, Meridian offered the only means of producing unique one-off CD-ROMs.

IV

The Future

It is no longer necessary for a company to buy expensive, dedicated hardware and specially train someone to be the CD-ROM expert in order to store information on CD-ROM. Meridian Data's NETSCRIBE is an integrated CD-Recordable system for Novell networks (see fig. 14.6). With NETSCRIBE, any workstation on a local area network has the capability of writing data to a CD-Recordable device.

Figure 14.6
Meridian Data's
NETSCRIBE.

The CD-Recordable drive appears as a storage device native to the network operating system. NETSCRIBE software runs under Windows, Windows for Workgroups, and DOS, and users can write data to CD-ROM as easily as printing files to a network printer, or storing data on a network hard drive. Meridian modifies the Philips model CDD521 CD-Recordable drive so that it appears as a dedicated workstation on a Novell network. NETSCRIBE software controls access so that only one user at a time can add data to a disc. NETSCRIBE is compatible with all DOS and Windows applications. Using NETSCRIBE Access software, MS-DOS, Windows, Windows for Workgroups, and Macintosh clients can transfer files to and from CD within their existing applications—just as they would with any other storage resource. With NETSCRIBE, there are no new applications or processes for the user to learn, and no stringent requirements for a high performance PC/workstation.

Trace's Report Tracer

Trace Mountain, Inc., in San Jose, CA, has manufactured floppy disk duplicators and other software duplication systems since 1981. The CD-ROM Products division, a Strategic Business Unit formed in 1992, is an international distributor of the Sony 900E CD-Recordable drive. Trace has developed Report Tracer, a software package comprised of authoring and retrieval modules for line printer or COM-ready (Computer Output Microfiche) data.

Data files can be imported from a mainframe computer or host to a PC using Report Tracer Authoring Software (RTAS) templates, specifying which fields are to be indexed and defined for each unique report format. Once the data has been indexed and compressed, it is written to CD-ROM. The Trace LH 2600 (Sony 900E) allows up to 16 recorders to be daisy-chained together to produce duplicate discs simultaneously. The recorded discs can then be individually labeled with Trace's CD-R printer, which uses a non-impact placement technology to print directly on the surface of special printable CD-R discs. Trace provides software templates to produce any desired graphics or text. Report Tracer Retrieval Software (RTRS) is available in stand-alone and network versions.

Trace has taken a truly novel approach in developing and testing Report Tracer— they use it internally. The MIS department uses Report Tracer to create reports for the various departments within the company. The Finance department uses Report Tracer for its general ledger, monthly and quarterly audits, customer revenue, accounts receivable, accounts payable, and sales tax reports. Trace estimates that by using networked CD-Recordable media instead of paper, they eliminate 15 to 18 boxes of paper per month for the finance department reports alone.

Other departments of Trace, such as purchasing, inventory, manufacturing, and shipping, use Report Tracer to keep track of current information generated by their MRP II and ASK order entry system. The data, which is printed and archived on CD-Recordable once a month, is also kept current and accessible at all times by using Report Tracer on-line on Trace's Novell network, ROM products division. Report Tracer replaces paper and computer output to microfiche. Previously, this type of application was done on WORM-type optical disc; doing it on CD-ROM takes advantage of low cost CD-ROM readers, emerging CD-ROM technology, and the worldwide ISO 9660 standard.

IV

The Future

Summary

The uses of CD-Recordable are many and varied. Recordable media prices are falling, making CD-R an attractive option for many uses. Seventy four-minute media are available for as little as $16. Archiving, backup, small production runs of compact discs in any format, and testing before replication are but a few of the uses for the new generation of CD-R drives. See Appendix G for information on companies that provide CD-Recordable drives, software, and media.

Part V

Appendixes

APPENDIX

CD-ROM Drives

This appendix lists companies that manufacture or integrate CD-ROM drives, multiple disc drives, multiple drive units, CD-ROM jukeboxes, and changers. Also supplied in this appendix are companies that sell CD-ROM drives by mail order. You also learn where you can get a damaged CD-ROM drive repaired.

Manufacturers

The following companies manufacture or integrate CD-ROM drives:

CD Technology, Inc.

766 San Aleso Avenue
Sunnyvale, CA 94084
408-752-8500
408-752-8501 (Fax)

Chinon America, Inc.

615 Hawaii Avenue
Torrance, CA 90503
800-441-0222
310-553-0274
310-553-1727 (Fax)

Hitachi Home Electronics

3890 Steve Reynolds Blvd.
Norcross, GA 30093
800-241-6558
404-279-5600
404-279-5696 (Fax)

Laser Magnetic Storage International (Philips)

4425 ArrowsWest Drive
Colorado Springs, CO 80907
800-777-5674
719-593-7900
719-531-0168 (Fax)

Legacy Storage Systems, Inc.

25A South Street
Hopkinton, MA 01748
800-966-6442
508-435-4700
508-435-3080 (Fax)

Liberty Systems, Inc.

160 Saratoga Avenue #38
Santa Clara, CA 95051
408-983-1127
408-243-2885 (Fax)

Mitsumi Electronics, Corp.

4655 Old Ironside Drive, Suite 130
Santa Clara, CA 95054
408-970-0700

Micro Design International

6935 University Blvd.
Winter Park, FL 32792
407-677-8333
407-677-8365 (Fax)

Micro Solutions, Inc.

132 West Lincoln Highway
DeKalb, IL 60115
800-890-7227
815-756-3411
815-756-2928 (Fax)

NEC Technologies, Inc.

1255 Michael Drive
Wood Dale, IL 60191
800-388-8888
708-860-9500
800-366-0476 (Fax)

Panasonic Communications

2 Panasonic Way, 7 G-1
Secaucus, NJ 07094
201-392-4603
201-392-4792 (Fax)

Pioneer

2265 East 220th Street
Long Beach, CA 90810
310-952-2111
310-952-2100 (Fax)

Plextor (Texel)

4255 Burton Drive
Santa Clara, CA 95054
800-886-3935
408-980-1838
408-986-1010 (Fax)

PLI, Inc.

47421 Bayside Parkway
Fremont, CA 94538
800-288-8754
510-657-2211
510-683-9713 (Fax)

Procom Technology, Inc.

2181 Dupont Drive
Irvine, CA 92715
800-800-8600
714-852-1000
714-852-1221 (Fax)

Reveal Computer Products, Inc.

6045 Variel Avenue
Woodland Hills, CA 91367
800-326-2222
818-340-3671 (Fax)

Sony Electronics, Inc.

3300 Zanker Road
San Jose, CA 95134
800-352-7669

Todd Enterprises, Inc.

224-49 67th Avenue
Bayside, NY 11364
800-445-8633
718-343-1040
718-343-9180 (Fax)

Toshiba America

9740 Irvine Blvd.
Irvine, CA 92713
714-583-3111
714-583-3133

Multiple Disc Systems

The following companies manufacture multiple disc CD-ROM changers or jukeboxes:

Hitachi Home Electronics

Jukebox—200 to 800 discs
3890 Steve Reynolds Blvd.
Norcross, GA 30093
800-241-6558
404-279-5600
404-279-5696 (Fax)

Pioneer Communications of America, Inc.

DRM 604 and 604X 6 disc changers
600 East Crescent Avenue
Upper Saddle River, NJ 07458
201-327-64002
201-327-9379 (Fax)

TAC Systems, Inc.

Jukebox—up to 720 discs
1031 Putman Drive
Huntsville, AL 35816
205-721-1976
205-721-0242 (Fax)

Multiple Drive Units

The following companies provide multiple CD-ROM drive units. These units range from 2 to 64 drives.

Business Automation Systems, Inc.

4652-A Haygood Road
Virginia Beach, VA 23455
804-464-4664

Communications Image Technologies

2222 Gallows Road, Suite 160
Dunn Loring, VA 22027-9805
800-944-2484
703-698-7050
703-698-0636 (Fax)

Future Echo

21414 Chase Street, #1
Canoga Park, CA 91304
818-709-2091
818-709-0489 (Fax)

Meridian Data, Inc.

5615 Scotts Valley Drive
Scotts Valley, CA 95066
408-438-3100
408-438-6816 (Fax)

Morton Management

12079 Tech Road
Silver Spring, MD 20904
301-622-5600
800-548-5744

TAC Systems, Inc.

1031 Putman Drive
Huntsville, AL 35816
205-721-1976
205-721-0242 (Fax)

Todd Enterprises

224-49 67th Avenue
Bayside, NY 11364
800-445-8633
718-343-1040
718-343-9180 (Fax)

Virtual Microsystems, Inc.

1825 South Grant Street, Suite 700
San Mateo, CA 94402
415-573-9596
415-572-8406 (Fax)

Sources for CD-ROM Drives

The following companies sell CD-ROM drives by mail order:

Bureau of Electronic Publishing

141 New Road
Parsippany, NJ 07054
800-828-4766
201-808-2700
201-808-2676 (Fax)

CD-ROM Direct

738 Main Street #378
Waltham, MA 02154
800-332-2404
617-332-2445
617-332-1783 (Fax)

CD ROM, Inc.

1667 Cole Blvd., Suite 400
Golden, CO 80401
303-562-7600
303-562-7395 (Fax)

Computer Integrated Technologies

57598 29 Palms Highway
Yucca Valley, CA 92284
800-779-2686
619-369-1222
619-369-0132 (Fax)

DAK Industries Incorporated

200 Remmet Avenue
Canoga Park, CA 91304
800-325-0800
818-888-8220
818-888-2837 (Fax)

Appendixes

Electrified Discounters

1066 Sherman Avenue
Hamden, CT 06514
800-678-8585
203-248-8680 (Fax)

Interaction: CD-ROM and Optical Storage

24705 U.S. Highway 19 North, Suite 308
Clearwater, FL 34623
800-672-3766

MultiMedia Direct

2105 South Bascom Avenue, Suite 290
Campbell, CA 95008
800-354-1354
408-371-5760 (Fax)

Multimedia Distributing, Inc.

123 South Woodland Street
Winter Garden, FL 34787
407-877-3807
407-877-3834 (Fax)

New Media Schoolhouse

Market Plaza Building
Box 390 Westchester Avenue
Pound Ridge, NY 10576
800-672-6002
914-764-0104 (Fax)

Peter J. Phethean Ltd.

1640 E. Brookdale Avenue
La Habra, CA 90631
714-990-5524
714-990-0137 (Fax)

System-One

226 Bellevue Avenue
Newport, RI 02840
401-847-0080
800-886-0080
401-596-6038 (Fax)

TigerSoftware, Inc.

800 Douglas Entrance
Executive Tower, 7th Floor
Coral Gables, FL 33134
800-666-2562
305-529-2990 (Fax)

Todd Enterprises

224-49 67th Avenue
Bayside, NY 11364
800-445-8033
718-343-1040
718-343-9180 (Fax)

Updata CD-ROM

1736 Westwood Blvd.
Los Angeles, CA 90024
800-882-2844
310-474-5900
310-474-4095 (Fax)

CD-ROM Drive Repair

Drive manufacturers repair drives that are out of warranty. Please check with your drive manufacturer for prices and turnaround time. Additionally, the following company repairs most models of CD-ROM drives.

CD-ROM Doctor

18642 El Carmen
Orange, CA 92669
714-538-3077

Multimedia

This appendix provides additional help if you want to develop a multimedia presentation. The companies listed in this appendix provide multimedia upgrade kits and authoring software.

Multimedia Upgrade Kits

The following manufacturers offer multimedia upgrade kits. These kits include a CD-ROM drive and controller that meet the MPC specification, an MPC-compatible sound card, and Windows 3.0 with multimedia extensions or Windows 3.1, which includes the necessary multimedia extensions features.

CompuAdd Corporation

CompuAdd Multimedia CD-ROM Upgrade Kit
12303 Technology Boulevard
Austin, TX 78727
800-627-1967
512-250-2530
512-331-6236 (Fax)

Creative Labs, Inc.

Sound Blaster Multimedia Upgrade Kit
Sound Blaster Discovery 8/Entertainment Upgrade Kits
Sound Blaster Discovery 16/Entertainment 16 Upgrade Kits
2050 Duane Avenue
Santa Clara, CA 95054
800-544-6146
408-986-1461

Focus Information Systems, Inc.

2theMax Opera
46713 Fremont Blvd.
Fremont, CA 94538
510-657-2845

Media Resources

Studio Pro MediaKit
StudioPro XL MediaKit
Studio MediaKit
640 Puente Street
Brea, CA 92621
714-256-5048

Media Vision, Inc.

Pro16 Multimedia System
Fusion CD 16 E
Fusion CD 16
47221 Fremont Blvd.
Fremont, CA 94538
800-845-5870
510-770-8600

NEC Technologies

1255 Michael Drive
Wooddale, IL 60191
800-NEC-INFO
708-860-9500
708-860-5114 (Fax)

Micro Express

Mulitmedia Upgrade Kit
1801 Carnegie Avenue
Santa Ana, CA 92705
800-989-9900

Procom Technology

Multimedia CD Station
Multimedia Station Pro
2181 Dupont Drive
Irvine, CA 92715
800-800-8600

Sigma Designs

WinStorm MM CD-ROM Upgrade Kit
WinSound 16 CD-ROM Upgrade Kit
47900 Bay Side Parkway
Fremont, CA 94538
510-770-0100

Sun Moon Star

1941 Ringwood Avenue
San Jose, CA 95131
408-452-7811

Technology Integrated Products, Inc.

MultiPro Photo CD Upgrade Kit
MultiPro Photo CD Advanced Kit
2323 Calla del Mundo
Santa Clara, CA 95054
800-886-4847

Turtle Beach Systems

MultiSound Full Upgrade Kit
Cyber Center, Unit 33
1600 Pennsylvania Avenue
York, PA 17404
717-843-6916

Multimedia Authoring Software

The following companies offer multimedia authoring software. The software title appears in boldface; the manufacturer's name, address, and phone number follow.

Ask Me 2000

Innovative Communication Systems
112 Roberts Street, Suite 14
Fargo, ND 58102
701-293-1004

Asymetrix Multimedia Toolbook

Asymetrix Corporation
110 110th Avenue NE, Suite 700
Bellevue, WA 98004
206-637-1500
206-455-3071 (Fax)

Authorware Professional for Windows

Authorware, Inc.
275 Shoreline Drive, 4th Floor
Redwood City, CA 94065
415-595-3101
415-595-3077 (Fax)

Guide 3.0

Owl International, Inc.
2800 156th Avenue SE
Bellevue, WA 98007
206-747-3203
206-641-9367 (Fax)

Hypercase

Interactive Image Technologies, Ltd.
700 King Street West, Suite 815
Toronto, Ontario, Canada M5V2Y6
416-361-0333

HyperWriter! 3.0

NTERGAID, INC.
2490 Black Rock Turnpike, Suite 337
Fairfield, CT 06430
203-368-1288
203-380-1465 (Fax)

IconAuthor

AimTech Corporation
20 Trafalgar Square
Nashua, NH 03063-1973
603-883-0220
603-883-5582 (Fax)

Linkway

IBM
Multimedia Information Center
4111 Northside Parkway
Atlanta, GA 30327
800-426-9402

Microsoft Multimedia Viewer
Microsoft Multimedia Development Kit

Microsoft Corporation
One Microsoft Way
Redmond, WA 98052
206-882-8080

Plus

Spinnaker Software
One Kendall Square
Cambridge, MA 02139
617-494-1200

TMM Producer

TMM
299 West Hillcrest Drive, Suite 106
Thousand Oaks, CA 91360
805-371-0500
805-371-0505 (Fax)

Sound Boards

The following companies supply sound boards for the PC:

Acer America

Acer PAC Magic
2641 Orchard Parkway
San Jose, CA 95134
408-432-6200

ACS Computer

Futura 16
260 East Grand Avenue #18
San Francisco, CA 94080
415-875-6633

Actix Systems

Lark
3350 Scott, Building 9
Santa Clara, CA 95054
408-986-1625

Addtech Research

Sound Pro II
4134 Christy Street
Fremont, CA 94538
510-623-7583

Advanced Gravis

Ultrasound
3750 North Fraser Way, Suite 101
Burnaby, BC, Canada Z5J 5E9
604-431-5020

AITech International

AudioShow
47971 Fremont Blvd.
Fremont, CA 94538
510-226-8960

V

Appendixes

Aztech Labs

Sound Galaxy
46707 Fremont Blvd.
Fremont, CA 94538
510-623-8988
510-623-8989 (Fax)

Calypso Micro Products

Audio Magician
160A Albright Way
Los Gatos, CA 95030
408-379-9494

Cardinal Technologies

Digital Sound Pro 16
1827 Freedom Road
Lancaster, PA 17601
717-293-3000

Criterion Computer

Sound Genie
5357 Rendell Place
Fremont, CA 94538
510-657-3898

Diamond Computer Systems

Sonic Sound
1130 East Arques
Sunnyvale, CA 94086
408-736-2000

DSP Solutions

Portable Sound Plus
2464 Embarcadero Way
Palo Alto, CA 94303
415-494-8086

Echo Speech

Echo DSP
Echo Speech Corporation
6460 Via Real
Carpenteria, CA 93013
805-684-4593

Genoa Systems

AudioBlitz Stereo
75 East Trimble Road
San Jose, CA 95131
408-432-9090

ImagiMedia

Audio Image 16
1991 Hartog Drive
San Jose, CA 95131
408-453-9911

Logitech

Sound Man 16
6505 Kaiser Drive
Fremont, CA 94555
510-795-8500

Media Magic

DSP 16
10300 Metric Blvd.
Austin, TX 78759
512-339-3500

Media Vision

Pro Audio Spectrum 16
47300 Bayside Parkway
Fremont, CA 94538
510-770-8600
510-770-9592 (Fax)

Meditrix Peripherals

Audiotrix Pro
4229 Garlock
Sherbrooke, Quebec, Canada
J1L 2C8
819-563-6722

Multiwave Innovation

Audiowave Platinum 16
747 Camden Avenue #D
Campbell, CA 95008
408-379-2900

New Media Corporation

.WAVJammer
15375 Larvanka Parkway #B101
Irvine, CA 92718
714-453-0100

Orchid Technology

SoundWave 32
45365 Northport Loop West
Fremont, CA 94538
800-767-2443
510-683-0030

Roland

RAP 10/A+
7200 Dominion Circle
Los Angeles, CA 90040
213-685-5141

Sigma Designs

WinSound 16
47900 Bay Side Parkway
Fremont, CA 94538
510-770-0100

Sun Moon Star

16-Bit Sound Card
1941 Ringwood Avenue
San Jose, CA 95131
408-452-7811
408-452-1411 (Fax)

Toptek Technology

Golden Sound Pro 16
14140 Life Oak Avenue
Bolding Park, CA 94076
818-960-9211

Turtle Beach Systems

Multisound Monterey
52 Grumbacher Road
York, PA 17402
717-767-0200
717-767-6033 (Fax)

Vision Enhancements

Vision Stereo Solution
29 West Thomas Road, Suite F
Phoenix, AZ 85103
602-265-5665

Wearnes Technology

Beethoven ADSP 16
1015 East Brokaw Road
San Jose, CA 95131
408-456-8838

Development

This appendix provides information to help you develop a CD. Company lists are provided for search and retrieval software, ISO 9660 formatting software, development systems, and packaging.

CD-ROM Build and Search and Retrieval Software

The following companies provide build and search and retrieval software for data indexing. For multimedia software, see Appendix B. Many of the packages listed below also enable you to create multimedia titles.

CDAuthor, CD Answer ReferenceSet

Dataware Technologies, Inc.
222 3rd Street, Suite 3300
Cambridge, MA 02142
617-621-0820
617-621-0307 (Fax)

DiscPassage

CMC ReSearch, Inc.
7150 SW Hampton, Suite 120
Portland, OR 97223
503-639-3395
503-639-1796 (Fax)

Folio VIEWS

Folio Corporation
2155 N. Freedom Blvd., Suite 150
Provo, UT 84604
800-54-FOLIO
801-375-3700
801-374-5753 (Fax)

FTR (full text) Questar (fielded)

Sony-PDSC
One Lower Ragsdale Drive
Monterey, CA 93940
408-372-2812
408-375-7130 (Fax)

Ful-Text

Fulcrum Technologies, Inc.
560 Rochester Street
Ottawa, Ontario, Canada K1S 5K2
613-238-1761
613-238-7695 (Fax)

Hyperwriter

NTERGAID
2490 Black Rock Turnpike, Suite 337
Fairfield, CT 06430
203-380-1280
203-380-1465 (Fax)

Hypoint

Logical Data Expression
5537 33rd Street NW
Washington, DC 20015
202-966-3393

I-Search
Windows Personal Librarian
DOS Personal Librarian

I-Mode Retrieval Systems, Inc.
7 Odell Plaza
Yonkers, NY 10701
914-968-7008
914-968-9187 (Fax)

KAware2

Knowledge Access, Inc.
2685 Marine Way, Suite 1305
Mountain View, CA 94043
800-252-9273
415-969-0606
415-964-2027 (Fax)

Knowledge Retrieval System (KRS)

KnowledgeSet Corporation
888 Villa Street, Suite 500
Mountain View, CA 94041
415-968-9888
415-968-9962 (Fax)

Lotus Bluefish

Lotus Development Corporation
55 Cambridge Parkway
Cambridge, MA 02142
800-554-5501
617-577-8500
617-225-1197 (Fax)

MediaBase
MediaBase Windows

Crowninshield Software, Inc.
1050 Massachusetts Avenue, 2nd Floor
Cambridge, MA 02138
617-661-4945
617-661-6254 (Fax)

MicroKey

MicroKey, Inc.
15415 Redhill Avenue, Suite B
Tustin, CA 92680
800-521-3575
714-258-3215 (Fax)

OPTI-WARE

Online Computer Systems, Inc.
20251 Century Blvd.
Germantown, MD 20874
800-922-9204
301-428-3700
301-428-2903 (Fax)

Personal Librarian (PLS)

Personal Library Software, Inc.
15215 Shady Grove Road, Suite 204
Rockville, MD 20850
301-926-1402
301-963-9738 (Fax)

Quicksearch

dataDisc
Route 3, Box 1108
Gainesville, VA 22065
800-328-2347
703-347-9085 (Fax)

Re:Search

MicroRetrieval Corporation
One Kendall Square, Building 300
Cambridge, MA 02139
617-577-1574
617-577-9517 (Fax)

ROMWARE

Nimbus Information Systems
Guildford Farm SR 629
Ruckersville, VA 22968
804-985-1100
804-985-4625 (Fax)

SearchExpress

Executive Technologies, Inc.
2120 16th Avenue South
Birmingham, AL 35205
205-933-5495

TEXTWARE

TextWare Corporation
347 Main Street
PO Box 3267
Park City, UT 84060
801-645-9600
801-645-9610 (Fax)

TMSFAX

Innerview
TMS, Inc.
110 W. 3rd St.
PO Box 1358
Stillwater, OK 74076
405-377-0880

TOPIC

Verity, Inc.
1550 Plymouth
Mountain View, CA 94043-1230
415-960-7600

Window Book

BOX Company, Inc.
63 Howard Street
Cambridge, MA 02139
617-576-0892
617-864-4512
617 868-4549 (Fax)

WinOnCD

CeQuadrant
Pennewartstrasse, #27
52068 Aachen, Germany
0241-963-1100
0241-963-1101

ISO 9660 Formatting Software

The following companies provide software that creates an ISO 9660
CD-ROM image:

CD-CREATOR

CSM, Inc.
211 N. El Camino Real
Encinitas, CA 92024
619-944-1228
619-942-5447 (Fax)

CD FORMATTER

Crowninshield Software, Inc.
1050 Massachusetts Avenue, 2nd Floor
Cambridge, MA 02138
617-661-4945
617-661-6254 (Fax)

CD FORMATTER

Online Computer Systems, Inc.
20251 Century Blvd.
Germantown, MD 20874
800-922-9204
301-428-3700
301-428-2903 (Fax)

CD GEN

CD ROM Strategies, Inc.
18 Chenile
Irvine, CA 92714
714-733-3378
714-786-1401 (Fax)

CD MAKE

Dataware Technologies, Inc.
222 3rd Street, Suite 3300
Cambridge, MA 02142
617-621-0820
617-621-0307 (Fax)

DisComposer

Trace
1150 Murphy Avenue, Suite 200
San Jose, CA 95131
800-872-2318
408-437-3375

ISO FORMATTER

Publishers Data Services Corporation (SONY)
1 Lower Ragsdale Drive, Suite 160
Monterey, CA 93940
408-372-2812
408-375-7130 (Fax)

KAware Pipeline Premastering System

Knowledge Access, Inc.
2685 Marine Way, Suite 1305
Mountain View, CA 94043
800-252-9273
415-969-0606
415-964-2027 (Fax)

Makedisc

Young Minds, Inc.
1910 Orange Tree Lane, Suite 300
Redlands, CA 92374
714-335-1350
714-798-0488 (Fax)

Personal Scribe

Meridian Data, Inc.
5615 Scotts Valley Drive
Scotts Valley, CA 95066
800-767-2537
408-438-3100
408-438-6816 (Fax)

TOPiX

Optical Media International
180 Knowles Drive
Los Gatos, CA 95030
800-347-2664
408-376-3511
408-376-3519 (Fax)

Development Systems

The following companies provide integrated hardware and software systems for
CD-ROM data preparation and premaster tape generation:

LH 2100

Trace
1040 East Brokaw Road
San Jose, CA 95131
408-441-3578
408-441-3399 (Fax)

Personal RomMaker

JVC Information Products Group
19900 Beach Boulevard, Suite I
Huntington Beach, CA 92648
714-965-2610
714-968-9071 (Fax)

TOPiX

Optical Media International
180 Knowles Drive
Los Gatos, CA 95030
800-347-2664
408-376-3511
408-376-3519 (Fax)

VR Publisher

Meridian Data, Inc.
5615 Scotts Valley Drive
Scotts Valley, CA 95066
800-767-2537
408-438-3100
408-438-6816 (Fax)

Packaging

The following companies provide custom packaging for CD-ROM discs:

DIGIPRESS

2016 Bainbridge Row Drive
Louisville, KY 40207
502-895-0565
502-893-9589 (Fax)

Optima Precision, Inc.

20 Authority Drive
Fitchburg, MA 01420
508-342-9626
508-343-0889 (Fax)

Reliance Plastics and Packaging Division

217 Brook Avenue
Passaic, NJ 07055
201-473-7200
201-473-1023 (Fax)

UNIVENTURE

6145 Scherers Place
PO Box 570
Dublin, OH 43017
800-992-8262
614-761-2669
614-793-0202 (Fax)

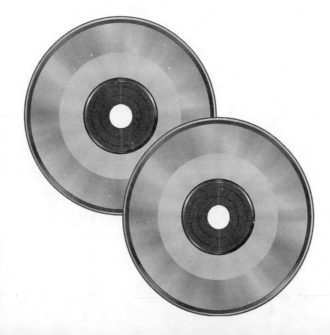

APPENDIX

CD-ROM Manufacturing

The manufacturing facilities discussed in this appendix can produce and replicate a CD-ROM from a premaster tape or other recording of an ISO 9660 image. Most manufacturing facilities accept nine-track tape for input, and most also accept Exabyte and DAT tape. Some accept WORM and MO cartridges and CD-R media. Call the manufacturing facility to see whether it accepts the particular media that you plan to output. Each manufacturing facility can send you precise information on the media it accepts, turnaround time, label specifications, and prices. Some manufacturing facilities perform other services that include premastering, custom development, marketing, and distribution.

Table D.1 illustrates a typical price list for services, although prices may vary from company to company. Many of these companies offer specials from time to time and also have "Developer" or "Express" programs that enable you to order a small number of discs at a low price. Disc manufacturing prices depend on a number of factors such as run size, turnaround time, the number of colors in the label, and packaging. Manufacturers also vary considerably in their pricing structures, so the prices are expressed as a range.

The term *turnaround* is used in the industry to indicate the number of days between receipt of the premaster tape and shipment of discs. The shorter the turnaround, the higher the cost. Five-day turnaround is standard, shorter turnarounds cost more, and longer turnarounds (10-day to two-week) are discounted.

The *mastering charge* is the charge to make the glass master and steel stamper. You also pay a per-disc replication charge that usually includes a two-color label if you supply the artwork. Some manufacturers will accept orders only for quantities of 500 or more discs. For larger run sizes, the mastering charge may be waived. Each additional color can cost from 10 to 20 cents per disc, and a label change—that is, the same disc produced with two or more different labels—costs extra. Discs can be serialized for about 50 cents each. Some companies insert each disc in a jewel case as part of the base per-disc price; other companies charge around 30 cents extra for this packaging.

Table D.1
Premastering

Service	Charge
Premastering (if required)	$200.00 - $400.00
Mastering	
Mastering—Five-day turnaround	N/C - $1,400.00
Quick turnaround	
One day	$700.00 - $1,650.00
Two day	$550.00 - $1,250.00
Three day	$250.00 - $970.00
Discount for long turnaround	
Six day	5%
Seven day	7.5%
Eight day	10%
Nine day	12.5%
Ten day	15%
Over ten days	Variable

Service	Charge
Disc Replication	
Replication, including packaging in jewel case and two-color label	<$1.00 - $2.00 per disc, depending on run size
Packaging	
Folders, booklets, liners—insertion	.05 per disc
Shrink wrapping	.05 per disc

Manufacturing (Replication) Facilities

Allied Records Corp.

6110 Peachtree Street
Los Angeles, CA 90040
213-725-6900
213-725-8763 (Fax)

Alshire International, Inc.

1015 Isabel Street
Burbank, CA 91506
213-849-4671
818-569-3718 (Fax)

Americ Disc Inc.

2525 Canadien
Drummondville, Que.
Canada J2B 8A9
819-474-2119
819-474-2870 (Fax)

American Multimedia Inc.

2609 Tucker Street
Burlington, NC 27215
910-229-5554
910-228-1409 (Fax)

ASR Recording Services of California

8960 Eton Avenue
Canoga Park, CA 91304
818-341-1124
818-407-9948 (Fax)

BQC, Inc.

2101 South 35th Street
Council Bluffs, IA 51501
712-328-8060
712-328-0490 (Fax)

Capitol Records

1 Capitol Way
Jacksonville, IL 62650
217-243-8661
217-243-6142 (Fax)

Cinram

2255 Markham Road
Scarborough, Ont.
Canada M1B 2W3
416-298-8190
416-298-9307 (Fax)

Cinram

1600 Rich Road
Richmond, IN 47374
800-927-7749
317-966-8041 (Fax)

Denon

1380 Monticello Road
Madison, GA 30650
706-342-3425
706-342-0637 (Fax)

Disctronics USA

2800 Summit Avenue
Plano, TX 75074
214-881-8000
214-423-2380 (Fax)

DMI

1120 Cosby Way
Anaheim, CA 92806
714-630-6700
714-630-1025

DMI

4905 Moores Mill Road
Huntsville, AL 35810
205-859-9042
205-859-4236 (Fax)

Evatone

4801 Ulmerton Road
Clearwater, FL 34622
800-382-8663
813-572-7000
813-572-6214 (Fax)

HRM/HMG

15 Bilpin Avenue
Hauppauge, NY 11788
516-234-0200

JVC

2 JVC Road
Tuscaloosa, AL 35405
800-677-5518
205-554-5535 (Fax)

KAO

41474 Christie Street
Fremont, CA 94587
510-657-8425
510-657-3208 (Fax)

KAO

1857 Colonial Village Lane
Lancaster, PA 17601
717-392-7840
717-392-7897 (Fax)

Metatec/Discovery Systems

7001 Discovery Boulevard
Dublin, OH 43017
614-761-2000
614-766-3146 (Fax)

Nimbus

PO Box 7427
Charlottesville, VA 22906
804-985-1100
804-985-3953 (Fax)

Pilz Compact Disc

PO Box 220
54 Conchester Road
Concordville, PA 19331
215-459-5035
215-459-5958 (Fax)

Polygram Manufacturing Distribution Centers, Inc.

PO Box 400
Grover, NC 28073
704-734-4100
704-734-4180 (Fax)

Print NW/Six Sigma

4101 Industry Drive East, Suite D
Fife, WA 98424
206-922-0990
206-467-0183 (Fax)

Sanyo Laser Products

1767 Sheridan Street
Richmond, IN 47374
317-935-7574
317-935-7570 (Fax)

Sonopress USA

108 Monticello Road
Weaverville, NC 28787
704-658-2000
704-658-2008 (Fax)

Sony DADC

400 N. Woodbury Avenue
Pitman, NJ 08071
609-589-8000
609-589-3007

Sony DADC

3181 N. Fruitridge Street
Terre Haute, IN 47804
812-462-8160
812-462-8776 (Fax)

Technidisc

2250 Meijer Drive
Troy, MI 48084
810-435-7439
810-435-7746 (Fax)

Technicolor

3233 East Mission Oaks Boulevard
Camarillo, CA 93012
805-445-1122
805-445-4340 (Fax)

3M

2933 Bayview Drive
Fremont, CA 94538
510-440-8161
510-440-8162 (Fax)

3M

1425 Parkway Drive
Menomonie, WI 54751
715-235-5567
715-235-4608 (Fax)

Uni Distribution

Highway 154 East
Pinkneyville, IL 62274
618-357-2167
618-357-3640 (Fax)

US Optical Disc

1 Eagle Drive
Sanford, ME 04073
207-324-1124
207-490-1707 (Fax)

Warner Specialty Records

210 North Valley Avenue
Oliphant, PA 18447
717-383-2471
717-383-9859 (Fax)

Zomax

5353 Nathan Lane
Plymouth, MN 55442
612-553-9300
612-553-0826 (Fax)

APPENDIX

Resources

This appendix provides lists of useful resources that you may need to contact if you choose to produce your own CD-ROM. The lists include companies that offer data conversion and companies that provide consulting services. Many of these companies also provide complete CD-ROM development services.

Data Conversion

The following companies offer data conversion services:

Access Innovations, Inc.

4314 Mesa Grande
Albuquerque, NM 87108
800-468-3453
505-256-1080 (Fax)

Computership International Data Services

125 Village Blvd., Suite 220
Princeton, NJ 08540-5703
609-452-2800
609-452-2875 (Fax)

D & L Conversion Services

670 East 3900 South, Suite 101
Salt Lake City, UT 84107
801-268-3708
801-268-9651 (Fax)

Data Development

3595 SW Corporate Parkway
Palm City, FL 34990
407-288-7226
407-288-2775 (Fax)

Data Horizons

4715 33rd Street
Long Island City, NY 11101
718-706-8400
718-482-0680 (Fax)

Documentation Development, Inc.

520 Eighth Avenue
New York, NY 10018
212-594-8001
212-594-8321 (Fax)

Equidata

3200 South Arlington Street
Akron, OH 44312
216-645-0004
216-645-0709 (Fax)

Innodata Processing Corporation

95 Rockwell Place, Dept. NF
Brooklyn, NY 11217
718-625-7750
718-522-7624 (Fax)

The Input Centre

320 N. Michigan Avenue
Chicago, IL 60601
312-269-0272
312-472-1888 (Fax)

Larkspur Digital, Inc.

70 Walnut Street
Arlington, MA 02174
617-643-6264
617-641-1125 (Fax)

NorthEast Scanning Technologies, Inc.

42 Pleasant Street
Watertown, MA 02172
617-926-6378
617-924-5914 (Fax)

Quadrant Technologies, Inc.

PO Box 7788
Nashua, NH 03060
603-888-5969
603-888-5322 (Fax)

Scan Text Corporation

12330 Northeast 8th Street, Suite 101
Bellevue, WA 98005
800-642-7226
206-451-3626
206-451-7955 (Fax)

Subsystem Technologies, Inc.

8150 Leesburg Pike
Tyson's Corner, VA 22182
703-442-7996
703-442-8131 (Fax)

West Coast Information Systems, Inc.

1901 Olympic Blvd.
Walnut Creek, CA 94596
510-930-7700
510-930-9316 (Fax)

CD-ROM Consulting and Development

The following companies provide consulting services for CD-ROM projects. Many of these companies also provide data conversion and preparation services as well as complete CD-ROM development services.

Applied Optical Solutions, Inc.

10551 Glen Hannah Drive
Laurel, MD 20723
301-498-2504
301-796-4565 (Fax)

Avtex Research Corporation

2105 South Bascom Avenue, Suite 290
Campbell, CA 95008
408-371-2800
408-371-5760 (Fax)

Boston Media Consultants

19 Damon Road
Scituate, MA 02066
617-545-2696
617-545-3464 (Fax)

Carl M. Rodia & Associates

13 Locust Street
Trumbull, CT 06611
203-261-1365
203-268-8071 (Fax)

Catalyst Software Systems

2720 Augusta Street
Eugene, OR 97403-2255
503-687-0606
503-344-7877 (Fax)

CD Consultants, Inc.

4404 Keswick Road
Baltimore, MD 21210
301-243-2755
301-243-9419 (Fax)

CD-ROM Solutions, Inc.

PO Box 9038-394
Charlottesville, VA 22906
800-487-3472
804-295-3978
301-977-7951 (Fax)

CD-ROM Specialists

PO Box 1337
League City, TX 77574
713-334-2363
713-334-1380 (Fax)

CD-ROM Strategies

18 Chenile
Irvine, CA 92714
714-733-3378
714-630-1025 (Fax)

Datavision Technologies Corporation

49 Stevenson Street, Suite 575
San Francisco, CA 94105
415-543-7903
415-543-9794 (Fax)

Digital United

282 Cabrini Boulevard, 6th Floor
New York, NY 10040
212-795-0403

Documentation Development, Inc.

520 Eighth Avenue
New York, NY 10018
212-594-8001
212-594-8321 (Fax)

Earth View, Inc.

6514 18th Avenue, NE
Seattle, WA 98115
206-527-3168
206-524-6803 (Fax)

Emerging Technology Consultants, Inc.

2819 Hamline Avenue, North
St Paul, MN 55113
612-639-3973
612-639-0110 (Fax)

Grafica Multimedia, Inc.

415 Ortega Street
San Francisco, CA 94122
415-759-7150
415-759-6974 (Fax)

Information Arts

PO Box 21726
Columbus, OH 43221
614-793-0771
614-793-0749 (Fax)

Information Workstation Group

501 Queen St.
Alexandria, VA 22314
703-548-4320
703-838-9271 (Fax)

Interactive Arts

3200 Airport Avenue, #20
Santa Monica, CA 90405
213-390-9466
213-390-7525 (Fax)

InterMedia

5025 Brookdale Avenue
Oakland, CA 94619-3205
510-533-5690
510-533-3364 (Fax)

Laser Storage Solutions

4520 Darcelle Drive
Union City, CA 94587
415-489-7732
415-964-2027 (Fax)

One-Off CD Shops (Several Locations)

International Head Office
237 8th Avenue, SE, 6th Floor
Calgary, Alberta, Canada T2G 5C3
800-387-1633

Palamar Communications

1444 Brookings Trail
Topanga, CA 90290
213-455-1002

Quick Source, Inc.

1010 Wayne Avenue
Silver Spring, MD 20910
800-888-0736
301-650-8865
301-565-9412 (Fax)

R.J. Bruno & Consultants

1209 South Main Street
Wheaton, IL 606187
708-469-1215
708-469-1452 (Fax)

Synectics Inc.

3030 Clarendon Blvd.
Arlington, VA 22201
703-528-2772
703-528-2857 (Fax)

Teachware

8901 South Santa Fe, Suite C
Oklahoma City, OK 73139
405-631-9205
405-631-3607 (Fax)

UniDisc, Inc.

4401 Capitola Road #4
Capitola, CA 94010
408-464-0707
408-464-0187 (Fax)

Young Minds, Inc.

1910 Orange Tree Lane, Suite 300
Redlands, CA 92374
714-335-1350
714-798-0488 (Fax)

Appendixes

CD-ROM Networking

This appendix lists companies that provide peer-to-peer networks with built-in CD-ROM support, hardware, and software for dedicated CD-ROM servers, and NLMs for CD-ROM support on Novell NetWare.

DOS-Based Peer-to-Peer Networks

The following list provides companies that offer peer-to-peer networks with built-in CD-ROM support:

EasyNetwork

Exzel Corp.
2003 E. Fifth Street, Suite 3
Tempe, AZ 85281
602-894-0795

GV LAN OS

Grapevine LAN Products, Inc.
8519 154th Avenue NE
Redmond, WA 98052
206-869-2707

Invisible EtherNet NET/30

Invisible Software, Inc.
1142 Chess Drive
Foster City, CA 94404
415-570-5967

LANtastic

Artisoft
575 E. River Road
Tucson, AZ 85704
602-293-6363

Map Assist

Fresh Technologies
1478 North Tech Boulevard, Suite 101
Gilbert, AZ 85234
602-497-4200
602-497-4242 (Fax)

Novell Lite

Novell, Inc.
122 East 1700 South
Provo, UT 84606
800-453-1267
801-429-7000
801-429-5775 (Fax)

POWERlan

Performance Technology, Inc.
800 Lincoln Center
7800 1H-10 West
San Antonio, TX 78230
800-327-8526
512-349-2000

Dedicated CD-ROM Server Hardware/Software

The following companies provide software and/or hardware for dedicated CD-ROM servers:

CBIS, Inc.

5875 Peachtree Industrial Blvd.
Building 100, Suite 170
Norcross, GA 30092
404-446-1332

Flex Sys Corporation

24 Graf Road
Newburyport, MA 01950
800-533-7756
508-465-6633 (Fax)

LANshark Systems, Inc.

6502 East Main Street
Reynoldsburg, OH 43068
614-866-5553

Logicraft

22 Cotton Road
Nashua, NH 03063
800-880-6544

Lotus CD-Networker

Lotus Development Corporation
55 Cambridge Parkway
Cambridge, MA 02142

Meridian Data

5615 Scotts Valley Drive
Scotts Valley, CA 95066
800-767-2537
408-438-3100
408-438-6816 (Fax)

Microtest, Inc.

4747 North 22nd Street
Phoenix, AZ
602-952-6400
602-952-6401 (Fax)

Online Computer Systems, Inc.

20251 Century Blvd.
Germantown, MD 20874
800-922-9204

SIRS

P.O. Box 2348
Boca Raton, FL 33427
800-232-7477
407-994-4707 (Fax)

NLMs for Novell NetWare

The following companies offer NLMs for Novell NetWare:

AHAccelerator NLM

Procomp USA
6777 Eagle Road
Cleveland, OH 44130
216-234-6387

CD Net

Meridian Data, Inc.
5615 Scotts Valley Drive
Scotts Valley, CA 95066
800-767-2537
408-436-3100
408-438-5816 (Fax)

CorelDriver Optical Disc Interface Kit

Corel Systems Corp.
1600 Carling Avenue
Ottawa, Ontario, Canada K1Z 8R7

Discport NLM

Microtest, Inc.
4747 North 22nd Street
Phoenix, AZ 85016
800-526-9675

Opti-Net NLM

Online Computer Systems, Inc.
20251 Century Blvd.
Germantown, MD 20874
800-922-9204

Procomm NLM

Procomm Technology
2181 Dupont Drive
Irvine, CA 92715
714-852-1000

SCSI Express

Micro Design International, Inc.
6985 University Boulevard
Winter Park, FL 32792
800-228-0891
407-677-8333

Serview NLM

Ornetix
1249 Innsbruk Drive
Sunnyvale, CA 94089
408-744-9095

CD-ROM Write-Once Hardware, Software, and Media

T his appendix lists companies that provide CD-ROM write-once units and CD-Recordable media. Also provided in this appendix is the address of a distributor of the CD-CATS CD-ROM test equipment.

CD-ROM Write-Once Hardware and Software

The following companies provide CD-ROM write-once units with software:

Austin InfoScience

1948 South IH 35, Building B
Austin, TX 78704
800-382-3766
512-440-1132
512-440-0531 (Fax)

CD-ROM Strategies, Inc.

6 Venture, Suite 208
Irvine, CA 92718
714-453-1702
714-453-1311 (Fax)

Crowninshield Software, Inc.

1050 Massachusetts Avenue, 2nd Floor
Cambridge, MA 02138
617-661-4945
617-661-6254 (Fax)

CSM, Inc.

211 N. El Camino Real
Encinitas, CA 92024
619-944-1228
619-942-5447 (Fax)

dataDisc

Route 3, Box 1108
Gainesville, VA 22065
800-328-2347
703-347-9085 (Fax)

Dataware Technologies, Inc.

222 3rd Street, Suite 3300
Cambridge, MA 02142
617-621-0820
617-621-0307 (Fax)

JVC Information Products Group

19900 Beach Boulevard, Suite I
Huntington Beach, CA 92648
714-965-2610
714-968-9071 (Fax)

Meridian Data, Inc.

5615 Scotts Valley Drive
Scotts Valley, CA 95066
800-767-2537
408-438-3100
408-438-6816 (Fax)

Microboards

308 Broadway
PO Box 130
Carver, MN 55315
612-448-9800
612-448-9806

Optical Laser

315 3rd Street
Huntington Beach, CA 92648
800-776-9215
714-536-7990
714-536-0817 (Fax)

Optical Media International

180 Knowles Drive
Los Gatos, CA 95030
800-347-2664
408-376-3511
408-376-3519 (Fax)

Philips Consumer Electronics

One Philips Drive
PO Box 14810
Knoxville, TN 37914-1810
615-475-8869

Publishers Data Services Corporation

1 Lower Ragsdale Drive, Suite 160
Monterey, CA 93940
800-654-8802
408-372-9267 (Fax)

Trace

1040 East Brokaw Road
San Jose, CA 95131
408-441-3578
408-441-3399 (Fax)

Young Minds, Inc.

1910 Orange Tree Lane, Suite 300
Redlands, CA 92374
714-335-1350
714-798-0488 (Fax)

CD-Recordable Media

The following companies supply CD-Recordable media:

dataDisc

Route 3, Box 1108
Gainesville, VA 22065
800-328-2347
703-347-9085 (Fax)

Eastman Kodak Company

343-T State Street
Rochester, NY 14652-3801
716-724-4000
716-724-0663 (Fax)

Microboards

308 Broadway
PO Box 130
Carver, MN 55315
612-448-9800
612-448-9806

MTC America, Inc. (Mitsui Toatsu Chemicals)

Two Grand Central Tower
140 East 45th Street
New York, NY 10017
800-367-2479
212-867-6330
212-867-6315 (Fax)

Optical Laser

315 3rd Street
Huntington Beach, CA 92648
800-776-9215
714-536-7990
714-536-0817 (Fax)

Pinnacle Micro

19 Technology
Irvine, CA 92718
800-553-7070
714-727-3300
714-727-1913 (Fax)

Trace

1150 Murphy Avenue, Suite 200
San Jose, CA 95131
800-872-2318
408-437-3375

CD-CATS CD-ROM Test Equipment

The following company distributes the CD-CATS CD-ROM test equipment:

Enterprise Corporation of America

120 West Towers Building
1200 Valley West Drive
West Des Moines, Iowa 50266
515-223-1290
515-223-7749 (Fax)

For further imformation on CD-Recordable technology, see:

The CD-Recordable Bible

by Dr. Ash Pahwa
Eight Bit Books
462 Danbury Road
Wilton, CT 06897
800-248-8466
203-761-1444 (Fax)

GLOSSARY

Glossary of Terms

A

access time

> The time required to deliver data from a CD-ROM disc. Access time consists of the time it takes for the optical head to travel to the desired location on the disc (seek time), plus the time it takes to focus the laser on the spiral track, plus the time it takes to transfer the data from the disc to the screen.

address

> The number of a particular computer memory location. Every byte of memory and every sector of a hard disk or a CD-ROM disc has its own address.

ADPCM

Adaptive Differential Pulse Code Modulation. A method of compressing audio data by recording the differences between successive digital samples rather than the full value of the samples. Many types of ADPCM standards exist. In this book, the standard used is as defined in the CD-ROM XA and CD-I standards.

algorithm

A mathematical formula or the instructions of a computer program. It is the orderly steps to be taken to solve a problem.

application

The use of a technology to achieve a specific objective.

archival

A medium that is readable and/or writable for an extended period.

authoring

Creation of a database including indexing and the provision of a retrieval application. Multimedia authoring packages include links to audio, graphics, and video elements.

B

binary

A counting system that is based on the number two. A number system comprised of zeros and ones, which represent off and on, absence or presence of a pulse. Used to store data.

bit

Binary digit; either a zero or a one. The smallest unit in computer information handling.

bundle

A package that includes several products for one price. For example, a CD-ROM drive with controller card, cable, software, and one or more CD-ROM discs.

bus interface

An electronic pathway between CPUs and input/output devices. A bus interface for a CD-ROM drive consists of a controller card and cable.

byte

A number of consecutive binary digits that are acted on as a unit. Usually, there are eight bits in a byte. A byte represents one character. Primary and secondary memory (RAM and magnetic media) are measured in kilobytes (1,024, or 2^{10} bytes) and megabytes (one million bytes).

C

cache

A holding area for data within the CD-ROM drive itself, on its interface board, or within standard RAM that provides a method for matching data transfer rates and presentation speed requirements.

CAV

Constant Angular Velocity. A disk that rotates at a constant rate of speed. Examples are hard drives, floppy disks, magneto optical discs, and some video discs.

CD audio

A laser-encoded optical disc that contains digitally encoded information, usually music, defined by the Red Book standard. Also called CD-DA (compact disc digital audio).

CD audio jack

An outlet on a CD-ROM drive that provides audio playback through speakers or headphones. Only Red Book or true CD audio sound can be heard from the audio jack on a CD-ROM drive.

CD-I

Compact Disc Interactive. A hardware and software system defined by the Green Book standard, which plays CD-I, CD audio, CD+G, and Photo CD discs. It connects to a television and stereo system.

CD-R

CD-Recordable, also called CD-WO (CD-Write Once). Term used to describe special players and media that enable the creation of a single CD-ROM in a desktop environment.

CD-ROM

Compact Disc Read-Only Memory. A laser-encoded optical memory storage medium, defined by the Yellow Book standard.

CD-ROM drive

A computer peripheral that plays CD-ROM discs.

CD-ROM XA

CD-ROM Extended Architecture. A compact disc standard that permits the interleaving of compressed audio and video tracks for sound and animation synchronization. Based on the Yellow Book, it also uses some elements of the Green Book (CD-I).

CD-WO

Compact Disc Write Once. A laser recorder that allows a compact disc (of special media) to be directly written, rather than mass produced. Recent developments allow CD-WO discs to be appendable. CD-WO media is physically defined by the Orange Book standard, Part II, and a proposal for the logical format has been submitted to the International Standards Organization by the Frankfort Group.

CIRC

Cross-Interleaved Reed-Solomon Code. A method of error detection and correction used on CD audio discs and as a basis for layered ECC on CD-ROM discs. Reed-Solomon codes are especially effective when errors occur in bursts, as on a scratched compact disc. Cross-coding and interleaving break long bursts of errors into smaller error bursts.

CLV

Constant Linear Velocity. A disc that rotates at a varying rate of speed. Examples are CD Audio, CD-ROM, CD-I, CD-ROM XA, and some video discs.

coaster

Slang term for a compact disc that is unreadable due to errors in content, manufacturing, or damage.

compatible

Describes different hardware devices that can use the same software or programs without modification or with appropriate software.

contiguous

Sequential. Describes the layout of sectors on a CD-ROM disc, which are placed end-to-end in a single spiral track.

controller

Specialized processor that controls the flow of data between a computer and one or more peripheral devices.

CRC

Cyclic Redundancy Check. A checksum calculated from data in a CD-ROM packet. It is used to generate EDC (Error Detection Code).

D

data

Denotes basic elements of information that can be processed or produced by a computer.

database

A collection of data, stored in electronic form.

decode

To convert information from machine or computer-readable format.

default

A standard setting or action taken by hardware or software if the user has not specified otherwise.

device driver

A program that contains the instructions necessary for a computer to control a peripheral device, such as a mouse or CD-ROM.

directory tree

A hierarchical database of files. Files are grouped together so that users and applications have access to subsets of files. A directory tree is useful for organizing large numbers of files. On CD-ROM discs, a directory tree and a path table comprise the file management system for the disc.

See *path table*.

disc

Used in reference to optical storage media, such as CD audio, CD-I, CD-ROM, video disc, or WORM.

disc caddy

A plastic container for CD-ROM discs that is inserted into a CD-ROM drive. All CD-ROM drives use the same kind of caddy, except for LMSI drives, which once used a two-piece caddy but now use a disk drawer with no caddy. A disc caddy resembles a square, flat box with a clear hinged lid.

disk

Used in reference to magnetic media, such as floppy and hard disks.

dongle

An electronic device or hardware key that plugs into one of the ports of a PC. Used to control access to licensed applications; the software checks the key for its serial number, without which the program cannot be executed.

double-speed drive

Refers to a CD-ROM drive that will read data faster than the standard requires (155KB/sec). Many drives now have 300KB/sec transfer rates (also known as twice the standard, or 2X); at least one claims 600KB/sec (4X).

drive bay

The opening in a computer chassis designed to hold a floppy drive, hard drive, CD-ROM drive, tape drive, or other device. The opening can be half-height or full-height, exposed or internal.

E

ECMA 168

A European Computer Manufacturers Association standard for CD-ROM and CD-WO. This standard is derived from the work done by the Frankfurt Group. It is a superset of the ISO 9660 standard.

EDC/ECC

Error Detection Code and Error Correction Code. A special, highly complex, and very efficient method of error detection and correction for CD-ROM discs, which is defined in the Yellow Book specification.

encode

To convert information into machine or computer-readable format.

executable

In MS-DOS, a file with the .EXE extension; a program that carries out commands. Executable is sometimes used to refer to .BAT and .COM files.

expansion slot

An internal connection on a PC's backplane or motherboard that can accept a printed circuit board.

F

FAT

File Allocation Table. Part of the MS-DOS operating system that keeps track of the location of files on a disk.

field

A piece of data. A group of fields makes a record, and a collection of records makes up a database. A record may include fields such as name, address, and phone number.

file server

A component of a Local Area Network, or LAN, which stores information for use by clients or workstations.

format

An established system standard in which data is stored.

fragmentation

Storing parts of a file in disparate, available space on a disk, rather than contiguously.

See *optimization*.

Frankfurt Group

An ad hoc group of compact disc industry researchers and developers who have written and submitted a proposal to the International Standards Association for a standard format for CD-WO appendable discs.

G

glass master

A highly polished glass disc, coated with photoresist or plastic and etched by a laser beam, that is used at the start of the compact disc manufacturing process.

graphics

Visual data. This data includes photographs, line drawings, computer-generated artwork, and graphs. Graphics can be entered into the computer by using scanners, drawing programs, cameras, and graphics tablets.

Green Book

The specification for the CD-I standard.

See *CD-I*.

GUI: Graphical User interface

A layer of software that allows the user to interact with the computer by choosing items from menus or selecting icons from the screen, usually with a mouse. The Macintosh Finder and Microsoft Windows are examples of GUI environments.

H

High Sierra format

The original format proposed by the High Sierra Group for organizing files and directories on CD-ROM. A revised version of this format was adopted by the International Standards Organization as ISO 9660.

High Sierra Group

An ad hoc group of CD-ROM researchers and developers who first gathered at the High Sierra Hotel in Lake Tahoe, California, to propose a standard CD-ROM file format. This proposal was later amended and approved as the ISO 9660 standard for CD-ROM.

I

icon

A pictorial, symbolic representation of a function or task. Used in GUIs (Graphical User Interfaces) such as Windows and Apple Macintosh Finder.

indexing

The act of creating a file or files that contain information about the location of specific pieces of data in the files being indexed.

interactive media

An application or program that requires a dialog between user and computer. Video tape and CD audio, for example, are not interactive media. They are designed to play sequentially from beginning to end. CD-ROM, CD-I, and CD-ROM XA are interactive because the user can choose a path to explore.

interface

The link between two pieces of disparate equipment, such as a CPU and a peripheral device. Also, a method of translating data from computer to user.

interleave

A method of storing information in an alternating sequence of frames.

International Standards Organization

Sets international standards for many technologies. Headquarters in Geneva, Switzerland.

ISO 9660

The international standard for directory structures and file layout on CD-ROMs, a logical, structural standard commonly used in conjunction with the Yellow Book physical standard for CD-ROM.

J-K

Janus disc

A CD-ROM disc that contains data tracks in two or more different formats, such as ISO 9660 and HFS (Macintosh Hierarchical File Structure).

jewel case

Hinged plastic box used to package, ship, and store compact discs.

jukebox

CD-ROM drive with a disc-changing mechanism that is capable of playing multiple discs.

keyword

A word in a database for which you can search. This word is in the index. Any word not contained in the index is called a stopword.

L

LAN

Local Area Network. A system connecting two or more personal computers to allow shared resources and communication.

lands

Microscopic flat areas on a compact disc that separate the pits.

laser

Light Amplification by Stimulated Emission of Radiation. Amplifies and generates coherent energy in the light region of the spectrum. Laser light contains waves that have the same phase, as opposed to conventional light, whose individual wave phases are unrelated to the phases of the others.

layered ECC

Layered Error Correction Code. Used to ensure the integrity of CD-ROM data. So called because it is used on top of the CIRC error correction of CD audio discs.

M

magnetic media

Any medium on which data is stored as variations in magnetic polarity; usually floppy disks, hard disks, and tape.

magneto optical

An information storage medium that is magnetically sensitive only at high temperatures. A laser heats a small spot, which allows a magnet to change its polarity. The medium is stable at normal temperatures. Magneto optical discs can be erased and re-recorded.

mastering facility

A manufacturing plant where compact disc "masters" are created for the mass production of compact discs.

megabyte

One million bytes, or 1,048,576 bytes.

See *byte*.

metal master

A metal disc created by plating an etched glass master disc with nickel. Used in a mastering facility to create metal stampers for the mass production of compact discs.

Microsoft Extensions

A program created by Microsoft Corporation that is used as an extension of the MS-DOS operating system to permit the reading of compact discs recorded in High Sierra or ISO 9660 format.

Microsoft Windows

A GUI operating environment developed by Microsoft for use on PCs running under the MS-DOS operating system.

MIDI

Musical Instrument Digital Interface. Industry standard for exchange of musical information between computers and musical instruments or music synthesizers.

mixed mode disc

A CD-ROM disc that contains both CD-ROM (Yellow Book) and CD audio (Red Book) tracks.

multimedia

Any application that combines text, graphics, audio, or video files.

Multimedia Extensions

Adds audio and video recording and playback capabilities to Microsoft Windows. Part of the MPC standard.

multisession

A drive that has the ability to read a CD-ROM that was recorded in at least two different recording sessions, or a disc that contains data that was recorded at different times.

N-O

network interface card (NIC)

Add-in circuit board that enables you to connect a PC to a Local Area Network (LAN).

network license

A license from a software vendor that allows an application to be shared by many users over a network.

operating system

A computer program that runs the computer and handles data traffic between the disks and memory.

Orange Book

Physical specification for CD-Recordable and appendable media.

P

path table

One of two tables contained in the volume descriptor of a CD-ROM which comprise the file management system for the disc. The path table contains the names of all directories on the disc and is the fastest way to access a directory that is not close to the root directory.

See *directory table.*

peer-to-peer

A type of LAN that treats all workstations connected to it as equals. It does not require a file server to hold shared files.

pits

Bumps which represent data, contained in the track of a compact disc.

platform

Refers to different computer types or operating environments. DOS-based, Macintosh, and CD-I are different platforms.

polycarbonate

Material from which compact discs are made.

premastering

The process of logically formatting data to create an image of a compact disc on tape or hard drive.

proprietary

A device or program designed and owned by a particular manufacturer or vendor, as opposed to a standard. CD-ROM drives are manufactured to read discs that comply with the Yellow Book standard, but their controller cards can be supplied by the manufacturer (proprietary) or based on the Small Computer Systems Interface (standard).

Pulse Code Modulation (PCM)

A method of converting analog sound into digital representation by the use of successive samples.

R

Red Book

The specification standards for Compact Disc Digital Audio.

See *CD audio*.

retrieval engine

A program that finds and presents data.

S

sampling rate

Sampling frequency. The number of samples taken per second of an analog signal, expressed in Hertz. A 44.1 kHz sampling rate, used for CD audio sound that represents 44,100 samples per second.

SCSI

Small Computer Systems Interface. Pronounced "scuzzy." A standard interface used to connect peripheral devices, such as a CD-ROM drive, to a computer.

search engine

Same as retrieval engine.

sector

A physical data block of a CD-ROM.

seek

In CD-ROM drives, the act of locating requested data on a disc.

servo

In CD-ROM drives, an electro-mechanical device that uses feedback to achieve precise starts and stops for movements of the optical head and to focus the laser beam.

single session

A drive that can read only discs on which data was recorded only once, or a disc on which data was recorded at one time.

See *multisession.*

sound card

An add-in card required by a DOS-based computer to access and/or create audio in .WAV, .SND, MIDI, and other digital sound formats.

spin up

Come up to speed. When a CD-ROM is inserted in a drive, it must reach a certain rate of rotational speed in order to be read.

stamper

In compact disc mastering facilities, the metal plate used to mass produce discs. It can stamp out thousands of copies of the disc in polycarbonate.

stopword

A word in a database that has not been indexed. Words such as "a," "and," "the," and "it" are examples of stopwords.

See *keyword*.

V-Z

videodisc

Thin, circular, double-sided 8- and 12-inch optical discs, which store motion video as an analog signal in a variety of formats. Their use and popularity has been largely eclipsed by VCRs using magnetic video tape cassettes.

WORM

Write Once Read Many. A type of permanent optical storage that enables the user to record information on a blank disc. Information can be added until the disc is full, but not erased or changed.

Yellow Book

The physical specification for CD-ROM discs.

See *CD-ROM*.

INDEX

INDEX

INDEX

INDEX

INDEX

INDEX

INDEX

INDEX

INDEX

INDEX

F

INDEX

INDEX

INDEX

INDEX

INDEX

INDEX

INDEX

INDEX

INDEX

INDEX

INDEX

INDEX

INDEX

INDEX

INDEX

INDEX

INDEX

INDEX

INDEX

INDEX

New Riders' Guide to CD-ROM, Second Edition
REGISTRATION CARD

Fill out this card to receive information about future CD-ROM books and other New Riders titles!

Name _____ Title _____

Company _____

Address _____

City/State/ZIP _____

I bought this book because: _____

_____

I purchased this book from:

☐ A bookstore (Name _____)

☐ A software or electronics store (Name _____)

☐ A mail order (Name of Catalog _____)

I purchase this many computer books each year:

☐ 1–5   ☐ 6 or more

I currently use these applications: _____

_____

_____

_____

I found these chapters to be the most informative: _____

_____

I found these chapters to be the least informative: _____

_____

Additional comments: _____

_____

☐ I would like to see my name in print! You may use my name and quote me in future New Riders products and promotions. My daytime phone number is: _____

New Riders Publishing 201 West 103rd Street • Indianapolis, Indiana 46290 USA

Fold Here

PLACE
STAMP
HERE

New Riders Publishing
201 West 103rd Street
Indianapolis, Indiana 46290
USA

WANT MORE INFORMATION?

CHECK OUT THESE RELATED TITLES:

	QTY	PRICE	TOTAL

The Graphics Coach. PCX, TIF, BMP—confused by the different graphics file formats? This book helps you figure out the file types that are compatible with your software and the file format that works best with your application. View, edit, and translate your graphics files with the DOS, Windows, and Macintosh shareware included with *The Graphics Coach.* ISBN: 1-56205-129-6.

           ____ $24.95   _____

The Fonts Coach. From the Personal Trainer Series, this book gives clear, concise explanation of how fonts work on different platforms. Includes a disk containing approximately 25 TrueType fonts and explains how to install these fonts. Provides font style guides to help you produce professional-looking documents. ISBN: 1-56205-130-x.

           ____ $24.95   _____

Inside Windows 3.1/Maximizing MS-DOS 5 Value Pack. *Inside Windows 3.1* earned a "Highly Recommended" rating in Byte's Essential Guide to Windows. CompuServe said *Maximizing MS-DOS 5* "...will guide you from the ranks of the confused to the expert." ISBN: 1-56205-140-7.

           ____ $44.95   _____

A Guide to Field Computing. The essential guide for linking managers, sales personnel, and other mobile workers with the office computer system. Examines the technologies available for networking mobile computers. Compares the types of computers best suited for field use. ISBN: 1-56205-091-5.

           ____ $29.95   _____

Name _____

Company _____

Address _____

City _____ State ____ ZIP _____

Phone _____ Fax _____

☐ Check Enclosed　☐ VISA　☐ MasterCard

Card #_____Exp. Date _____

Signature _____

Prices are subject to change. Call for availability and pricing information on latest editions.

Subtotal   _____

Shipping   _____

$4.00 for the first book and $1.75 for each additional book.

Total   _____
Indiana residents add 5% sales tax.

New Riders Publishing 201 West 103rd Street • Indianapolis, Indiana 46290 USA

Orders/Customer Service: 1-800-428-5331
Fax: 1-800-448-3804

WINDOWS TITLES

ULTIMATE WINDOWS 3.1

FORREST HOULETTE, JIM BOYCE,
RICH WAGNER, & THE BSU
RESEARCH STAFF

The most up-to-date reference for
Windows available!

Covers 3.1 and related products

ISBN: 1-56205-125-3

$39.95 USA

INSIDE WINDOWS NT

FORREST HOULETTE, RICHARD WAGNER,
GEORGE ECKEL, & JOHN STODDARD

A complete tutorial and reference to
organize and manage multiple tasks
and multiple programs in Windows.

Windows NT

ISBN: 1-56205-124-5

$34.95 USA

WINDOWS FOR NON-NERDS

JIM BOYCE & ROB TIDROW

This helpful tutorial for Windows
provides novice users with what they
need to know to gain computer
proficiency…and confidence!

Windows 3.1

ISBN: 1-56205-152-0

$18.95 USA

INTEGRATING WINDOWS
APPLICATIONS

ELLEN DANA NAGLER, FORREST HOULETTE,
MICHAEL GROH, RICHARD WAGNER, &
VALDA HILLEY

This book is a no-nonsense, practical
approach for intermediate- and
advanced-level Windows users!

Windows 3.1

ISBN: 1-56205-083-4

$34.95 USA

To Order, Call 1-800-428-5331

GRAPHICS TITLES

INSIDE CORELDRAW! 4.0, SPECIAL EDITION

DANIEL GRAY

An updated version of the #1 best-selling tutorial on CorelDRAW!

CorelDRAW! 4.0

ISBN: 1-56205-164-4

$34.95 USA

CORELDRAW! SPECIAL EFFECTS

NEW RIDERS PUBLISHING

An inside look at award-winning techniques from professional CorelDRAW! designers!

CorelDRAW! 4.0

ISBN: 1-56205-123-7

$39.95 USA

CORELDRAW! NOW!

RICHARD FELDMAN

The hands-on tutorial for users who want practical information now!

CorelDRAW! 4.0

ISBN: 1-56205-131-8

$21.95 USA

INSIDE CORELDRAW! FOURTH EDITION

DANIEL GRAY

The popular tutorial approach to learning CorelDRAW!...with complete coverage of version 3.0!

CorelDRAW! 3.0

ISBN: 1-56205-106-7

$24.95 USA

OPERATING SYSTEMS

INSIDE MS-DOS 6.2, 2E

NEW RIDERS PUBLISHING

A complete tutorial and reference!

MS-DOS 6.2
ISBN: 1-56205-289-6
$34.95 USA

DOS FOR NON-NERDS

MICHAEL GROH

Understanding this popular operating system is easy with this humorous, step-by-step tutorial.

Through DOS 6.0
ISBN: 1-56205-151-2
$18.95 USA

INSIDE SCO UNIX

STEVE GLINES, PETER SPICER,
BEN HUNSBERGER, & KAREN WHITE

Everything users need to know to use the UNIX operating system for everyday tasks.

**SCO Xenix 286, SCO Xenix 386,
SCO UNIX/System V 386**
ISBN: 1-56205-028-1
$29.95 USA

INSIDE SOLARIS SunOS

KARLA SAARI KITALONG,
STEVEN R. LEE, & PAUL MARZIN

Comprehensive tutorial and reference to SunOS!

**SunOS, Sun's version of UNIX for the
SPARC workstation, version 2.0**
ISBN: 1-56205-032-X
$29.95 USA

NETWORKING TITLES

#1 Bestseller!

INSIDE NOVELL NETWARE, THIRD EDITION

DEBRA NIEDERMILLER-CHAFFINS &
DREW HEYWOOD

This best-selling tutorial and reference has
been updated and made even better!

NetWare 2.2, 3.11 & 3.12

ISBN: 1-56205-257-8

$34.95 USA

MAXIMIZING NOVELL NETWARE

JOHN JERNEY & ELNA TYMES

Complete coverage of Novell's
flagship product…for NetWare system
administrators!

NetWare 3.11

ISBN: 1-56205-095-8

$39.95 USA

NETWARE: THE PROFESSIONAL REFERENCE, SECOND EDITION

KARANJIT SIYAN

This updated version for professional
NetWare administrators and technicians
provides the most comprehensive
reference available for this phenomenal
network system.

NetWare 2.x & 3.x

ISBN: 1-56205-158-X

$42.95 USA

NETWARE 4: PLANNING AND IMPLEMENTATION

SUNIL PADIYAR

A guide to planning, installing, and
managing a NetWare 4.0 network that
best serves your company's objectives.

NetWare 4.0

ISBN: 1-56205-159-8

$27.95 USA

To Order, Call 1-800-428-5331

Installing the New Riders'
Guide to CD-ROM Bonus Disc

To use the disc, remove it from its plastic package and place it in your CD-ROM
drive. Open Windows Program Manager and select Run from the File menu.
Assuming that your CD-ROM drive is drive L, type L:\SETUP.EXE and click OK.